Since it was founded in 1969, the Booker Prize has established itself as Britain's foremost literary award. Each October, for one dramatic night, the judges assemble at the Guildhall, London, to present their choice of best novel of the year. The list of winners – often challenging and controversial at the time – reads like a rollcall of great modern fiction.

From the beginning Jonathan Cape dominated the shortlist. It has won the prize no fewer than five times – more than any other publishing house. Now, to celebrate the Booker's twenty-fifth anniversary, Cape is proud to republish its five winners, *The Conservationist, Saville, Midnight's Children, Hotel du Lac* and *The Famished Road*, in a special anniversary edition. Each one is an enduring classic of fine writing and imagination.

THE CONSERVATIONIST

A wealthy industrialist, attractive to women and not yet fifty, Mehring wants nothing that white privilege in a black country can bring him. But the presence of a dead man, in a distant field of his 400-acre farm, asserts that Africa, in the end, is something a white man can't buy.

The Conservationist is a study of a man both reckless and calculating, who clings to the patterns that reassure him of his power to conserve his way of life.

'The author of this gravely beautiful book has transcended her considerable talent and produced one of those rare works of imaginative literature that command the special respect reserved for artistic daring and fulfilled ambition. Nadine Gordimer has earned herself a place among the few novelists who really matter. *The Conservationist* reads as if it had to be written.'

Paul Bailey, *Observer*

'This book makes practically every other novel I've reviewed in the past few years look like indulgent trifling . . . A novel of enormous power.'

Paul Theroux

Nadine Gordimer was born and lives in South Africa. Her writing has received numerous awards, including the Malaparte Prize in Italy, the Nelly Sachs Prize in Germany, and the Grand Aigle d'Or in France. In 1991 she was awarded the Nobel Prize for Literature.

THE CONSERVATIONIST

NADINE GORDIMER

JONATHAN CAPE
LONDON

First published in this edition in 1993

1 3 5 7 9 10 8 6 4 2

Prose quotations are from the Reverend Henry Callaway's *The
Religious System of the Amazulu*, dealing with Unkulunkulu, or the
Tradition of Creation: Amatonga, or Ancestor worship; Izinyanga
Zokubula, or Divination; and Abatakato, or Medical Magic and
Witchcraft, originally published by the Springdale Mission Press.
Acknowledgements are made to the facsimile edition published by
C. Struik (Pty) Ltd, Cape Town, 1970

Acknowledgements are made to Richard Shelton for permission to
quote part of his poem 'The Tattooed Desert', first published in *The
New Yorker Magazine*, © 1970 The New Yorker Magazine, Inc.,
and subsequently included in Mr Shelton's collection of poetry, *The
Tattooed Desert*, University of Pittsburgh Press, 1971

First published in the United Kingdom in this edition in 1993 by
Jonathan Cape
Random House, 20 Vauxhall Bridge Road, London SW1V 2SA

Random House Australia (Pty) Limited
20 Alfred Street, Milsons Point, Sydney,
New South Wales 2061, Australia

Random House New Zealand Limited
18 Poland Road, Glenfield,
Auckland 10, New Zealand

Random House South Africa (Pty) Limited
PO Box 337, Bergvlei, South Africa

Random House UK Limited Reg. No. 954009

A CIP catalogue record for this book
is available from the British Library

ISBN 0-224-03831-1

Printed and bound in Great Britain by
Mackays of Chatham PLC, Chatham, Kent

I must have been almost crazy
to start out alone like that on my bicycle
pedalling into the tropics carrying
a medicine for which no one had found
the disease and hoping
I would make it in time

I passed through a paper village under glass
where the explorers first found
silence and taught it to speak
where old men were sitting in front
of their houses killing sand without mercy

brothers I shouted to them
tell me who moved the river
where can I find a good place to drown

Richard Shelton, 'The Tattooed Desert'

P ale freckled eggs.
Swaying over the ruts to the gate of the third pasture, Sunday morning, the owner of the farm suddenly sees: a clutch of pale freckled eggs set out before a half-circle of children. Some are squatting; the one directly behind the eggs is cross-legged, like a vendor in a market. There is pride of ownership in that grin lifted shyly to the farmer's gaze. The eggs are arranged like marbles, the other children crowd round but you can tell they are not allowed to touch unless the cross-legged one gives permission. The bare soles, the backsides of the children have flattened a nest in the long dead grass for both eggs and children.

The emblem on the car's bonnet, itself made in the shape of a prismatic flash, scores his vision with a vertical–horizontal sword of dazzle. This is the place at which a child always appears, even if none has been in sight, racing across the field to open the gate for the car. But today the farmer puts on the brake, leaves the engine running, and gets out. One very young boy, wearing a jersey made long ago for much longer arms but too short to cover a naked belly, runs to the gate and stands there. The others all smile proudly round the eggs. The cross-legged one (wearing a woman's dress, but it may be a boy) puts out his hands over the eggs and gently shuffles them a little closer together, letting a couple of the outer ones roll back into his palms. The eggs are a creamy buff, thick-shelled, their glaze pored and lightly speckled, their shape more pointed than a hen's, and the palms of the small black hands are translucent-looking apricot-pink. There is no sound but awed, snuffling breathing through snotty noses.

He asks a question of the cross-legged one and there are giggles. He points down at the eggs but does not touch them, and asks again. The children don't understand the language. He goes on talking with many gestures. The cross-legged child puts its head on one side, smiling as if under the weight of praise, and cups one of the eggs from hand to hand.

7

Eleven pale freckled eggs. A whole clutch of guinea fowl eggs.

The baby at the gate is still waiting. The farmer goes back to the car, switches off the ignition, and walks away in the direction he has driven from. He has left the road and struck out across the veld, leaping the dry donga to land with a springy crackle on dead cosmos and khaki weed that bordered it last summer. Over the hard ground his thick rubber soles scuff worn scrubbing-brushes of closely-grazed dead grass. He is making for the compound; it is up beside the special paddock where the calves are kept at night. But the neat enclosure with oil drums cut in two to make feed troughs is empty; no one is about. From a line of rooms built of grey breeze-blocks the sound of radio music winds like audible smoke in the clean fine morning: it's Sunday. A woman appears from behind the lean-tos of wire and tin that obscure or are part of the habitations. When she sees him approach, she stands quite still, one of those figures with the sun in its eyes caught in a photograph. He asks where the chief herdsman is. Without moving, but grimacing as if she strains to hear, she makes an assenting noise and then answers. He repeats what she has said, to be sure, and she repeats the assenting noise, long and reassuring, like the grunting sigh of a satisfied sleeper. Her gaze steers his back in the direction she has indicated.

He is crossing a lucerne field. The last late cutting of autumn must have been made some time that week; although the shrivelled scraps that remain (dirt-rolls rubbed between finger and thumb, or bits of bust balloon) have lost their clover-shapes and faded to grey-green, underfoot they give out now and then a sweetish whiff of summer—breath from the mouth of a cow, or the mouth of a warm sleepy woman turned to in the morning. Involuntarily he draws it deep into his lungs and it disappears into a keener pleasure, the dry, cool and perfect air of a high-veld autumn which, shut up in the car that carried with it the shallow breath of the city, he has not yet taken. Not this morning, not for a week. As the air plunges in him, his gaze widens and sweeps: down along the river the willows have gone blond, not yet at their palest, combed out into bare strands, but still lightly spattered and delicately

8

streaked with yellowed leaves. Around them is a slight smudgy ambience, a mauvish-smoky blend between their outline and the bright air...

A whole clutch of guinea fowl eggs. Eleven. Soon there will be nothing left. In the country. The continent. The oceans, the sky.

Suddenly he sees the figure of the black man, Jacobus, making for *him*. He must have come out of the mealies on the other side of the road beyond the lucerne and is lunging across the field with the particular stiff-hipped hobble of a man who would be running if he were younger. But it's *he* who's looking for Jacobus; there's a mistake somewhere—how could the man know already that he is wanted? Some semaphore from the kraal? The farmer gives himself a little impatient, almost embarrassed snigger—and continues his own progress, measuredly, resisting the impulse to flag the man down with a wave of the hand, preparing in his mind what to say about the guinea fowl.

Although it is Sunday Jacobus is wearing the blue overalls supplied him and although there has been no rain and none can be expected for five months, he has on the rubber boots meant for wet weather. He's panting, naturally; but stops, as if there were a line drawn there, ten feet away from the farmer, and goes through the formalities of greeting, which include a hand-movement as if he had a hat to remove. The farmer approaches unhurriedly.
—Jacobus, I was coming to find you. How's everything?—
—No—everything it's all right. One calf he's borned Friday. But I try to phone you, yesterday night—
—Good, that's from the red cow, eh?—
—No, the red cow's she's not ready. This from that young one, that ones you buy last year from Pietersburg—
Each is talking fast, in the manner of a man who has something he wants to get on to say. There is a moment's pause to avoid collision; but of course the right of way is the farmer's. —Look, Jacobus, I've just been down at the third pasture, there—
—I'm try, try to phone last night, master—
But he has in his mind just exactly how to put it: —The children are taking guinea fowl eggs to play with. They must've

9

found a nest somewhere in the grass or the reeds and they've taken the eggs.—

—There by the river...you were there?— The chief herdsman's lips are drawn back from his decayed horse-teeth. He looks distressed, reluctant: yes, he is responsible for the children, some of them are probably his, and anyway, he is responsible for good order among the dependants of the farm workers and already the farmer has had occasion to complain about the number of dogs they are harbouring (a danger to the game birds).

—It's not as if they needed them for food. To eat. No, eh? You've got plenty of fowls. They're just piccanins and they don't know, but you must tell them, those eggs are not to play games with. If they find eggs in the veld they are not to touch them, you understand? Mustn't touch or move them, ever.— Of course he understands perfectly well but wears that uncomprehending and pained look to establish he's not to blame, he's burdened by the behaviour of all those other people down at the compound. Jacobus is not without sycophancy. —Master—he pleads—Master, it's very bad down there by the river. I'm try, try phone you yesterday night. What is happen there. The man is dead there. You see him.— And his hand, with an imperious forefinger shaking it, stabs the air, through chest-level of the farmer's body to the line of willows away down behind him.

—A man?—

—There—there— The herdsman draws back from his own hand as if to hold something at bay. His forehead is raised in three deep wrinkles.

—Somebody's died?—

The herdsman has the authority of dreadful knowledge. —Dead man. Solomon find it yesterday three o'clock.—

—Has something happened to one of the boys? What man?—

—No. Yes, we don't know who is it. Or what. Where he come to be dead here on this farm.—

—A strange man. Not one of our people?—

The herdsman's hands go out wide in exasperation. —No one can say who is that man.— And he begins to tell the story again: Solomon ran, it was three o'clock, he was bringing the cows back. —Yesterday night, myself I try sometime five time—he holds up his spread fingers and thumb—to phone you in town.—

—So what have you done?—

—Now when I'm see the car come just now I run from that side where the mealies are—

—But with the body?—

This time the jutting bearded chin as well as the forefinger indicate: —The man is *there*. You can see, still there, master, come I show you where is it.—

The herdsman stumps past. There is nothing for the farmer to do but follow. Why should he go to look at a dead man near the river? He could just as well telephone the police at once and leave it to the proper channels that exist to deal with such matters. It is not one of the farm workers. It is not anyone one knows. It is a sight that has no claim on him.

But the dead man is on his property. Now that the farmer has arrived the herdsman Jacobus has found the firmness and support of an interpretation of the event: his determined back in the blue overalls, collar standing away from slightly bent neck, is leading to the intruder. He is doing his duty and his employer has a duty to follow him.

They go back over the lucerne field and down the road. A beautiful morning, already coming into that calm fullness of peace and warmth that will last until the sun goes, without the summer's climax of rising heat. Ten o'clock as warm as midday will be, and midday will be no hotter than three in the afternoon. The pause between two seasons; days as complete and perfectly contained as an egg.

The children are gone; the place where they were might just as well have been made by a cow lying down in the grass. A coyly persuasive voice blaring a commercial jingle is coming out of the sky from the direction of the compound...YOUR GIANT FREE... SEND YOUR NAME AND ADDRESS TODAY...

The two men have passed the stationary car and almost reached the gate. The tiny boy in the jersey bursts from nowhere but is disconcerted at the sight of the herdsman. Hanging from his plump

II

pubis his little dusty penis is the trunk of a toy elephant. He stands watching while Jacobus unhooks the loop of rusty wire that encloses the pole of the barbed fence and the pole of the gate, and the gate, which is just a freed section of the fence, falls flat.

The road has ruts and incised patterns from the rains of seasons long past, petrified, more like striations made over millennia in rock than marks of wheels, boots and hooves in live earth. There was no rain this summer but even in a drought year the vlei provides some moisture on this farm and the third pasture has patches where a skin of greenish wet has glazed, dried, lifted, cracked, each irregular segment curling at the edges. The farmer's steps bite down on them with the crispness of biscuits between teeth. The river's too low to be seen or heard; as the slope quickens his pace through momentum, there is a whiff in the dry air (the way the breath of clover came). A whiff—the laundry smell of soap scum. The river's there, somewhere, all right.

And the dead man. They are jogging down to the willows and the stretch of reeds, broken, criss-crossed, tangled, collapsed against themselves, stockaded all the way to the other side—which is the rise of the ground again and someone else's land. When it is not a drought year it is impossible to get across and the cows stand in midstream and gaze stupidly towards islands of hidden grass in there that they scent but cannot reach. The half-naked willows trail the tips of whips an inch or two above the threadbare picnic spot, faintly green, with its shallow cairn of stone filled with ashes among which the torn label off a beer carton may still be read by the eye that supplies the familiar missing letters. With the toe of his rubber sole the farmer turns, as he goes, a glint where the bed of the river has dropped back; someone lost a ring here, last summer. The blue overalls are leading through dead thistle, past occasional swirls of those swamp lilies with long ragged leaves arranged in a mandala, among the amphibian tails of a patch of tough reeds that keep their black-green flexibility all winter. The two men plunge clumsy as cattle into the dry reeds, exploding a little swarm of minute birds, taking against their faces the spider-web sensation of floss broken loose, by their passage, from seeding bulrush heads. There lying on his face is the man.

12

The farmer almost ran on to him without seeing: he was close behind his herdsman and plunging along doggedly.

The dead man.

Jacobus is walking around the sight. There is a well-trampled clearing about it—the whole compound must have been down to have a look. —How is happen. What is happen here. Why he come down here on this farm. What is happen.— He talks on, making a kind of lament of indignation. The farmer is circling the sight, too, with his eyes.

One of them. The face is in the tacky mud; the tiny brown ears, the fine, felted hair, a fold or roll where it meets the back of the neck, because whoever he was, he wasn't thin. A brown pin-stripe jacket, only the stubs of button-shanks left on the second-hand sleeves, that must once have been part of some white businessman's suit. Smart tight pants and a wide belt of fake snakeskin with fancy stitching. He might be drunk, lying there, this city slicker. But his out-dated 'stylish' shoes are on dead, twisted feet, turned in stiff and brokenly as he was flung down. Except for the face, which struck a small break or pocket between clumps, his body isn't actually on the earth at all, but held slightly above it on a nest of reeds it has flattened, made for itself. From here, the only injury he shows is a long red scratch, obviously made by a sharp broken reed catching his neck.

The farmer bats at something clinging at his face. No mosquitoes now; bulrush gossamer. —He was dead when Solomon found him?—

—Dead, dead, finish.— The herdsman walks over delicately towards the object and bending, turns his face back at his employer and says confidentially, rather as if he had been listening —And now already is beginning to be little bit... He wrinkles his nose, exposing the dirty horse-teeth.

The farmer breathes quite normally, he does not take in the deep breaths of dry clear air that he did up on the lucerne field, but he does not reduce his intake either. There is nothing, really nothing; whereas, up there, that sweetish whiff.

—You'd better not touch him. You're sure nobody here knows him? It's got nothing to do with any of you here?— He looks very

13

deeply at his herdsman, lowering his head and hooding his eyebrows over his eyes.

Jacobus puts a hand dramatically on his own breast, where a stained vest shows through the unbuttoned overalls. He swings his head slowly from side to side. —Nobody can know this man. Nothing for this man. This is people from there—there— He points that same accusing finger away in the direction of the farm's southern boundary.

The skin of the palm of a hand is too insensitive to detect the gossamer but still it clings. The farmer projects his lower lip and blows sharply, upwards over his face. And now he notices a single fly, one of the lingering, persistent kind, hovering just above the neat brown ear down there. The fly is on the side to which the head is fractionally turned, although it is full-face in the mud, the side on which the mouth must be close to being exposed. The fly hovers and lands, hovers and lands, unmolested.

—Just leave it as it is. The police must come.—

—Ye-e-es Master—the herdsman says, long-drawn-out in sympathy for the responsibility which is no longer his. —Ye-e-es …is much better.—

There is a moment's pause. The fly looks as if it ought to be buzzing but cannot be heard. There is the customary silence down here among the reeds, broken by the rifle-crack (so it sounds, in contrast) of a dry stalk snapped by the movement of some unseen bird. The seething of the wind through the green reeds in summer is seasonal.

They turn and thrash back the way they have come, leaving the man. Behind them he is lying alone on his face.

The farmer takes the car to get up to the farmhouse and Jacobus accompanies him, sitting carefully with feet planked flat on the carpeted floor and curled hands together on neat knees—he has the house-keys, anyway, so that he can always get in to telephone if necessary. The house is closed up because no one lives there or uses it during the week. They enter through the kitchen door and the farmer goes straight to the telephone in the living-room and turns the little crank beside the receiver. The party line is busy and while he waits he frees from the thin tacky mud on his soles the slivers of dry reed that are stuck in it. He prises one sole against

14

the other and the mud wrinkles and blobs, like droppings, to the shiny linoleum patterned with orange and brown roses. The table is laid ready with hardware for a meal, under a net weighted at the hem with coloured beads; an authoritative refrigerator, placed across the angle of a corner, hums to itself. The ring that he is waiting for makes him start. The line is free now and the exchange connects him with the police station.

He always talks the white man's other language to officials; he is speaking in Afrikaans. —Listen, Mehring here, from Vleiplaats, the Katbosrand Road. You must send someone. There's a dead man been found on my farm. Down in the vlei. Looks as if he's been dumped there.—

There is a blowing noise, abrupt, at the other end, air is expelled in good-natured exasperation. The voice addresses him as if he were an old friend:—Man...on Sunday...where'm I going to get someone? The van's out on patrol at the location. I'm alone here, myself. It's a Bantu, ay?—

—Yes. The body's lying in the reeds.—

—Your boys have a fight or what?—

—It's a stranger. None of my boys knows who it is.—

The voice laughs. —Yes, they're scared, they'll always say they don't know. Was it a knife-fight I suppose?—

—I tell you I've no idea. I don't want to mess about with the body. You must send someone.—

—Hell, I don't know what I'm going to do about that. I'm only myself, here. The van's in the location...I'll send tomorrow morning.—

—But this body was found yesterday, it's been lying there twenty-four hours already.—

—What can I do, sir? Man, I'm alone here!—

—Why can't you get hold of some other police station? Let them send someone.—

—Can't do that. This's my district.—

—Well what am I to do about a dead body on my property? The man may have been murdered. It's obvious he's been knocked on the head or something, and dumped. You can see from his shoes he didn't walk a step in that vlei.—

—There's injuries on the head or where?—

—I've told you, that's your affair. I don't want my boys handling someone who's been murdered. I don't want any trouble afterwards about this business. You must get a man here today, Sergeant.—

—First thing in the morning. There won't be any trouble for you, don't worry. You're there by the vlei, just near the location, ay? It comes from there, all right, they're a terrible lot of kaffirs, we're used to that lot... —

The farmer replaces the receiver and says in English, *Christ almighty*; and snorts a laugh, softly, so that Jacobus shall not hear.

The herdsman is waiting in the kitchen. —They'll come early tomorrow. I've told them everything. Just keep people away. And dogs. See that no dogs go down there.— The herdsman doesn't react at all although he has no doubt thought the farmer didn't know that the dogs which were supposed to be banished from the compound have quietly reappeared again, not the same individual animals, perhaps, but as a genus.

—Excuse, my master—he indicates that he wants to pass before him into the living-room and tramps, tip-toeing almost, across to a piece of furniture that must have once featured as the pride of a dining-room 'suite' but is now used as bar (a locked cupboard to which Jacobus has not got a key) and also repository (unlocked drawers) for farm documents, and pulling out one of the stiff drawers by its fancy gilt handle, feels surely under the feed bills tossed there. He has found what he apparently had hidden for safekeeping: he brings in the bowl of his palms a huge, black-dialled watch with a broad metal strap, and a pair of sunglasses with a cracked right lens. He waits, indicating by the pause that his employer must put out his hand to receive, and formally gives over the property. —From him?— And the herdsman nods heavily.

—All right, Jacobus.—

—All right, master.—

—Send Alina up about one to make some me lunch, eh—he calls after him.

So they have touched the thing, lifted the face. Of course the dark glasses might have been in a pocket. No money. Not surprising; these Friday murders are for money, what else. Jacobus took the objects (the Japanese-made steel watch is the kind of stolen goods black men offer surreptitiously for sale on street corners) into safekeeping to show that the people here've got nothing to do with the whole business.

Going to the drawer Jacobus has just shut, he finds a foolscap window-envelope, already franked, that has carried some circular. The watch with its flexible steel-mesh strap wrapped close fits in easily, but the glasses prevent the flap from closing. He doubles a rubber band over his fingers and stretches it to secure envelope and contents. He writes on it, Watch and Glasses, property of dead man. He adds, For the Police, and places the envelope prominently on the table, on top of the net, then moves it to the kitchen, putting it on the draining-board of the sink where it cannot fail to be in the line of vision as one walks into the house.

Outside the kitchen door he distends his nostrils distastefully at the smell of duckshit and three or four pallid kittens whose fur is thin as the bits of duckdown that roll softly about in invisible currents of air, run from the threatening column of his body. *Psspsspss* he calls, but they cower and one even hisses. He strides away, past the barn, the paddock where the cows about to calve stand hugely in company, and the tiny paddock where the old bull, used less and less now, with the convenience of artificial insemination available, is always alone, and he continues by way of the mealie fields the long walk around the farm, on a perfect Sunday morning, he was about to begin when he drove down to the third pasture.

The matter of the guinea fowl eggs has not been settled. He's conscious of this as he walks because he knows it's no good allowing such things to pass. They must be dealt with. Eleven eggs. It would have been useless to put them under the Black Orpingtons; they must have been cold already. A red-legged partridge is taking a dust bath where it thinks it won't be spied, at the end of a row of mealies reaped and ready to be uprooted. But there are no guinea fowl feeding down in the far field where they usually come. Those bloody dogs; their dogs have probably been killing them off all summer. Eleven freckled eggs, pointed, so different from hens' eggs made to lie in the standard depressions of plastic trays, in

17

dozens, subject to seasonal price-fluctuation. Soon there will be nothing left. No good thinking about it; put a stop to it. The hands of the child round the freckled eggs were the colour of the under-side of an empty tortoiseshell held up to the light. The mealies are nearly all reaped, the stalks stooked in pyramids with dry plumy apexes, the leaves peeling tattered. Distance comes back with these reaped fields, the ploughed earth stretching away in fan-shaped ridges to its own horizon; the farm grows in size in winter, just as in summer as the mealies grow taller and thicker the horizon closes in, diminishes the farm until it is a series of corridors between walls of stiff green higher than his head. In a good year. If there is going to be a good year, again. A tandem harrow has been left out to rust (no rain, but still, the dew can be heavy). Now is the time to clear the canker weed that plagues this part of the field, near the eucalyptus trees which have made a remarkable recovery, he can scarcely notice, for new branches, the stumps where they were always chopping them for firewood until a few years ago.

Although he had no sign of it when he set out this morning, a Saturday night headache is now causing pressure on the bridge of his nose; closing his eyes against the light he pinches the bone there between thumb and finger. He feels pleasantly, specifically, thirsty for water. He makes for the windmill near an old stone outbuilding. The cement round the borehole installation is new and the blades of the windmill are still shiny. He puts his head sideways to the stiff tap and the water sizzles, neither warm nor cold, into his mouth. The windmill is not turning and he releases the chain and arm that brake it in order to set it going, but although it noses creakily, it does not begin to turn because there is no wind today, the air is still, it is a perfect autumn day. He sets the brake again carefully.

A little after one, passing the servant Alina's room beside the fowl-run, on his way up to the house, he sees Jacobus talking to her. He and the herdsman do not seem to see each other because they have seen each other before and no greeting is exchanged. He calls out: —You'd better take something—to put over, down there. (His head jerks towards the river.) A tarpaulin. Or sacks.—

18

Mehring was not a farmer although there was farming blood somewhere, no doubt. Many well-off city men buy themselves farms at a certain stage in their careers—the losses are deductible from income tax and this fact coincides with something less tangible it's understood they can now afford to indulge: a hankering to make contact with the land. It seems to be bred of making money in industry. And it is tacitly regarded as commendable, a sign of having remained fully human and capable of enjoying the simple things of life that poorer men can no longer afford. As the chairman of an investment fund, of which Mehring was a director, said—You get a hell of a kick out of a place like that, don't you? I know that when I go off Friday afternoon and find a nice field of my hay being baled, I haven't a worry in the world. Of course, if hail arrives and batters the young mealies, the end of the bloody world's come— A special boyish grin reserved for the subject of farming showed how remote that disaster was from any reality that might originate in the boardroom in which they were chatting.

Mehring went to his farm almost every weekend. If he had put his mind to it and if he had had more time, he knew he could have made it pay, just the same as anything else. But then there would be an end to tax relief, anyway; it would be absurd. Yet land must not be misused or wasted and he had reclaimed these 400 acres of veld, fields and vlei that he had probably paid a bit too much for, a few years ago. It was weed-choked, neglected then (a dirty piece of land, agriculturally speaking), yet beautiful—someone who was with him the first time he went to look at it had said: —Why not just buy it and leave it as it is?—

He himself was not a sucker for city romanticism and he made sure the rot was stopped, the place cleaned up. A farm is not beautiful unless it is productive. Reasonable productivity prevailed; he had to keep half an eye (all he could spare) on everything, all the time, to achieve even that much, and of course he had made it his business to pick up a working knowledge of husbandry, animal and crop, so that he couldn't easily be hoodwinked by his people there and could plan farming operations with some authority. It was amazing what you could learn if you were accustomed to digesting new facts and coping with new situations, as one had to do in industry. And as in the city, you made use of other people—the farmers round about were professionals:—I'm not proud, I'll go over and sit on the stoep and pick their Boer brains if I need to.—

He took friends to the farm sometimes at weekends. They said what a marvellous idea, we adore to get out, get away, and—when they debouched from their cars (the children who opened the gate at the third pasture the richer by a windfall of cents)—how lovely, how lucky, how sensible to have a place like this to get away to. There would be a sheep roasted on a spit rigged up over the pit and turned by one of the boys from the compound, and bales of hay to sit on, lugged down on instructions over the phone to Jacobus. The wine was secured to keep cool in the river among the reeds at the guests' backs and the picnic spot was carefully chosen to give the best view of the Katbosrand, a range of hills on the north horizon, over which, once or twice at least in a lazy Sunday, a huge jet-plane, travelling so high it seemed slower than the flights of egrets or Hadeda ibis, would appear to be released and sail across the upper sky on its way to Europe. To people like those on the grass drinking wine and eating crisp lamb from their fingers, the sight brought a sensation of freedom: not the freedom associated with a great plane by those who long to travel, but the freedom of being down there on the earth, out in the fresh air of this place-to-get-away-to from the context of stuffy airports, duty-free drinks and cutlery cauled in cellophane.

Sometimes he went out alone on weekdays. It was an easy forty-minute drive at most, even through the five o'clock traffic. Once out of the city, there was another industrial area to get through, one of those Transvaal villages whose mealie fields had disappeared into factories with landscaped gardens, and whose main street was now built up with supermarkets, discount appliance stores and steak houses, but it was useful to be able to stop for cigarettes or delicatessen at the Greek's on the way. After that it was a clear run beside the railway until you reached the African location, where they were inclined to come hurtling out of the gates—big, overloaded buses, taxis, lorryloads of people, bicycles and children all over the show. The location was endless; the high wire fence, sloping inwards and barbed at the top, cornered the turn-off from the tarred main road and followed the dirt one. The rows of houses were not yet built up to the boundary. In fact, on this side, they were still far across the veld, ridge after ridge of the prototype shelter that is the first thing little children draw: a box with a door in the middle, a window on either side, smoke coming out of a chimney. In the evenings and early mornings this smoke lay over them thick and softly; from one of those planes, one wouldn't be able to make out the place at all. Then the road did a dog-leg away from the location. In the angle, old Labuschagne and his sons had their house; their cowsheds, fields and labourers' shacks spread on both sides of the road. There was a windmill like a winged bird they never repaired. The next landmark he would tell his Sunday lunch-party visitors to look out for was the Indian store about two miles up, on the left. An enamel sign on the roof advertising a brand of soft drink long off the market, a wire stand with potatoes and withered cabbages on the verandah. From that point on, you could see the farm, see the mile of willows (people remarked that it would have been worth buying for the willows alone) in the declivity between two gently rising stretches of land, see the Katbosrand in the distance, see the house nobody lived in. No one would believe (they also said) the city was only twenty-five miles away, and that vast location just behind you. Peace. The upland serenity of high altitude, the openness of grassland without indigenous bush or trees; the greening, yellowing or silver-browning that prevailed, according to season. A landscape without theatricals except when it became an arena for summer storms, a landscape without any picture-postcard features (photographs generally were unsuccessful in conveying it)—a typical Transvaal landscape, that you either find dull and low-keyed or prefer to all others (they said).

The farmer and Jacobus and young Izak, who is good only for holding things steady, are repairing the pump. Jacobus said over the telephone, yes, the police had come—but now something was wrong with the pump and the Japanese radishes that were being grown for winter cattle-feed were drying up. Jacobus is pretty conscientious, really; he was even able with some difficulty to spell out the name and number of the new part needed for the repair.

It is dark and dank in the pump-house near the eucalpytus trees and they work in the intimacy of light from a gas-lamp, exchanging nothing more than instructions and occasional grunts of effort as a bolt refuses to yield. They emerge holding filthy hands away from their bodies, the afternoon sun touches their faces, and the rock pigeons that the farmer sometimes amuses himself by shooting are beginning to fly.

—So there was no trouble? On Monday?—

—Yes, was no trouble. They say to me I know who is this man. I say—me, I don't know who is, the master tell you nobody here can know. The master tell you already. Then they ask me, who is find him? And I bring Solomon and they ask him, same, same, you know who is this man? Solomon he say, no, I can't know. I give them that things in the kitchen, I tell them if you want you can phone master—(Mehring nods in approval towards his boots)— you can phone master in town.—

—Nobody phoned.—

—No, I know. Then the white policeman he go down there with the van.—

—Good. So they took everything away. And they didn't say you must come to the police station—he makes the gesture of signing a statement—that's fine.—

Jacobus stops, with the effect of making the farmer turn to him. Jacobus is frowning, he stands a moment forgetting to walk on.

22

—He's *there, there*. The white one send the native policeman to find me in my house, he's ask for spade. They dig and they put him in, down there where we was, Sunday. Then they go away. They don't see me, they don't tell me nothing.—

As so often in dealing with petty officialdom, again the first reaction is derisive. Good God, should one laugh, or get angry? Does one want to bang their thick heads together or hand it to them—a shining example of the splendid pragmatism of laziness, the cunning of stupidity, cutting through red tape with the dirty penknife idly used to take the black line from beneath fingernails? The supremacy of ignorance, confusing audacity with authority, the policeman in khaki gaberdine with the blindfold lady? Who do they think they are? As a story (already, at once, it has become a story to be told over drinks and at the dinner-table) really it is in the same class as the chestnut about the dead horse dragged from Commissioner Street to Market Street because the policeman couldn't spell Commissioner.

Who the hell do they think they are? He *is* angry; his farm isn't a public cemetery. If they don't want to be bothered to find out who killed the man, let them at least dispose of him themselves. But no. Just dig a hole and shovel him in, out of the way. On someone else's property. It's no good phoning that idiot. Better go to police headquarters at John Vorster Square and see someone responsible.

The days are getting shorter. Giant shadows of the eucalyptus lie felled across the road. Now that the sun is down a cellar-chill comes up from the river, there is no stored warmth from the day to hold it back. He opens the gate of the third pasture (the children do not usually appear for people on foot) and goes down under the yellowed willows. He pictures the place as very near, to be picked out from the banks of the picnic spot, almost. But light is going and he doesn't find it. The cows trample everywhere; there are so many places flattened among reeds and bulrushes leaning this way and that. The strong, shrill, sleepy chattering of the weaver-birds surrounds him. He hears his own crashing footfalls as if he were being followed. A pair of partridge hear them, too, and stop, necks lifted, far up in the field where they have been pecking their way slowly on their way to roost. Up at the kraal, Jacobus and Phineas are surrounded by the young calves in their paddock, and he stands leaning on the wooden crossbars a while, stared at by small stupid creatures with their legs planted defensively and wide-spaced eyes glinting backwards. One of them has cut itself on barbed wire and Jacobus is anointing the place with salve. He swings his legs over the palings and helps hold the little beast down. The white faces and other varicoloured red markings of the calves make a new pattern of blotches of light and dark in place of the fading outlines of their bodies. He takes the opportunity to speak to Jacobus about guinea fowl eggs, emphasizing that he has seen very few of the birds on the farm recently. Jacobus stands up, hands on his hips, done with the calf, and laughs, assuring expansively—Plenty, plenty guinea fowls here on the farm, early in the morning I'm see them where we plough those mealies, every morning...

But *he* isn't there early in the morning. Or rarely.

Of course—no investigation means no time wasted for Jacobus and Solomon at the police station, no policemen sticking their noses into the kraal bothering people and asking questions. There is always some poor devil whose pass is non-existent or irregular whose illegal status would come to light if the police started kicking over stones. And if there were to be a court case, the next thing, he'd find himself dragged in to give evidence, since this is his property—a day or even days wasted hanging about the bloody magistrates' courts waiting to say he knows nothing. The poor devil—that other poor devil—is dead anyway. In that enormous location these things happen every day, or rather every weekend, everyone knows it, they are murdered for their Friday pay-packets or they stab each other after drinking. A hundred and fifty thousand of them living there. He opens a can of beer up at the house before going back to town and while he drinks it telephones the sergeant at the local police station again, after all.

—What's the idea? Is my farm a dumping-ground or cemetery or what?— It is no good talking to them on any other level.

—No man—it was just a—you know, for health and that—it's not healthy to leave a body lying there, and the van from the

24

mortuary couldn't come. We'll fetch him properly, maybe even tomorrow.—

—Before the weekend?—

—Oh yes, don't worry, it's just the mortuary van couldn't...—

He does not want to hear the whole explanation over again. He has to get back to the city and change before going to one of the dinner parties for which, as a man in the age group of married friends but restored to bachelor status for some years now, he is much in demand.

So close by! You must be pretty vulnerable to stock-theft?—
—Oh yes. There's a high fence all round to keep them from
getting in and out except through the location gates, but
there're great big gaps where they cut the wire and come out at
night. I haven't lost anything yet but an old chap, De Beer,
reckons to lose a couple of head a year. In spite of his dogs. And
his reputation for shooting on sight.—

—Ughhh—fancy digging someone up again.—

—It's too beautiful—haven't you ever been out there?— She
was a good-looking woman whom he had known for fifteen years.
She always seated him on her right at her dinner-table. Now she
asserted long friendship through making clear to others her
family's familiarity with his possessions and way of life.

—Ah well—there are possible advantages, whatever happens.
There's a rumour they're going to establish a township for
Coloureds, adjacent to the location, out towards the Katbosrand
side.—

—Oh no! How ghastly— She put her palm down a moment on
his wrist, just as he was breaking off a piece of the roll on his side-
plate.

—Not at all, I'll be expropriated, sell to the government, make
a fortune. And that'll be the one and only success in my farming
operations!— While they laughed, he popped the bit of bread into
his mouth, and as he did so, caught on the back of his hand the
perfume of the woman beside him. She dutifully divided her
attention between the men on her left and right, but when it was
his turn she talked in a low voice, with many questioning murmurs,
as if words were not always necessary, and a special shy but open
gaze in her blue-green eyes. He knew that look; was surprised he
had not noticed it before, because it was obvious that it must have
been there, for him, on other occasions, come to think of it.
We've been aware of each other a long time, it said. We'll soon be
old, or dead. But he, who was not accustomed to passing over such

26

opportunities whenever or however they presented themselves, felt nothing of his usual swift reaction to pounce in discreet response. A little later, when her daughter, whom he used to fetch to play with his son a few years ago, and who was now sixteen or seventeen, came to give him the good-night kiss on the cheek that was the relic of childhood politeness, he made a discovery. It was she, among the females present, whom he wanted to meet and undress in a hotel room.

The breeze-block quarters that had been put up on this farm kept the rain out better than the mud-houses the people were used to making for themselves, but they were colder in winter. They had begun to be cold already, as soon as the sun went down; the coughing of the children went on incessantly and ignored inside, while the men squatted or stood with hunched shoulders round the brazier. Jacobus had made his own arrangements: did not live down at the compound at all, actually—he and his wife and youngest child occupied Alina's room in what was supposed to be the domestic servant's quarters near the house, while Alina and her man had fixed up the shed as their room—but Jacobus came to the compound often for the company, in the evenings, as well as going back and forth for one reason or another, during the day. He was speaking of a dog, the need of a fierce dog to keep intruders off the farm at night. —Like the India's dogs at the shop. Something everybody will be afraid of. I'll keep it chained up all day, then it will get mad at night. That's the way to have a good dog.—

—Ask him.—

—I told you—many times, I've said it to him.—

—What can you do then.—

—Many times. You know how it is. You say one thing, and they just use it to say another. He looks past my face: how many dogs already on this farm? They are killing everything, the compound dogs. So I tell him it's not true about the dogs. Then he says, then people must be putting traps for the birds, where have the birds gone?—

—Even the eggs—someone said.

Jacobus made a soft, long ah-sound of exasperation and defeated contest, and the others made similar sounds, a kind of laughter. He clicked his tongue against his palate in a glottal snap-of-the-fingers.

—Even the eggs...—

But Jacobus did not respond and so the laughter died; he could not encourage this talk too much—he was himself half on the side

28

of the authority it mocked, he earned his privileges by that authority and also protected *them* against its source. He had told the women to warn the children not to collect eggs where they could be seen; he had remarked to *him* that there were plenty of guinea fowl about if you had to be up at work early enough to see them.

—He won't bring—(a gesture of the head to indicate the police) —from town?—

Jacobus grinned out of inside knowledge. —He doesn't like those Dutchmen!—

The man called Witbooi who had come from Rhodesia illegally seventeen years before rocked slightly, reassured, on his haunches. If he had no pass, it was not that he, whose real name was Simon Somazhegwana, had no papers: in the plastic fertilizer bag that held his clothes and possessions there was an old wallet full of paper—expired work permits from areas where he had been endorsed out, pages torn from school exercise books inscribed *Bearer, Witbooi, is a good boy*...TO WHOM IT MAY CONCERN... *This is to say that Bearer, native Witbooi*...with the barely-literate signatures of white housewives and farmers as reference. He produced them to employer after employer, over the years, preserving them carefully against a day when they would meet the pair of eyes in which surely they would find validity, like that of any other document given out by white people; like that of the bits of paper issued officially at the pass office.

The farm people bought their paraffin, matches, tobacco, soap, tea and sugar from the Indian store at the turn-off of the farm road; the weekly mealie-meal ration was part of their wages, doled out from sacks by Jacobus. The children made expeditions to the store when they had cents from the gate to buy sweets with, or found bottles on which they could claim the deposit. Jacobus, his own master most of the week, used the tractor to drive down when he pleased.

—What's going on at your place there?—

—Why? Why 'what is going on'?— Jacobus did not talk to the Indian as he did to a white man, nor as he would to one of his own people.

The Indians behind the counter were three: the old one—the

father's father—the father himself, who had spoken, and a slim young son. The old one had a beard, bluish lips on which two worn brown teeth rested, wore a round white cap, and sat all day on a kitchen chair. The full contours of the middle one's face shone with stubble and he was always in shirtsleeves; this son (there were several) wore tight bell-bottom pants and jackets with a back vent or lurex thread—sometimes farm workers would touch and marvel, half joking: —Where you buy this? In town?— On Saturdays and Sundays Indians still younger served—schoolboys of the family, who began to help in the shop as soon as they were old enough to distinguish the different denominations of coins.

—You know. You've been fighting there.— The challenging, aggressive way of speaking was something that meant nothing to farm people; a convention of the barriers between them and the Indian proprietor; they were used to him.

Jacobus fell in with the rules of the game. —Me! I didn't do nothing. Me, fight! What for?—

—Come on, man! The police was there on your farm. Someone killed there.—

—The police was here? To you?— Jacobus screwed up one eye, leant forward just a little across the counter.

—They came here, they came here. They talked to my boys— my boys don't know anything, what do they know about your place.—

The Indians had blacks of their own working for them.

—No, they don't know our place. That's right.—

The Indian threw the money into the till expertly, banged it shut with a shrill ring. —You make trouble down there, you bring the police to make trouble for everybody.—

—We don't make.— Jacobus shook an open hand in the direction of the location. —The people *there*—

—Trouble for everybody!—

But the old man did not open his half-closed eyes or move his folded hands whose right index finger twitched all the time like a winged insect come to rest, and the young one leant S-shaped against the counter and seemed not to have been listening.

—No, everything it's all right. That man he was dead, the police

30

come and take it away. Finish. Is not our trouble.— The 'our' took in the shopkeeper, his *ménage*, Jacobus himself, and the farm people.

The shopkeeper cut off his attention abruptly; already his hand with the little red-eyed ring had put on his glasses and taken up the suppliers' invoices he was checking. His lips moved sternly over words: 12 only gents' plastic watch straps. The shop was empty after Jacobus's clumsy shape sauntered out of the light of the door and the old man and the young watched their son and father keeping vigil, as it was necessary to do over everything and everyone with whom they had dealings.

The Indians had a house snugly contiguous with the store, with beans trained up the walls and marigolds behind the barbed-wire fence. Except for the façade of the store the ten-foot fence enclosed their whole property, right around the partly-bricked-in yard, taking in the tin hovels supported by the yard wall down where their blacks lived. The fence was shored up here and there with sheets of corrugated iron and even an old bedstead—the blacks had built it for their employers, to keep blacks out. The two great dogs—cross-breeds of the white men's favourite watch-dogs, Alsatian and Dobermann Pinscher—who were chained to runners along the fence had worn a shallow ditch inside the length of it, bounding, racing and snarling at everything that passed within their hearing and vision. They barked now at an approach, but when Jacobus came up to the high gate, stopped, claws splayed tensely in the dust, sniffed. He stood a moment or two, his fingers hooked through the diamond mesh, exchanging greetings with a woman who was pumping water from the well. The dogs stood by with swinging tails while the woman let him in and she and he strolled over to the tin houses. He and the people there greeted each other with 'brother', 'sister', 'mother', 'uncle', a grammar of intimacy that went with their language; one of the women was doing the Indians' washing, a visitor was eating half a loaf and drinking a bottle of Coke, an old man as well as several other women were home. The doors of the houses were open and gave directly onto the dirt, the broken chairs, empty bottles and cooking pots proclaiming the outside as much a living area as the inside.

Perhaps in response to a message run by a child, one of the men who worked in the store appeared, too. He and Jacobus had not seen each other when Jacobus was in the store. His hands were dusty with some whitish grit: he had been at the back, weighing mealie-meal into paper bags.

—They were here?—

—The same day.—

Jacobus was comfortable on an up-ended box. He was offered, but did not take, a pinch of snuff from the old man's tin. —What's he so worried about? Do you ever hear that an India kills people.—

—Frightened about the shop. You know they're not supposed to stay here, this place is for white people. The Indians can't have a shop here. They pay.— He put out his black hand, pollened with white, and rubbed the thumb along the close-held fingers. He smiled at the thought that this was something Jacobus didn't know.

The old man said—Yes, plenty of money, these people. They pay and then everyone is quiet. Nice and quiet. They leave them alone. No trouble. No trouble and they won't come, they won't ask anything if it's Indians or a white man in the shop.—

Jacobus smoked the half cigarette he had taken from his pocket; exclaimed amusedly, a comment to himself on the exchange he had had in the shop, and then was distracted by the visitor's new bicycle that was lying beside him: how much did a bicycle like that cost, nowadays? It was a third as much again as Jacobus had paid for the same make some years ago, before he had begun to use the tractor for transport. They talked of money; it led, inevitably, to talk of work. Someone's relative working on a farm round about had been told to go—that was how dismissal happened and no one questioned the bluntness any more than the purpose of mentioning the matter to Jacobus.

—We don't need anybody.—

But they knew Jacobus was the boss of the show, he ran that farm while the white man lived in town. —All right, tell him to come. But not Sunday. Before Sunday or after Sunday. I don't know— perhaps I can... It's nearly winter, there's not so much work, you

32

know. Perhaps I can say...I can tell him I need another boy for the cows.—

A woman who had not spoken turned out to be the man's wife: Hallo, sister, hallo, brother. —She's staying here, but she can't stay—someone said. One of her children carried the baby of the family like a hump on its back. The baby's hair was reddish, the usual symptom of nutritional deficiency when infants become too old to be satisfied by the breast and are given mealie porridge instead. It was crying and the child joggled it until its yelling head rolled. Children followed Jacobus through the gate and climbed on to the tractor but he chased them off and they watched him drive away at the majestic pace of the iron caterpillar, laughing, pummelling each other, falling about in the dust.

I pray for corn, that many people may come to this village of yours and make a noise, and glorify you.

Mehring read in the paper how hippos were aborting their foetuses in dried-up pools. It was the fourth (fifth?) year of drought. Of course, it didn't affect him; the river, if reduced in volume, was perpetual, fed by an underground source. The farm didn't depend on surface water. He didn't depend on the farm. He would have to buy a considerable amount of supplementary feed for the cattle, but that could all go down as a tax loss.

He has just flown to Japan for a week; his frequent travels are of the kind where luggage consists of a couple of new shirts and whole files of papers to be studied on the plane. There seldom is time—chance—for any pleasure. A dinner with the Japanese or Germans or Canadians and their wives is part of the business schedule. They all have boats or summer places about which, as a change from base metals, it is protocol to talk over food and drink. —I'm not in the yacht-owning class, I'm afraid (it was charming of him to say). I have my bit of veld and my few cows. And that's all I want.—

In Africa! A farm in Africa! How he must love Africa. And were there any wild animals there?

A week's absence in Japan finds everything just as it was. Past the location entrance, the lurching buses and second-class taxis are a menace, and the location people wait for them in the litter of beer cartons and orange peel, women sitting on their bundles, the men dolled up and full of drink. The children are spending the day picking over the dirt on the stretch of open veld opposite that is used as rubbish dump. Because it's Sunday, the Indians are on the verandah of their house, even the women in their pink and yellow trousers and tunics. Poor bloody chained dogs still racing up and down; the blacks from the farm trudging or zig-zagging on bicycles along the dirt road. The man in the tatters of dungarees who skips aside and stands at something between a bow and attention, lifting a purple knitted cap in greeting, doesn't know him: just had a few too many.

They are banging away at their drums somewhere over the river.

36

The usual beer-drinks. But his own, up at the kraal, are pretty quiet. The thudding and distant shouts are no more than a smudge on the perfect silence that stretches to his horizon, which is first of all, while he walks, the rise of the next farm beyond the river, and then, when he lies down at the willows, the maze of broken reeds. The willows dangle at him from the sky. A wan yellowed leaf taken between thumb and forefinger is pliable, like thin kid-skin. He rolls onto his belly and, remembering a point he ought to have made clear in Tokyo, making a mental note to make a note of it (there is a tape-recorder in his briefcase but the briefcase is in the car) his presence on the grass becomes momentarily a demonstration, as if those people on the other side of the world were smilingly seeing it for themselves: I have my bit of veld and my cows... Perhaps he has dozed; he suddenly—out of blackness, blankness—is aware of breathing intimately into the earth. Wisps and shreds of grass or leaf stir there. It is the air from his nostrils that moves them. To his half-open eye the hairs that border it and the filaments of dead grass are one.

There is sand on his lip.

For a moment he does not know where he is—or rather who he is; but this situation in which he finds himself, staring into the eye of the earth with earth at his mouth, is strongly familiar to him. It seems to be something already inhabited in imagination.

At this point his whole body gives one of those violent jerks, every muscle gathering together every limb in paroxysm, one of those leaps of terror that land the poor bundle of body, safe, in harmless wakefulness. The abyss is no deeper than a doorstep; the landing, home.

He must have dropped off face-down and his head has sagged off his forearm; a dribble of saliva has made the earth stick to his lip. He's had complaints that he's inclined to sleep open-mouthed and make noises.

He rolls onto his side, where he has the impression the reeds facing him hide him as drawn curtains keep out day. The sense of familiarity, of some kind of unwelcome knowledge or knowing, is slow to ebb. As it does, it leaves space in his mind; or uncovers, like the retreat of a high tide, carrying away silt.

37

He lies for what seems a long time. This place—his farm—really is what everyone says of it, he himself as well (and he can hear, as if rehearsing, the jokes about tax deductions, the serious remarks that reveal how surprisingly much he knows of husbandry). A high-veld autumn, a silvery-gold peace, the sun lying soft on hard ground, the rock pigeons beginning to fly earlier, now, the river he can hear feeling its dark tongue round the watercress and weeds, there inside the reeds. As if he hasn't been away. As if nothing had ever happened; as if there never has been—is not—someone dead, down there. Just as everyone believes—he himself has long ago come to believe—that the farm was acquired as a good investment. Yet when he brought her here that day, the first time he saw the place, and they were walking over the very piece of ground on which he is stretched now, allowing that distant first time to return to him, he was possessed only by the brilliant idea of the farm-house as a place to bring a woman.

—I'm in pig-iron.— Confident enough to clown a little: these were the preliminaries, the exchange-of-unvital-information stage.

—No ordinary pig-iron dealer—she said. But it was not flattery, not her—ironic, sarcastic even, condescending, weighing him up.

That ugly little *plaas* house—he hadn't even been inside it yet, but he could visualize the flowered linoleum on the floor and the dead flies against the bedroom windows—it was only twenty-five miles or so from town and she had a car. Much safer than a flat, and a hotel room was probably out of the question, with a woman like her. (Though one never knew; the ones who fancied themselves brainy were often the least fastidious when roused.) All the time they were walking about this place (he is sitting up, in a slight buzz of dizziness—has lit a cigarette and is inhaling deeply), while his tongue was busy talking, his body responding, taking her hand and momentary weight across dongas, his real attention was on the lucky existence of a house. Only twenty-five miles from town and she the sort of woman who drives about in her little car all over the show. No one would ever know where she was going. The hairdressers'; the dressmaker's, a girlfriend. The house would have the minimal luxuries essential to its purpose, and none of the

38

unnecessary domestic essentials. It would not be in the least like home, anybody's home, and she would love it. Whisky and Danish beer, good cheese and fresh bread bought on the way; cologne and huge towels in the bathroom. Yes, his mind raced ahead planning while they walked and talked, tried to cross the river, pored, close enough to smell each other's warmth, over the boundary map the estate agent had given him, waded through khaki-weed whose barbed seeds changed their trousers into a bristly hide. He talked of clearing weeds, fencing, ploughing, draining, irrigating. She pulled the seed needles off herself with the concentrated pleasure of a dog de-fleaing: —Why not just buy it and leave it as it is?—

How could she know how close she came to the light in which he was actually considering acquisition of the place? Undoubtedly a thousand times better than any flat in town, from the point of view of discretion, and the farm servants no problem at all since, as he had no wife, they would assume she was that person, *the missus*. My God, what a state of heat, over that bitch, what excitation of secret plans he had indulged himself with. Had he ever bought the bath towels and the cologne?—that he does not remember. But he paid 100 rands an acre; high at the time, must be worth more than double by now.

He has got up, stiffly, and picked up the Sunday paper which he had been reading before he fell asleep. Having your back scrubbed by a professional Japanese is no substitute for exercise. The paper is folded into the sort of wad you make to swat something with, and is a nuisance to carry. But he never leaves so much as a cigarette butt lying about to deface the farm; it's they—up at the compound —who discard plastic bags and put tins beside tree-stumps. He's forever cleaning up after them. There the children are now, shouting in their thin voices as they come over the veld carrying those endless paraffin tins of water from the pump. Some of them are so small they appear to be paraffin tins with legs. But the parents don't care. Just back from Japan, he feels himself to look a lonely man, walking along beside the reeds. So many of them are dried out and trampled down by cattle that you can walk quite a way farther in among them than was possible a few weeks ago. The weaver-bird nests (like balls of dusty hair-combings women leave behind them)

are knocked off and deserted and the vlei is dry; the river has re-
treated to a passage he can't see. Dried-up water plants web and
scum the hard mud. He bats his way through the margin of over-
laid reeds, using the newspaper. Hippos aborting their foetuses in
dried-up pools, places like this. It's extraordinary how nature
isn't squeamish about what to do in desperation. The shallowest
covering of earth is enough. The part of the river bed he is standing on seems to be somewhere about the place that Jacobus took
him. Cows break up and tamp down the surface, some small
creatures (rats?) make their holes, reeds fall; it looks no different
from anywhere else. No way of telling. The biggest willows were
away over to the left, from where that thing lay... What a tremendous fuss she would have made over it, a woman like her! For
instance once, just after he'd closed the deal for the land, he mentioned to her some incident concerning one of the farm boys he'd
taken on.
—What was it you call him?—
—Witbooi.—
Her face. —How old is he?—
—How would I know? Don't suppose he knows, either.—
She would refer to 'that herdsman of yours, Swart Gevaar'.
Her face was—is?—the smooth pale sallow colour he supposes
you call olive-skinned, although olives are green, brown or black.
The sort of monotoned skin that has no shades nor gradation of
texture; fascinating. From the nose-wings to the ears, the chin to
the hairline. Her hair began very clearly, too—he likes that. No en-
croachment on the oval, neither at the temples nor in the form of
wispy growth in front of the ears. Straight hair, dark dull brown in
colour, coarse and shiny. In her thirties, she ostentatiously does—
did?—not pull out one or two single white hairs that, visible from
the fount of the crown all the way down, seem transparent, like
nylon fishing line. —Trouble—she said, leaning across the café
table so that not only the dark tanned V but also the paler flesh at
the top of her breasts showed in the unbuttoned neck of one of
those shirts she wore. He'd seen her eyes, staring at nothing while
she waited for him, before she caught sight of him: staring at fear.

Witbooi = White boy   Swart Gevaar = Black danger

40

But as she gabbled her story she began to show off, as such people always did. When she forgot the fear, by pretending to him she wasn't afraid, she was enjoying herself. It should have been quite obvious to her that what had happened would happen: she filled her house with blacks, and white parsons who went around preaching Jesus was a revolutionary, and then when the police walked in she was surprised. *No ordinary pig-iron dealer:* it suited her, telephoning him mysteriously to meet her in some Greek café, to make that a kind of flattery, now, to use the implications to make some claim on him. He was to speak to a good lawyer—a respectable, shrewd company lawyer, the kind he would know; it was no good being represented in court by one of her own set. While she talked he could picture her saying to them: I know someone, one of those tycoons who know how to do things. One of those tycoons they despised. The *naïveté* of them all, her kind! The high-minded stupidity. Written all over her 'intelligent' face.

If she were here now her body would be beginning to be foreshortened, that's what happens to women in a few years, the space between hips-and-belly and breasts gets less and less, as if age presses down upon them from the top of their heads. It is happening to the beautiful woman—the friend of fifteen years who asks him to dinner too often. Coming to a fence that cuts across the field to the reeds, he stops a moment; a week's absence in Japan isn't a bad way to have begun cooling that old friendship. A week can become weeks, a month. I've been away a lot… It happens that people drift apart. Everyone drops someone from time to time. He stands watching a black and white stork, over the fence. The daughter—the little girl no longer a little girl—is an impossibility. She will have the space between hips and breasts, even dressed it is obvious she has no belly, absolutely flat. That stork should have left for Europe long ago; it jerks along with hunched wings and eyes on the ground, as if it has lost something valuable. The ring, last year; never turned up; he realizes that although that ring, even if not in his mind, is usually in the reflex with which the tip of his boot flips over stones when he walks about the farm, today he has forgotten it. The stork is taking no notice of his presence. The drought changes the pattern of migration, perhaps? The birds hang on, where there's water, to the last dried-up pool where the hippos abort their half-formed young. There were atrocities in Cambodia, no maize crop at all, the second year running, in the Transkei, the paper also said—the Sunday paper that is a nuisance to him to be carrying. He has turned up along the fence, plodding towards the road and eucalyptus trees, as inattentive to the earth as the stork is attentive. It is fatal to fall asleep in the afternoon. Sometimes he wakes up with the words of an old dance number—he can't even sing in tune, that's how much he knows of music—going round in his head like a trapped bluebottle fly. Sometimes there's the presence of an extreme irritation over something trivial that has floated up from some obscure corner of experience. Sometimes, as now, he seems to be addressing someone. It is only a step away from the aberration of talking to oneself. Atrocities in Cambodia. Not a good idea to take the Metallgesellschaft Germans to the Kruger Park because of the possibility of stinking hippo foetuses. Across the empty irrigation ditch and on to the road, he meets the pot-bellied black brats with tins on their heads, standing aside for him on their way to fetch more water. This is what they're doing all day, every day. And do you think I don't know? You think I don't know? —He even slaps at his thigh with the folded newspaper; if anyone on the road or the newly-ploughed field, where the mealie stalks are piled into tepees, is looking at him, it may be interpreted as the brisk gesture of a man enjoying exercise. But the children ignore him as he ignores them. What percentage of the world is starving? How long can we go on getting away scot free? When the aristocrats were caught up in the Terror, did they recognize: it's come to us. Did the Jews of Germany think: it's our turn. Soon, in this generation or the next, it must be our turn to starve and suffer. Why not? And did you think my respectable company lawyer, defending the just cause of your jolly parties with blacks, your posters discovering injustice as if you'd invented it—did you think he could save you from that?

Earth in his mouth.

There is grit between his teeth; as he swallows and the heavy upper and lower molars meet they grind some microscopic boulders. Earth in his mouth. Although he did wipe his lips. He gathers saliva with his tongue and drops a string of spit into the dust.

Half-grown, half-wild cats in the roof-gutter above the kitchen door; there's plenty of milk, but they probably don't ever bother to feed them. —No, there is a scummy dish beside the step. *Psspsspss.* He will wash out his mouth in the bathroom. The screen door squeaks open and bangs, swinging again of its own momentum and banging a second time behind him. The kitchen smells of burned porridge and soured milk and the plates of the electric stove, although switched off, give heat like a flushed face; they cook here, of course, although they are not supposed to. In the rest of the house the floors are thick with diligently-applied polish that no one walks on.

A place to bring a woman.

The shower is dousing warm soda water over his face and turns colder and more forceful as it runs, blinding and deafening him. Once in the bathroom, it seemed a far better idea than just rinsing his mouth. The chromium snake and rose, which may be secured in a bracket on the wall above the bath or held in the hand, are in brilliant contrast to the chipped tiles decorated with peeling Bambi transfers which were the previous owners' level of bathroom luxury. A thousand needles of water are breaking down the immobility of his face. He holds his breath and then gasps, and the water prickles delightfully into his mouth, pinging his tongue. He hears bells ringing; water beating on your head always gives the sensation of ringing. But no; something is ringing, outside his head. The telephone. It has taken several years for his aural sense to learn to respond only to the particular combination of rings on the party line—three short and one long—that is his. He goes naked down the passage, his spoor beading wet on the impermeable layer of wax polish.

Whenever he hears the voice of one of the locals on the phone (it is not that he knows any of them well enough to distinguish one from the other, but he recognizes the strong Afrikaans accent they all have if they speak English, and the authentic mother-tongue intonation if they speak Afrikaans) his own response takes on the firm pleasantness of the defensive, because they usually phone to complain. A straying cow has got into their lucerne or the boys have disregarded the rotation of days on which the river may be used for irrigation. But today the rather hesitant telephone voice that announces itself as De Beer (the old De Beer himself) has the slightly wheedling tone these Boers use when they want something. Afrikaans, with all its homely turns of phrase and its diminutives comfortingly formed by rounding off a word with a suffix instead of preceding it with an adjective such as 'tiny' or 'little', is better suited to this tone than English, but these people seem to ignore his ability to speak Afrikaans. Their insistence on

44

talking to him in English demarcates the limit of his acceptance, out here, outside the city from which he comes and goes. At the same time, there have been moments when they seek to claim him: —Mehring?— A smiling, prodding, inculpatory look, as a Jew takes note of the curve of a nose, perceptible only at a certain angle in an otherwise innocent face. —Then you're an Afrikaner, nê?— breaking into the mother tongue. They are answered in the same tongue. —It's a German name, perhaps. From South West. A long way back.—

—Look, Mr Mehring—old De Beer is very concerned not to trouble him—Are you people at home?—

The 'you people' is the usage of delicacy; the farmers know there isn't a wife around, but they also know there are sometimes carloads of visitors, and in any case, they cannot conceive of a man without a family of some sort. If he hasn't got one, they will invent one for him, by compassionate assumption.

—Man, it's all right then if we come over to your house? Just to have a little chat or so. It won't be long. Perhaps you'll be able to help us out.—

There has been a whole preamble of small talk about the weather, the drought, the usual thing before getting to the point. Because he is naked, Mehring feels like hopping with impatience. It is born of the nervous apprehension his body feels that someone may walk in: his mind is aware that no one lives in the house, there is no one to enter. Yet while he listens, smiles exasperatedly into the telephone in his right hand, his other hand plays with himself the way a small boy seeks reassurance by touching his genitals—his fingers comb the damp springy hair, draw down the foreskin that has been pushed back during the shower, weigh the uneven balls, absently tender to the one that is smaller and lighter than the other.

He dresses very quickly. It's hardly the prospect of the visit from Meneer De Beer: it's the shower that's done it, got rid of that curious awakening down at the reeds and returned him to the ordinary plane of his existence. 'You've got out of bed the wrong side', the old saying; it is true that one can wake up in the wrong place. The acupuncture of water needles has restored the face with which he will meet the Boer from down the road, and the Metallgesellschaft people, tomorrow morning; meets himself in the mean rectangle of bathroom mirror. He brushes his hair. Sideburns are brindled with grey. Even naked: the face is the kind Metallgesellschaft would recognize.

Alina! He yells out the back door.

Alina!

It's a nuisance that the very day he needs them—Sunday—is naturally the day they want to gallivant off. In the sitting-room he struggles to push up the rusty wire flyscreens and open some windows. Any visitors he may have from the farms round about will always look more at home in here than he does; he bought the house *voets-toets*, lock, stock and barrel, nylon pile 'suite', rickety three-legged coffee tables, Rhodesian copper firescreen with embossed Flame Lily, wrought-iron plant stand—except for family photographs it is exactly their own sitting-rooms. There is even an upright piano with holes where candle-brackets must have been screwed; occasionally when one of his own friends strays up to the house, a key will be struck, in amusement: sometimes there is a note, sometimes just the small thud of the hammer's pad. He has offered to give the heirloom away to anyone who will come and take it—an offer that brings a laugh. He keeps a transistor radio on the sideboard that is his bar and the receptacle for farm accounts, and now he switches on to hear the news, forgetting that it is broadcast at a later hour on Sundays. The full panoply of a noisy symphony distends the whole house; it seems, when the entourage troops in through the front door (he has forgotten it hasn't been used for months, there is a delay while he opens up for them) that truly the house is peopled, throughout the rooms they don't see, with movement and voices.

They are quite a delegation; the whole family expects to go along if there's an outing of any kind on a Sunday afternoon. Old De Beer has brought young De Beer, and young De Beer has with him young Mrs De Beer and child. There is also an adolescent girl who looks like young Mrs De Beer, probably a sister. He has seen them all, or a similar combination of the family, looking out from under ceremonious hats, when their car passed on their way home

46

from church on the farm road, this morning. That's how they knew he'd be at the farm.

They are people who won't dispose themselves about a room until you tell them to. Come in, come in, sit down... They stand grouped slightly behind old De Beer. Please come inside.

Even when they are settled (looking round at the chair seats before placing their backsides, as if they're afraid of sitting on something or doing some damage) they remain hidden behind his shirt-tails—they don't speak. The child is so bashful, she's a vine wound to her mother's thick, young, knees-together legs. Hansie De Beer runs the farm, he's the one Mehring usually deals with, but in his father's presence he ventures no opinions unless the old man turns his face to him. Old De Beer is a handsome man, his clothes filled drum-tight with his body; there ought to be a watch-chain across it, but there isn't, he wears on his wrist instead the latest Japanese electronic watch with a dial like something off an instrument panel. The retaining wall of belly and bunch of balls part the thighs majestically. Oh to wear your manhood, fatherhood like that, eh, stud and authority. The coatsleeves are stuffed with flesh that gives the arms the angle to lie monumentally on chair-arms—Mehring is going over these stock points, forgetting his duty to offer beer. The old man's Kaiser face, Edward VII face, regards him unyieldingly a moment; the son and the woman don't respond. Christ, they probably don't drink on Sundays, the son is afraid to say yes.

The old man's hoarse slow voice: —Perhaps if you've got brandy. I'll take a brandy.—

Easy now, for Hansie. —Thanks very much, beer.—

—Have you perhaps got a cold drink?— The wife makes a soft, little girl's request, she wouldn't be allowed to drink in front of the father-in-law anyway, Sunday or no Sunday.

—Just a drop of water in it. That's enough. No, that lucerne of yours was not so bad you know, not so bad at all. But why don't you plant the top veld there—you know, by your boys' kraal, right up to Delport's fence—before, you know, when (he looks to his son, who supplies the name)—when Jacobs had this place, it was always lucerne there. It'll do well, man. There's not much frost

47

there. With your water you can keep it going right through the winter.—

—Oh I've had mealies there. They did exceptionally well.—

—Mealies! Yes man...but now the mealies are all reaped. If you had lucerne, now. You'll get a good price for lucerne if you've got it in winter.— He speaks to the city business man, he even smiles under the sweep of moustache that hides his lip: —That's the law of supply and demand, hey?—

Mehring gives a hostly laugh, and the son backs it up. The young woman is whispering fiercely all the time in asides to the children, who are occupied sharing out a Coke that, despite the traffic in his kitchen, has been lying in the refrigerator untouched for weeks. —Just a minute, maybe I can find another bottle.—

—No, no, it's plenty for them.—

The child will sink, she will drown if she lets go of her mother, yet her clinging is flirtatious, she tries to make him look at her so that she may at once hide her head against the mother's thigh. She's a beautiful child as their children often are—where do they get them from?—and she'll grow up—what do they do to them?— the same sort of vacant turnip as the mother. —Sorry, I've run out, I've been away.— To go into one of those women must be like using the fleshy succulent plants men in the Foreign Legion have to resort to.

—Not so bad. The only thing, the bales didn't weigh fifty pounds...isn't that so...— (Now addressing, calling in Hansie when he needs him.)

—No, it's true, it was a bit less than you...it doesn't matter...—

They bought lucerne from him—before Japan; six weeks ago?—before that, or later?

—We lost about ten per cent on it— Hansie is forced by a look to nod confirmation of this.

—It must have dried out. Because it wasn't the boys who weighed, I know I did it myself.—

It was the week before that business with the police. He hadn't come out to the farm at all. Perhaps they knew; the old man with his intelligent brown eyes might know. They expected it of a city man like himself to leave things to the boys.

48

—You can't trust a kaffir about the scale, I can tell you that. You can teach them as much as you like. It doesn't matter to them, you see, if it's so much or so much. To them it seems the same. They'll know better just by picking it up on their backs. I've had some boys who can tell how much you'll get, just picking the bales up.—

They are all laughing quite admiringly, even old De Beer himself, even young Mrs De Beer, tossing her head piled with Grecian curls behind a nylon scarf, her chin pressed back against her pink neck with exactly her child's bashful gesture —It's true, you know, that's quite true what my father-in-law say—

Putting out a hand to stop the angle of the bottle over his glass in indication that the second tot should rise no farther, old De Beer is in full command, now, not even Mehring will break in on him unless he chooses to make way. —But what I wanted to ask—you can p'raps do me a favour, you know. I've got a lot of building material and stuff that I've got to pick up. A mass of stuff. And there's only that small van, except for the milk truck, and I can't take that, you see, the milk's got to go into town every morning—

They want to borrow the little pick-up, of course. It's not necessary to wait for them to ask, not neighbourly. He is used to the conventions of open-handedness, sauna baths and trips to the Kruger Park. —But take my Toyota, why not? I'll tell my boy. What day d'you want it?—

—Two days or so—Hansie ventures to put in.

—You see it's out in Rustenberg, my late uncle's place— Young Mrs De Beer cannot resist being expansive about something that must be recognized as within her province of interest. —He just passed away. Mmm, it was terrible, for a long time now he couldn't—you know—couldn't hold down his food. Not even water.—

The old man does not so much as acknowledge her as the source of prattle. He is looking sideways under his lids as if the interruption were something that has just walked through the room, his hand is raised and his lips are open, taking breath between sentences. —Monday will do. Monday will be all right.—

—My auntie wants to give up the place, yes, shame.—

—With pleasure. You just tell my boy, whenever it suits you. I don't think we'll be needing it for anything this week.—

—Oh that boy of yours— Two palms convivially flat on spread thighs, old De Beer allows another smile under the moustache. —He uses the tractor when he wants to go around to his friends, he doesn't need the truck.—

He takes the joke against himself appreciatively; it is anyway at the same time a gesture of solidarity, from them, one employer telling another what he ought to know.

The old man refuses a third brandy. It looks as if they are going to go; but they don't. The children have tripped out into the yard and returned with a captured kitten bunched up against the little one's chest along with her skirt.

—You're a man who travels all over. You must know about these things—there's a family bible and other old stuff. Very old. Antique. Antique, hey? I think people pay a lot of money for old things these days. For investment, hey? You must come over to our place. I'll let you have a look at it, when we bring it here.—

—Interesting, yes.—

—I collect myself. I have signed photographs of all our prime ministers. Since General Botha. My *father* fought with General Botha—you know that? And *his* father (a pause for attention) my *grandfather*—he fought in the Kaffir Wars. I have a coloured portrait of the late Dr Verwoerd, personally signed for me. I met him in Pretoria in July, nineteen-sixty. Yes. And I've got one signed by John Vorster, too.—

The terrified kitten escapes, skittering across the linoleum and under the sideboard. The mother is sucking the first joint of the child's finger to take away the sting of a scratch. The child's reddened face threatens them all with tears.

—Five chairs that belonged to my mother's mother. They say they came from the Cape. Originally. But I'm interested in history—you understand. That's my hobby. The history—of—the—Afrikaner. That's what I like. Not furniture and so on. General Botha gave the photograph to my father himself, my father's name is written on it—Henrik Barend De Beer, in General Botha's handwriting—

50

The elder girl, motherly towards smaller ones as only black or Afrikaans children are, waggles the distraction of something she has picked up from the fireplace, and the threat dies down, but Hansie says in Afrikaans—No, she'll break it, put it back.—

What is it anyway? There is nothing in the room, the house, that he values. What the elder girl is holding, uncertain whether to replace it or not, is one of those crude carvings of a black warrior with a spear and miniature hide shield that people buy in souvenir shops or airports all over Africa. He doesn't know how it got into the house; the spear's missing from the hole in the hand where these things are usually stuck. —Let her take it. It's nothing.—

—But don't you want to keep it?—the mother says, knowing he's a travelled man.

—I don't know how it got here. You can buy them anywhere.—

—My grandfather—old De Beer is saying, risen from his chair without difficulty, considering his weight—My father's father, had a kaffir doll they took from the chief's place, there when they burned it in the war. Did you ever hear of Modjadji's Kraal? Just near there.—

—A kaffir doll?—

—There in the Northern Transvaal. You know about the kaffir rain queen? Well, up in those parts. One of their dolls they used for magic. It's not much left of it; there were feathers and little bags of rubbish tied to it, but it's old now.— The big shoulders move to indicate it is still somewhere around.

—You should hang on to that, Meneer de Beer. Museums in America pay fortunes these days to get hold of those things.—

—Say thank you nicely to the uncle.—

They take a detour, by way of the paddock where newly-calved cows are confined, to their car, trailing along behind Mehring and old De Beer. Hansie gives some advice about a calf. Jacobus has appeared in his gum-boots and torn overalls and is carrying feed; fortunately he always seems to remember you can't drink and work at the same time. The vet has been to look at the calf; hardly off the plane from Tokyo when there was Jacobus on the phone, wanting the vet to be sent for.

—But is it taking the milk, now?—

51

Yes, baas, she's eat now.—

—But why does it still lie down all the time? Doesn't it walk about?—

—Yes, baas, she's walk.—

Jacobus, before the neighbouring farmer, agrees with everything that Mehring says, rather than gives an independent answer. He stands as if he has been called up in front of a class. Then, as though demonstrating what he has been taught, as though he didn't do this every day when these men who are watching him are not there, he slops the mash with balletic accuracy into the troughs, spreads the hay in the byres.

—You've got this place going nicely.— Old De Beer graciously condescends by pretending to defer.

—This master will take the pick-up tomorrow or some other day this week. You'll look out for him and give him the key, eh?—

With a sort of skip, knees bent, Jacobus has come to attention again. He agrees: Yes, baas.

While they are getting into the car a black man is trudging past carrying a plastic can; the endless Sunday traffic from compound to compound, every farm is a thoroughfare for them, nothing can be done about it: it is the same at De Beer's place. But this one hails Mehring, he's only a little drunk: *Mina funa lo job?* The tone is more threat than question. —No job!— Mehring throws up his hands.

Hansie is at least allowed to do the driving. —There's a lot of loafers about. It's that location. I can wish we were a hundred miles away from that location. Honestly. And you even had some skelm lying murdered in your place. It's not safe.—

Old De Beer dismisses womanish speculation.

—My boys know I'll shoot anyone I find coming near my cattle at night. They know that. They let their friends know that.—

The small child is prompted by the mother to wave from a window as the car drives away.

—What's he going to do with the pick-up?—Jacobus follows at

a short distance, back to the house, the way he does when he's about to make a request. The farmer has turned round; they are facing each other, not really close enough for a conversation.

—He's got some things to fetch from Rustenberg.— He turns back and is walking on while he speaks. They reach the screen door together and Jacobus comes in behind him: —Why he doesn't take his brother's lorry?—

—I don't know. What brother? Has he got a brother here?—

A snort and a smile. —That's his brother, at Theronshoop.—

They know everything about us. He wonders whether he should say something about the tractor. Oh what the hell, if it gives the old devil a thrill; so long as it doesn't harm the tractor. There will be another time, sometime, when he feels more like delivering himself of a reproach. —Well, what's your trouble, Jacobus?— Like a dog, the man scents he's in the mood to hand out something. To get at the cigarettes in his trouser-pocket, he has to lift his body by expanding his chest, he takes three from the pack and the cupped hands are immediately there to receive them. With two fingers Jacobus puts them into the breast pocket of his overalls.

All serious discussions of farm business are held here in the kitchen, standing up. —Master, we must have another boy for the cows.—

—For the cows! But what's wrong with Solomon and Phineas and Witbooi?—

—Witbooi he's...master, he's getting little bit old.— But it sounds as though the notion has just presented itself to be seized upon as a reason.

—Have you been quarrelling, you boys? What's Witbooi done?—

—No, no, Witbooi he's all right. We are nice together. You know that long time. *Another* boy. He can help Witbooi.—

—No more boys! The winter's coming. Hey, Jacobus? What d'we want more boys for, there's nothing much growing! No, no, you tell Witbooi to carry on.—

He is smiling, laughing almost, chivvying. The black man is slowly pushed into smiles, too, first nodding his head, then shaking it, slowly, but still smiling, distressed, half laughing.

—All right, Jacobus.—

He locks the door of the sideboard where the liquor is kept; stands looking round a moment in this room that so seldom holds people: they have left their dents in the chair cushions. The well-regulated demands and responses between the Boers and himself, the usual sort of exchange between his black man and himself have re-engraved the fine criss-cross of grooves on which his mind habitually runs. The empty space that was clear in him this afternoon is footprinted over, it exists no more than does a city pavement under the comings and goings of passing bodies that make it what it is. He recognizes with something like pleasure the onset of the usual feeling he has on Sunday night—a slight anticipatory impatience to set off for the city. Just as on Sunday morning he is ready to get out of it. The rhythm of these alternating feelings is simple and dependable as the daily cognisance of peristaltic activity that presages his bowel movement, along with the after-breakfast cigarette. As he's about to leave the house, he thinks of that kitten. Down on his knees, face tightened and reddened by the bending, he peers under the sideboard. Dust there, the tidemark where the wax polish, describing the arc of the polishing cloth, ends. Well, he's got something better to do… He'll tell Jacobus to tell Alina, on the way out. There was a marble in the dust against the wainscot. He has picked it up for his son; finds it in his hand. He is negotiating the dip where the road turns out of the farm entrance, past the post where a mealie-cob and a white rag flag are still stuck up to indicate the mealies that were for sale six weeks ago, and the marble presses like a cyst between his right palm and the steering wheel. His son is sixteen now. He tries awkwardly to wind down the window on that side, still holding the marble. When the window is open the hand hesitates. He has tossed the marble not out of the window, but into the open shelf under the dashboard.

54

*... I ask also for children, that this village may have a large popu-
lation, and that your name may never come to an end.*

Jacobus had six pieces of brown paper torn from a sugar bag from the Indian shop, spread on the ground before his haunches. He took three cigarettes out of the breast pocket of his overalls. His hands were slender and long-boned but the finger-tips were calloused and they seemed to juggle the white tubes like the sensitive but hard points of a crab's claws; there was only one nail, the thumbnail, long enough to slit the cigarettes open, and it was too thick to do so without spilling the contents. Dismissing his own laziness at trying to do things the amateurish way, he took out of the trouser section of the overalls, that were very large and folded over on themselves under a belt, so that the fly ran diagonally from where the division between his legs must be to where his left hip must be, a lozenge tin containing the proper equipment. In it was a broken razor blade; he slit the three cigarettes neatly and divided their tobacco onto the six bits of brown paper.

—What about the Dutchman at the other farm? The brother of the one who came yesterday. He can try there.—

They were resting; they had been feeding the dry and stripped mealie plants into a machine that chopped up the stuff for cattle fodder; tissue-thin fragments of leaf, millimetre strips of bamboo-smooth stalk, flecks of pith like spit, clung lightly to them in a dust complex as snow-flakes. Their old hats protected the heads of three, but the bare wool of the fourth, whose possibilities of finding a job were in question, was linted with it.

—That's no good.—

—He went there.—

The first bit of brown paper with its pile of tobacco was rolled, licked, handed out. —He'd better try town.—

It was not necessary to remind Jacobus that a farm labourer has no papers for town. He must have something in mind.

—They're short at the abattoir.—

—Who told you that?—

—Alina's daughter's husband said.—

The man was given a smoke, too. He had not worked with them the whole morning but had come to look for them, down from the compound, falling into the rhythm of their work, an hour or two ago.

Someone made a loud tongue-click, followed by a sharp, grunted squeak of scepticism, and another click.

—That's the municipality, isn't it? they're going to take someone without a town pass? I've never heard of it. The municipality?—

—We can all go to earn money in town then!—

—Yes—Jacobus offers for what it's worth, his voice rising slightly—You can ask the daughter's husband, he'll tell you. They are short. They'll take you on. That's what he said once.—

A figure went by on a bicycle, pumping regularly from left leg to right, singing without words as a man does when the wind of his own passage, in his ears, makes him confident that because he can scarcely hear himself, no one else can, either. One of them called teasingly after him; he had not noticed them under the open shelter of the barn.

—I can go and ask on the telephone.— For Jacobus, if not for them, it was simple as that.

—Who will you ask on the telephone?—

The young man had propped his bicycle nearby, and joined them, without interruption, respectful of a conversation he could not at once expect to follow. He was wearing his black and white checked cap, green bell-bottoms, shoes and socks, yellow orlon-knit shirt; the day-off clothes set him apart like a bridegroom among his familiars.

—Come on. I can go up to the house now and phone William at the India's. William can come to the phone. They'll call him. He can ask Alina's daughter.— Jacobus reeled off answers to all their doubts and objections before they could formulate them.

Still they hesitated. He laughed. They knew that he had the keys of the house, that he could go in and out when he liked. Perhaps it was true that he could even phone the Indian shop and ask to speak to one of the men who worked there. Perhaps the Indian would agree to let him come to the phone.

57

—Let's go. I'm going to the house.— It didn't matter to him whether they accompanied him or not.

While they walked past the stall where the bull was ruminating and the shed where the spike-tooth cultivator and other combinations of steel teeth and blades lay half-disassembled (Jacobus stepped aside to push some vulnerable part nearer its fellow components) someone said—Why didn't those people say anything about it when he was staying there with them?—

This time the man answered for himself. —They didn't tell me. I don't know.—

—I only say, I remember what Alina's daughter's man said to me. Perhaps it's too late. We can find out, eh, we can ask. On the telephone.—

He went into the open garage and took the kitchen door key from his hiding-place strung up with the bundles of onions that he was drying from the rafters. The house stank of cat's pee. They trooped into the livingroom behind him, walking softly, with slightly bent knees. The elderly Rhodesian, Witbooi, took off his hat. They stood while Jacobus's finger went down numbers written on the margin of a calendar with a picture of a white woman without clothes. He turned the crank of the telephone, picked up the receiver, all the time keeping the forefinger of his other hand on the number, and then, after a hesitant beginning, repeated the first digit and spelled out all four to the operator. He did not look at them while waiting for the call to be connected. The Sunday paper was lying on the floor of the room. There were empty bottles beside the chairs. The ashtrays were full.

Speaking English, which not all of them could do, not only his words were different now. He stuttered, he kept lifting one foot and putting it down again, he was crouched round the hand in which he held the receiver. —Please...please I want speak William. William. The boy, there. Ye-es. Ye-es. William. No, no, I'm his brother want speak with him.—

Another silence. The youngster, Izak, picked up a beer bottle, tipped it, put it down. Now Jacobus began to talk again, fast, loud, in the language they all spoke, and they all listened. They could tell from what he was saying what the man at the other end had

58

said: it was true that sometimes the abattoir took people without papers to work in town. Jacobus was bellowing down the machine and the other voice was bellowing back. —You mean he can go there with Dorcas's husband any day? But what do you mean then? Not now? But why did you say—oh yes, all right, if you're not sure. He comes home when—six o'clock? Seven o'clock. All right. All right, *boetie*—

Jacobus put the phone back firmly and carefully, rang off by turning the crank, presented the accomplishment of the piece of business to them. —He'll find out when that one comes home.—

Izak had lifted the lid of the piano; smiling at them to look at him, his hand was above the keys as if he were about to capture a butterfly.

Jacobus gave a jerk of the head to indicate the lid must be closed. As they all went out he paused, in this room, and collected from the ashtrays a half-smoked cigarette and the butts of several cigars. The butts were all smoked down to precisely the same length—like the ones the children knew they must deliver to him whenever they found them in the grass.

Rusty scales of long-dried blood gilded the gum-boots. Izak, who was sent over to buy beer at the shanty town behind De Beer's farm, recognized the blood-coated boots before he separated the faces of the men in the drinking-place, a one-roomed house with a roof held down by rocks and pumpkins. Izak had a milk-can with a lid secured by a chain, for the beer; it jingled its early-morning sound as the two men cycled back together in the half-dark.

—That husband of Dorcas came past with Izak.— Jacobus's wife brought him a mug of tea.

Jacobus coaxed the last of the pap round his flowered plate, with his fingertips, and made it into a final mouthful. —You can see in the dark.—

She put sugar in the tea.

—Where'd Izak find him?—

—How do I know. Eight o'clock, nine o'clock—when they work in town they come when they like. They go where they like.— She and Alina spent a lot of time together complaining about their children and their children's husbands and wives.

Jacobus passed the paddock where the calves were lying down for the night. One or two staggered to their feet and he murmured something soothing. From here he could see the light of the braziers at the compound, reddening the walls of the breeze-block.

—So you went off to go and get him from the India's?— He treated young Izak with the tolerant amusement of an older man for a youth.

—He was there where I went to fetch beer for Thomas.— Izak was wearing his cap, smiling.

—That place!—Why do you people send Izak there?—

—You go yourself sometimes.—

—*I* go. He's a child. That place is worse than the location, for him. They'll take your money. If they don't do it themselves, with a knife, they'll get those dirty women to steal it out of your trousers.—

Izak looked softly from side to side, enjoying attention.

The fowls were quarrelling for places to roost on stumps of a tree hung with loops of iron and bits of wire; someone made as if to beat at them and the dark shape of the tree blew up.

—They'll take something else out of his trousers—

—That's nice, Izak? Ay? He likes that—

Jacobus said to the quiet face of the man without work—Well, what does he say?—

But the man in the blood-gilded gum-boots whom they all thought of simply as Dorcas's husband, since she was the daughter of one of them, of Alina—answered directly, in his place. —Even if he had a pass it's no good, man. There's no work now. That time when I talked to you…but not now. It was the time at Christmas, before they stopped the farmers sending so many cattle. It was when too many cattle were coming at once. They were dying at the station. You remember? The slaughter-house was full up, we couldn't do anything. The farmers were sending more and more… because of no rain…

The man who was looking for work shook his head slowly before them all. The black and white checked cap defined young Izak's head clearly, but this head was still dusty from the morning's work, it had a mothy dimness, half-effacing itself into the perimeter of the firelight. The fowls settled again; the children coughed in their sleep; a woman brought round the last of the beer.

—You keep away from there, Izak. No one should send you, soon you'll begin going on your own and I tell you, that's the beginning of trouble for you. You'll give *me* trouble and that will be the end of it, for you.—

Nobody laughed. Nobody said anything. Jacobus was speaking and he must be heard through.

—That's where they came from, not from the location; the people who left that—down there at the river.—

Nobody spoke but the quality of their presence had changed; quite suddenly, drawn away at the touch of these words, clenched as the tendrils of a sea-anemone move with dumb-show recoil deep under water.

—I'm telling you.—

Izak looked from one to the other, for a clue, quite forgetting. For the moment the withdrawal seemed another reproof directed at himself—what had he done now?— Then the touch reached him, too. He remembered.

Jacobus took a gulp of beer, releasing them from the necessity to bring among them something no one spoke of. But just as they were beginning to talk about other things, he broke in again—I don't ask anyone there. I won't say this one or that one. Who or who. But all the same— He rapped four fingers at the bony plate of his breast, behind which this knowledge, for all of them, was thrust away.

This house smells of cat. For weeks now. Every time he comes, he is greeted by it. It's because the place is shut up all week.

She never ever came to the house.

Although he has spoken to the servants nothing seems to be done. There are too many cats around and God knows how they keep alive, anyway. He has suggested to Jacobus that there are too many cats, but being Jacobus, he just grins and counters with another positive statement: There are too many rats. Cattle apart, you can't get them to care for any animal. He would like to keep a beautiful dog on the farm, a collie or a pointer, but there's no one to look after it during the week.

The smell is strongest in the bathroom. Of course, if a cat gets shut inside, it will often do its business in the bath. There is no disinfectant to pour down the plughole. He keeps forgetting to buy something. Even cologne would do.

'I'm sending you to fetch a most charming and beautiful woman.' 'A most delightful man will be coming to fetch you.'—So that people are already embarrassed and prepared to be bored with each other before they are thrown together in this calculated, voyeur's match-making game. He asked his passenger to get from the glove-box the slip of paper with the address where the lunch-party was being given, and she read out solemnly from some company report that he'd stuck in there: '...and its wholly-owned subsidiaries, Tube Manipulations, Hot-Dip Galvanizers...' The voice she assumed was pompous, the sort of voice she wanted him to think she thought company chairmen must use—she who, of course, couldn't be expected to know because she belonged to another world.

—I'm in pig-iron.—

—No ordinary pig-iron dealer.—

If, when he telephoned her a few days later, he had suggested meeting for a drink or taking her out to dinner she might have been

63

able to say no, the approach somehow confirming they 'had nothing in common', as dinner-party sexual mores would have put it. But the fact that here is a man who phones with the rather odd idea of asking a woman he's recently met at lunch, casually somewhere, if she'd like to drive with him to look at a farm he's thinking of buying—that was the right sort of move with a woman like her. Out of their own set of conventions they allowed themselves that a tycoon—not merely a petty businessman, mind—might have some imagination and dash quite amusing to toy with, in a detached way, never forgetting what sort of person such a man was. The agent did not give him the key of the house. He looked in at the windows, cupping his eyes against the reflections on the glass that prevented him seeing properly into the rooms that, indeed, he could imagine...if he were to buy the place, bring her there. It was perhaps then, exactly, that the purpose of buying had come to him, taken him up, and exactly because they had not been able to get into the house that day. What it was meant for, for him, was defined and set aside by the fact that it was closed against anything else. She showed no interest in the house; she stood by with her hands full of silver rings spread on her trousered thighs, gazing, with the sleepy look city people take on in the country, away down over the weed-high fields to the willows. —If I had your money, I'd buy it and leave it just as it is.—

—No farm is beautiful unless it's productive.—

—You hear these things and believe them because they sound 'right'. That's your morality.—

The flirtatious sneer in her voice unexpectedly gave him an erection. (Even then, perhaps?...the beginning of these—inappropriate—reactions now, being pecked on the cheek by some child he's known since she was in napkins.)

—And what's yours, my dear? You're so concerned about those pot-bellied piccanins on the way here, don't you think land ought to be growing food?—

He knew all the answers she could have given, knew them by heart, had heard them mouthed by her kind a hundred times: On starvation wages? For whose benefit? For your profit? Or your loss, in a bad year, to reduce your supertax? But she decided to

64

play culpable. They sense when they've had that effect on you, it flatters them even if it doesn't excite them, even if they're aware, as a thirty-something-year-old woman must have been, that it can happen to you in response to all sorts of stimuli, few of which they'd find it flattering to be associated with. Smiling, pulling a face: —Yes I know—I know. I want to change the world but keep bits of it the way I like it for myself. If I had your money...—

That is why you will never change the world or have my money. Wherever she's landed up, marching on embassies, enjoying heroic tussles with nice London bobbies who don't even carry a gun. She will have thrown her bra away by now, like the others, tits wobbling as she is dragged off. A face full of intelligent stupidity, just as the very last time he saw it, not in the slightly shiny olive-coloured flesh but put together by the black dots of a newsprint photograph, recorded looking back from the steps of the aircraft. What was it her kind always said—*I love my country deeply and I am heart-broken at having to leave.* But the highly-respectable company lawyers employed and the contacts with the British government implored for a foreign passport to get away! The intelligent-stupid face so indignant after police interrogation; shit-scared. What did they expect?

—You've bought that farm!—

—Come out to celebrate with me.—

—Where?—

Not yet the house; but soon, soon there. —Wherever you like. The Carlton.—

—Oh God, no. Not champagne and smoked salmon.—

—An Italian place?—

—No, no. Parma ham and melon.—

—All right, you don't like restaurants.—

—We can eat here. Better than those lousy expensive places where you go. I prefer my own cooking. But you must bring wine, I've got nothing worthy of celebrating your farm.—

—My latest property deal.— It was part of the tone of their getting together for him to guy her attitude towards him, in *his* turn to assume her assumptions.

Where she lived looked inside as he would have thought,

65

glimpsing it once from the front door when he fetched her for that
lunch. A large secretive, overgrown garden and small rooms with
books and her husband's family furniture in need of repair. Native
pots. Leftist newspapers. She stopped him sitting in a chair that
could take light people only. The whisky was low because her husband was 'on loan' to an Australian university for linguistic
research.

—Dusty subject, Bushmen and aborigines. Deserts you have to
go to, to find them, the whole thing's dry, from the past. I'm more
interested in people who aren't just about safely extinct.—

He was always good at understanding what women really were
saying to him when they were talking about their husbands.

—People with a future. If I had your money—

They laughed together across the table. A funny thing, the
simple pretty ones disintegrate when they drink, the clever handsome ones become more beautiful, their sex comes to the surface.
She shone, on wine; not the way a woman has a shiny nose, but
like one of those satiny stone eggs, striped brown agate that come
from the desert back where he was a child: warmed in armpit or
groin, breathed on by the body's heat, when the bloom was rubbed
off again against the leg of his khaki shorts a graining of alluvial
light would come up beneath the glassy brown skin. —You would
build a school for the piccanins.—

—A charity school on your farm? A Mehring Mission? Not on
your life!—

But of course: it would be 'perpetuating the system'. For Christ's
sake! He should have had more sense than to give her the opening.
But—then—what did it matter. They were drinking, and laughing
at everything. —You're the sort who has *too much*. You've brought
too much wine.— She was very natural, she belched behind a
frown and tightened lips, she said what she thought.

A little brass chandelier suspended over the table held candles
that were already burned half-way down before they were lit. She
despised elegance. They lasted exactly through the meal, to the
coffee. He was watching them; through everything he said and
that was being said by both of them. There was a little brass hand-
bell with the figure of a stork-like bird to shake it by, and the meal

66

was punctuated by stages when she tinkled it to summon the servant, but the candles kept an unbroken kind of time. He witnessed how they burned out, one by one. Each flame was a yellow lotus with a brownish shape exactly like it, within it. Within that, at the base, was the same shape, still smaller, and incandescent blue. The blue rests on the wick. When the wax reaches the brass lip of the holder, the wick suddenly collapses over it. It sticks out sideways, as if gasping for air. The flame snuffs; then puffs into life again (no brown kernel—the wick is buried in wax—just the yellow aureole and the blue base, intenser blue now). Out; and then silently exploding into flame (she doesn't hear it) once more. And again. It dies finally in the form of a thread of dark smoke that rises straight to the ceiling.

He drew her tongue into his mouth as he would suck the flame of a match up into his cigar. Perhaps she deliberately used half-burned candles, knowing they would always last exactly the duration of one meal for two people—the interplay of conversation with more guests would extend the time taken, of course.

Under the net weighted with beads, Alina has today, as usual, set out tomato sauce, marmalade, honey, mustard, uncertain what category of meal it is that he eats when he comes here. The variety assembled goes further than that: it expresses the mystery of eating habits, unimaginable choices of food not open to her. There is also a jar of pickled onions he bought the other weekend from one of those roadside lorries that sell home produce and handcrafts, fireside pouffes made of off-cuts of fake leather, stuffed cotton toys. It is true, lately he quite often eats at the farm, and at odd times—he may work through lunch and then, on impulse, leave the office at three and pick up provisions whose nature is determined by whatever shop's convenient, on the way. There are no lunch parties down at the river. Not since before he was in Japan. The willows have moulted entirely and the grass, grazed down to earth, anyway, has a layered, slippery covering of narrow brown leaves. Dead, and buried, down there—the summer. Whenever he thinks of bringing some friends out from town... it would amount to the same old crowd, the good friend of fifteen years and her set, the daughter who was the playmate of his son.

On the farm it is the time for conservation—buildings to be repaired, fire-breaks cleared, he must go round all the fences with Jacobus. The sort of jobs they'll never think to do unless you push them to it. A place must be kept up. His energy rises in inverse proportion to winter slackness: sitting there warming themselves against the wall of the kraal, while the weekly bags of mealie meal are sure to be doled out and their poor little devils trail to the pump for water. Jacobus reports that there has been frost already: he has him up on the roof of the shed, hammering down a dog-eared sheet of galvanized iron, sniffing raucously, drawing mucus back into his running nose as he will all winter. On the fences they work together, as they do, from time to time; it is the only way to get the job done properly. Jacobus calls out some reproach, in their language, to chase away the children who are hanging around, not really noisily, just scuffling and stiffling giggles, and, of course, coughing all over the place. —Here, wait!— There seem to be more of them every time he comes out. He has got rid of the two- and one-cent pieces in his pocket and they are happy.

Yes, happy. His hand comes into contact, in the pocket, with the letter addressed in a schoolboy hand that he has not opened.

—Why you don't ask that master what he do? Why he break that light in the back? Is long time now, then he going say somebody else you break you pick-up—

The letter crepitates against the lining of the pocket with every movement of the right thigh. —*You* worry about what you do to the tractor, using it like a location taxi.—

—Me!— But the wire is held steady, no fool; presence of mind, that one.

—Yes, you know what I'm talking about.—

The job is finished in the silence of wire squeaking under strain round the new creosoted posts, twanging like broken guitar strings when released.

—The India he's speak about me.— He's been working it out.

—I don't go to the Indians to talk about my farm. But I know what goes on. Remember that. And if you come and tell me next time the tractor's broken—

He hasn't got an answer to that one. But when he and Solomon

68

and the youngster, the one who affects fancy headgear, are clearing up the roll of barbed wire and the unused posts, they are busy complaining about *him* in the safety of their own language, they retreat into it and they can say what they like. This slightly tautens the muscles in the thickness between his shoulder-blades, a fibrosis, as he feels them behind him, leaves them behind him.

The farm is large. He can go off anywhere. (Quite frankly, I can't wait to get away to my old *plaas*.— There is a mica-glitter of malice in the polite refusal of weekend invitations. He is still in demand; he's needed at table. What a pity, and I had such a charming woman for you.)

Four hundred acres. But like an old horse, he... Everything has its range. Even the most random-seeming creatures are shown by studies to have a topography of activity from which they never really depart, although they may appear to casual observation to weave and backtrack aimlessly, almost crazily, free. From the flat to the car to the office, from tables to beds, from airports to hotels, from city to country, the track like the etching something (worms? ants?) has left on this tree-trunk amounts to a closed system. No farther. Wherever he sets out for or from, or however without direction he sets out to roam, on his farm, it's always here that he ends up. Down over the third pasture at the reeds. Peaceful, of course. They don't come down here any more, for some reason or other; not even the piccanins. He is here alone; there is a sensation he can't place, it's as if, sitting down, he has taken a (non-existent, since he hasn't been wearing one) hat off—it's because the willows have no leaves at all now, they leave the brow and eyelids without any shield against light and space. He is alone with the letter between pocket lining and thigh, not the sort of letter—a letter from a woman—that must be taken away to be read in some special private place. But a letter that has to be read sometime. A shallow grave of stones is under his eye for a few seconds of absent lack of recognition—of course it's not the grave, there is no grave: the pit where sheep were roasted in the summer. Every feature is made simple and prominent by the purity and dryness of winter. The hump of the bank here where, when it is higher, the river flows out of the reeds, has emerged from its plump rump of summer green, the bony hip of an Amazon torso under his shoulder. The muscles round his mouth and the cleft pad of his chin briefly compress the flesh into dimpled bloodlessness in one of those tics developed by men accustomed to conceal their irritation with subordinates. The dead reeds are never quite silent and once he has slit the envelope the unfolding rustle of the two thin sheets within is a fingering in the reeds.

'I don't know how you can say so. There isn't plenty of time at all. You know we had to fill in the registration form last year. They've got my name and everything. You know that when I went with the school tour I couldn't even get a passport to go overseas without you writing to Pretoria for permission from the Defence Force. As soon as the exams are over at the end of the year—this year—(underlined twice) they'll call me up. Please, dad, I know you're busy and that but I must know. Am I going to America in December or not. That's what I must know. (Crossed out.) All I can tell you, that if anyone thinks I am going into their army to learn to "kill kaffirs" like a *ware ou*, well I'm damn well not. Thank you very much—you say it will be an experience for me to meet all sorts of people I don't normally, being sent to a good—I'd call it snob, by the way—school. What sort of people? I don't see anything good (crossed out) anything to be gained by living for nine months as a cropped head with a bunch of loyal South Africans learning how to be the master race because you've got the guns. It would be a good experience, too, I suppose, to be sent up to the Caprivi Strip to shoot Freedom Fighters. About the August holidays. Thanks, but I don't feel like Johannesburg. Mummy suggests that I come to New York to her, but she'll have David and Erica, she won't really be lonely, and it's such a lot of money to ask you. And as you know I hope to be going over in December. But you know Mummy—she always thinks you're a millionaire! Anyway, what I want to do—I thought I'd like to go to South West, to Swakopmund. Will you write to Emmy and Kurt and tell them it's all right? I wrote and they said fine, okay, but would like to hear from you, etc. Don't send an air ticket or the train-fare. I'll hitch.'

Oh fine, okay, cast off the things of this world for those jeans with the hems carefully cut ragged and take your begging bowl on the road to South West Africa. No one's going to know that the old couple who're waiting to anoint the little lordling's feet at the other end are living on a pension from your father.

If I had your money. Of course, his mother didn't want him when she left him, eight years old, but she would fly him back and forth ten thousand miles twice a year to be with her new American brood, why not?

If I had your money... I'd pretend it doesn't exist; on the road, not even the train-fare to my name.

I'd leave it all just as it is. And if I had children, I don't believe in inheritance of property, unearned possessions, the perpetuation of privilege.

—You've got a son? He lives with you?—

—I've always had sole custody. He's away at school. Almost a man. As tall as I am. He said to me last holidays, 'Why did you marry?' And I said to him, what's the reason we go after them—she was pretty. She had a smashing figure.—

It was the hour for a cigarette and confidences, after love-making. Suddenly she was up on one elbow, the olive-brown face with smeared eye-paint was looking down on him with an admiring disgust, an expression he had seen once before under different circumstances, on the face of a woman he had taken to watch a wrestling match. —About his mother?—

—He's not a child.—

—You used exactly those words? As if you were talking of buying a woman in a bar or off the street.—

—Shall I tell you something, Antonia? You don't know it, but there's a special pleasure in having a woman you've paid. Now and then. I can't explain it. It's very clear-cut. For that one night, or that one afternoon or day, whatever it is. You've bought and paid for everything.—

—There will be absolutely no unfulfilled emotional obligations on either side, hanging on afterwards.—

—No, no, you see deep meanings in everything. Sorry to disappoint you. Just the feeling that you're not only taking this woman, you've also paid for her.— His forefinger was stirring with

71

gentle regularity in the black fur in the cup of her armpit, while they talked, as he would scratch a cat just under the ear.

—My god, you want to convince me you can buy anything. Mehring and his wholly-owned subsidiaries.—She began to caress him somewhere, too, to assert that she was not the passive partner in whose role people like him would cast her.

—No, just that there are some good things to be bought.—

A plover has landed within a few yards of his feet, tipping from beak to tail for balance. Its exquisitely neat black and white markings take his eye into visual discipline. The winter landscape of the high-veld is supposed traditionally to be harsh but here it is harsh only to the touch—the bristles of broken grass tussocks, the prickly dead khaki-weed, the snagging knife-edge of dead reeds— everything his gaze has been resting on except the ink of the letter and the shapes of the grave-stones, over there, is soft and tonal. The range of distant hills is laid, pale and gentle, along his horizon. The willows, when he sees them as a destination, from the house or up on the road, are caught like smoke over the reeds. The fact is that all this softness is the result of smoke; particles of smoke that hang in the still winter air; smoke from that location that lies between the farm and city. It's a cataract over the fierce eye of the sun; it's even possible, some days, to look straight at the sun as if you are staring at the prism deep in the under-water radiance of a star sapphire.

He has torn up the letter. Not angrily but not without a self-conscious indifference. Now he doesn't know what to do with the pieces. Paper is organic; it would rot, in the reeds, if he threw them there, no one comes here, no one would understand the jig-saw of words, anyway—'I must know', 'you're busy and that', 'cropped head', 'kill kaffirs'. —Imagine if she were to be walking unknowingly over an undiscovered grave on a farm but she made out, on a scrap of paper, the words 'kill kaffirs'—oh my God, the story she could concoct on *that* bit of evidence of casual heartlessness and brutality, etc!

What do they want, anyway, who only know it's not what he's got? What is it *he* wants—a special war to be started for him, so that he can prove himself the conscientious objector hero? The

72

way he once longed for a bicycle with racing handlebars? The way *you* wanted to end up sending for me to come to you in the Greek café: —Trouble—you said, your eyes changing from fear to idiotic arrogance and excitement the instant you looked up and saw me. No wonder those back-veld oafs in uniform slapped your face; I felt like doing it myself, once or twice. Free spirit, bold gipsy in bed (her name was Mancebo before she married her professor, an old Romany name from Spain or France, she said; more likely just some Jewish blood somewhere); but you were not so free and bold when answering questions about your poor bloody black friends at John Vorster Square. Speak to a good lawyer, a respectable, shrewd company lawyer, and keep out of jail the conscientious objector hero with the straight white-blond hair and that brownish fuzz round the chin that he's produced surprisingly young (he'll be virile, in spite of himself, like his papa, chase women, whether he approves of himself or not).

What is it they think they can have? What do they think's available? Peace, Happiness and Justice? To be achieved by pretty women and schoolboys? The millennium? By people who want good respectable company lawyers?

Change the world but keep bits of it the way I like it for myself—who wouldn't make the world over if it were to be as easy as that. To keep anything the way you like it for yourself you have to have the stomach to ignore—dead and hidden—whatever intrudes. Those for whom life is cheapest recognize that. Up at the compound, Jacobus and his crowd. The thousands in that location. Face down under the mud somewhere, and cows trample and drop their pats overhead, the dry reeds have fallen like rushes strewn to cover, it's all as you said when you suggested: Why not just leave it as it is?

He has them up, arraigned, before him and they have no answer. Nothing to say. He feels inside himself the relief and overflow of having presented the unanswerable facts. To prevail is to be recharged. For a moment there's an impulse to put the bits of paper under one of the stones in the pit; he even stubs at it with the toe of his boot, although he knows (he carried some of them there) it would take two hands to lift it. But he opens the slit envelope and

73

carefully shakes the flakes of paper back into it, making a kind of spout of the angle of fingers from cupped palm. Not one piece escapes to lie about.

—The Dutchman can take the pick-up and break the light at the back and scratch the door. Yes.—

—What kind of man is that? Like a stray dog running in from town and running back. Where's his child? His woman? He doesn't seem like a rich white man.— Dorcas's husband stood among them and followed the figure with the eyes of a town-dweller; on Saturdays and public holidays farm labourers worked but he did not.

—Oh he's got a son. He comes here sometimes.—

—'Terry'. His son said he doesn't want to be called master—he told Jacobus, didn't he? You mustn't call me Master Terry. He just wants us to call him by his name.— Izak gave his young laugh.

Jacobus dismissed irrelevancies, dropping his voice although he knew his words, even if audible at this distance, wouldn't be understood. —Does it break the tractor if I take it up to the shop?—

—You should take the pick-up. Use the pick-up when you like. He wouldn't know the difference. How could he know? He's running in from town and running back. You're a fool, old man.—

—I'm the one who oils and looks after the tractor, I'm the one who looks after all his machines, *all* his machines, everything, all his cattle, every day. Saturday, Sunday, even Christmas.—

They are raking down cattle feed from the bunker silo. A great show of industry—no one looks up except a visitor (the constant stream of Saturday and Sunday visitors, drunk and sober) who is gossiping with them. He must have imagined it, composed out of the cadences of their language what was somewhere in his mind, but did he hear the name 'Terry', quite distinctly, it seems to him, as he passed? Very unlikely. It was some other word that has a similar sound. The round lid of the dustbin outside the kitchen door lifts like a cymbal in his hand (the letter drops into the mess of

74

burnt mealie-meal and potato peelings giving up a smell of fermentation) and clangs closed.

As usual, just as he is about to drive away Jacobus is seen hurrying over with an urgent request. The car engine is running. A bag of cement; this time it's a bag of cement. No matter how thoroughly the question of the farm's needs has been gone into, there will always be this compulsion of Jacobus to think of just one more thing, hardly more than a delaying tactic, as if he doesn't want to be left behind here where he belongs, doesn't want to be left to it, the farm. The responsibility; he really is responsible, old Jacobus, in his way. He has his usual worried grin, head on one side, showing those few rotten tusks; no sign of any offence. He could say to him, take the pick-up on Monday and go to the builders' suppliers; but there's no telling how far the interpretation of such authorization can be taken. The next thing, they're piling in for a beer-drink or a funeral and the pick-up's smashed somewhere, a dead loss because the driver was unlicensed and insurance won't pay. These are the sort of easy concessions that don't do anybody any good; all they do is threaten the organization of a place like this.

Who wouldn't make the world over, if it were easy as that.

—The rise and fall of currencies, of stock exchange prices, of imports and exports, of the supply of labour and the cost of raw materials—

—Of pig-iron.—

—Yes, pig-iron.—

—Ah, I see you do believe in something—you are one of those whose Baal is development—

—What d'you mean 'Baal'?—

—Because you're a pagan, you have to invest some concrete object—a thing—with power outside yourself—

—Coming from a lapsed-Catholic gipsy or whatever it is you are...—

She put her hand on him, just under the left pectoral muscle, half patted, half slapped, half caressed. —This is what I believe in—flesh-and-blood people, no gods up in the sky or anywhere on the ground. 'Development'—one great big wonderful all-purpose god of a machine, eh, Superjuggernaut that's going to make it all

75

all right, put everything right if we just get the finance for it. The money and the know-how machine. Isn't that it, with you? The politics are of no concern. The ideology doesn't matter a damn. The poor devils don't know what's good for them, anyway. That's how you justify what you condone—that's what lets you off the hook, isn't it—the Great Impartial, Development. No dirty hands or compromised minds. Neither dirty racist nor kaffir-boetie. Neither dirty Commie nor Capitalist pig. It's all going to be decided by computer—look, no hands! Change is something programmed, not aspired to. No struggle between human beings. That'd be too smelly and too close. Let them eat cake, by all means—if production allows for it, and dividends are not affected, in time.—

The farm, to justify its existence and that of those who work on it, must be a going concern. These are the facts.

... once at night he was told to awake and go down to the river and he would find an antelope caught in a Euphorbia tree; and to go and take it.

Thousands of pieces of paper take to the air and are plastered against the location fence when the August winds come. The assortment of covering worn by the children and old people who scavenge the rubbish dump is moulded against their bodies or bloated away from them. Sometimes the wind is strong enough to cart-wheel sheets of board and send boxes slamming over and over until they slither across the road and meet the obstacle of the fence, or are flattened like the bodies of cats or dogs under the wheels of the traffic. The newspaper, ash, bones and smashed bottles come from the location; the boxes and board and straw come from the factories and warehouses not far across the veld where many of the location people work. People waiting at the roadside for buses cover their mouths with woollen scarves against the red dust; so do the women who sit at their pitches selling oranges or yellow mealies roasting on braziers. The scavengers are patient —leisurely or feeble, it's difficult, in passing, to judge—and their bare feet and legs and the hands with which they pick over the dirt are coated grey with ash. Two of the older children from the farm go to school in the location. They could return as they come, across the veld and through the gap cut in the fence by gangs who bring stolen goods in that way, but they lengthen the long walk home by going to have a look at what people are seeking, on the dump. They do not know what it is they would hope to find; they learn that what experienced ones seek is whatever they happen to find. They have seen an ash-covered forefinger the size of their own dipping into a sardine-tin under whose curled-back top some oil still shone. When the oil was licked up there was still the key to be unravelled from the tin. There have been odd shoes, casts of bunions and misshapen toes in sweat and dirt and worn leather; a broken hat. The old tyres are hardest to get because people make sandals out of them. From hoardings along the railway line, which also runs through the industries, providing sidings, black men with strong muscles and big grins look down, brushing their

78

teeth, drinking canned beer or putting money in a savings bank. Industries and factories announce themselves—gas welding, artistic garden pots, luxury posture-corrective mattresses, THIS IS THE HOME OF FIAT.

The location is like the dump; the children do not know what there is to find there, either. It is not at all like the farm, where what you will find is birds' eggs, wire, or something (a coin, a pocket comb, cigar stumps) white people have dropped or thrown away. A ring was lost; the children were told to look for a shiny stone in the grass. Once there was a tortoise, and the parents ate it and the shell is still in Jacobus's house.

They roamed the streets of the location seeing in to houses that had furniture, like the white farmer's house, and peach trees fenced in, with dogs like the India's barking, and they passed other kinds of houses, long rows of rooms marked off into separate dwellings by the pink and blue paint used on the exterior, where a lot of men from the factories lived and made mounds of beer cartons on the waste ground around. Outside a hall as big as a church they saw the huge coloured pictures of white men shooting each other or riding horses but they had never paid to go inside. They went into little shops like the India's and bought five cents' hot chips wetted with vinegar, and hung about against the glass walls of the biggest store in the location with thousands of different coloured bottles of liquor behind its fancy steel burglar grilles. They saw men in clothes better than anything Izak had, white caps and sunglasses, wonderful watches and rings on hands resting on coloured fur-covered steering wheels of cars. There were women wearing the straight hair of white people and hospital nurses in uniforms clean and stiff as paper. There was an abundance of the rarities carefully saved, on the farm: everybody here had boxes and carriers and bottles and plastic cans in their hands or on their heads. A child had a little three-wheeled bicycle; a shopkeeper chased a screaming girl who had taken a pineapple. They played in the streets with some children who suddenly snatched their chips off them and disappeared; a balloon was handed to them from a van with a voice like Izak's radio, telling people to buy medicine for their blood. Looking on at boys their own age

79

gambling they saw one pull a knife and thrust it into the back of the other's hand. They ran. But they went back; always they went back. One had once been farther, actually into Johannesburg, lying on a manure hawker's cart and seeing the buildings, enormous, jolting all round as if about to topple with the movement of the frightened horse and uneven axles in the traffic.

Walking home after school from the location, the dirt road gathered itself ahead or behind, rolling up its surface into a great charge of dust coming at them; there was a moment when they saw a car and a face or faces at the fuming centre, and then they were whipped into turmoil, it lashed round them a furry tongue of fiery soft dust spitting stinging chips of stone. When they could breathe and see again, the fury was already gathering up the road on the other side, smoking against the sun and blocking the other horizon. Sometimes it was Mehring whom they found in that split second when they saw into the core of the storm.

Two men came out of the dark, unafraid of the cowardly dogs. The cooking fires were dead and Izak saw two uprights casting hoods of shadow across the kraal yard in the winter moonlight. They were pressed forward, driven within the circle of yelping and snarling. They asked for Solomon.

Solomon was somewhere within the room stored with sleeping bodies whose strong smell was brought out by the warmth of a tin of live coals. He had a woman in his iron bedstead and rose on one elbow beside the head tied in a cloth; he wore, against the cold. the shirt that he worked in and it took enough glow from the fire to show his face. He said nothing, as a man will do when he is neither alarmed nor puzzled. But he made no move, either to get up or lie down again, and Izak turned away. He stepped round those who slept on the floor.

He did not speak to the waiting men and was not surprised that they did not speak to him; he was young, no one consulted him yet. Solomon came out of the room with trousers and shoes on; they said—Your brother says you must come.—

—Tonight?—

—You must come now.—

—I'll come tomorrow.—

—He says tell you to come tonight.—

His movements had stirred children in the room behind him and they began to cough in their sleep.

—I am in bed. We are all sleeping.—

But they were not; they were standing there.

He argued with them for a while.

—No, not tomorrow. Tonight. He's in trouble, you must come, man. There are people making trouble for him. Tonight.—

Solomon went back into the room and returned wearing his pullover. When he walked away with the others Izak could still distinguish him by the light stripes at the neck and waistband.

He was not there to drive the cows to pasture with Phineas and

81

Witbooi in the morning. Jacobus thought he must have slept at his brother's in the shanty town past De Beer's farm and would be late. Jacobus was neither concerned nor annoyed: Solomon was not a drunkard and if his brother had been caught without a pass he would have to find out in which police station he was being held and go there to bail him out. It could take a day.

At twelve o'clock Jacobus went to investigate a blockage in the irrigation pipes and himself discovered Solomon lying naked except for a vest, in the veld. His hands and feet were cold and scaly as a reptile. He had lost a lot of blood from a wound in the head; the spilt blood was frozen, a thin pink ice diluted with frost on the dead grass, where his body had kept off what warmth there was in the morning sun blown glassy by the wind. He was deeply unconscious and did not rouse to cries, voices, or the journey to the location hospital, wrapped in blankets from his bed, in the back of the pick-up. Jacobus and Solomon's woman and Izak went to the shanty town from the hospital but Solomon's brother was not there and had not been seen for three days. They had started their inquiries at the most likely source for news, the drinking-place, and then been sent on the route of rumour from one person to another. Izak could not describe the men because he had not seen their faces. He repeated again and again, for each group or individual, exactly what had been said. Some asked, as if it were Izak's fault, But why did he go with those people? And others pressed, But did he know those men? Izak could only say again exactly what had happened. As the account and the response it brought became ritualized, Jacobus began to add, at the point where Izak's silence began, a remark. —If he had called me, it would have been different.—

They looked at Izak; only a boy.

Solomon's woman wept; he hadn't spoken to her when he came back to fetch the pullover. She was not his wife, he did not tell her things. Back at the farm, Izak showed where he had stood and where the men had appeared, and people testified whether they had heard anything or not. The fowls picked where the men had stood and the dogs who had whined and barked but not prevented their approach lay twitching their bony haunches in daytime sleep.

The children lingered around in the place where something had happened as people who have missed a train continue to stand about. The water was still not coming through the irrigation pipes; but about half-past three it began to run again—Jacobus and the other men got up from the pot of hardened mealie porridge where they had shared some sort of late meal, and went off to set the jets going. The women and children could hear the men's voices, still in discussion, as they went slowly up the fields.

Later Jacobus took the house key from the nail among the hanging onions and telephoned to town. But the office was closed, and there was no reply from the flat. The next afternoon, he tried again.

—I see why it is no water. Is getting too much cold down there by the river. Is coming ice in the pipe; again this morning. Yesterday the same, and again this morning.—

—What do you mean 'again'? Did it flow at all, yesterday?—

—When it's coming little bit warm, in the afternoon, yes—

The voice has no time for this. —Oh all right, I suppose I can get some packing for the pipe—which pipe is it?—directly from the pump-house or where?—never mind—I'll see on Sunday. I just hope it doesn't burst before then. Jacobus, *don't* use any irrigation in the meantime, that's the safest, just leave it, eh? But let the pipe empty while the sun's on it, be sure there's no water there, then disconnect it. Do you understand? Don't irrigate.—

—Yes, yes, much better. And Solomon is very sick in the hospital.—

—Oh my God, what now. And what's wrong with Solomon?—

—In the night he's go over there to the other farm, the Dutchman's farm, to look for his brother. Somebody come fetch him late in the night; I think more than eleven. Now in the morning he's not here for the cows and lateron I myself I see Solomon's all the time in the veld, there, down there, where—you know ... ?

—The third pasture, you mean?—

—...Yes. Someone's take his clothes, everything, cut his head, he's blood there in the veld. He doesn't hear me when I'm take him in the pick-up—I fetch the pick-up and carry him to the location.—

There is no reaction to the mention of the pick-up, although

83

when Jacobus says the word he leaves a fractional pause before he continues; a white man will never refuse you if he has proof that someone is ill or dying; the pause is just to remind him of what he said about using the tractor.

—And what happened at the hospital, Jacobus? Is he all right?—

—He was sleeping, sleeping. They say he's very bad but perhaps he can come all right.—

—Well, that's terrible, Jacobus. He's lucky he didn't die, in this weather, out all night.—

—But I think he's all the time sleeping, don't know nothing, yes …—

—Heavy frost, eh? What are the radishes like? Gone black?—

—They still coming nice…and I find another boy, then, from another place, he can hold Solomon's job for him. Good boy, he know cows well.—

Again a pause. And the response falls into the place that has been made ready for it, just as, at the telephone exchange that connects the two voices, certain metal levers have had to drop into their slots in order to establish the communication. —All right. I suppose so. If it's necessary. I'll try and come tomorrow. If not, Sunday. Don't forget—no irrigation, ay, Jacobus.—

Jacobus looked round before he left the house; nothing there that would be cause for complaint: the pair of boots cleaned and standing beside the refrigerator, the windows closed and curtains drawn. The glass bowl Alina had put in the middle of the table with three shrivelled oranges left over from last time. Nobody had touched anything. He sniffed: no smell, not that he could detect, anyway. He locked up and from the kitchen door, recognizing the head of the man beside Witbooi, hailed the tractor as it was passing the barn. Witbooi called back; their cries rose and died away across each other, nocturnal calls beginning with the cold shadow of sunset. The house behind him was dark; on each window a sun, rouged with smoke and dust, slipped down the blind glass.

The tractor propelled itself over the contours of the darkening earth like a cripple. Witbooi and the other sat a moment when it came to a halt, Witbooi leaning slightly towards Jacobus. Jacobus's one hand was feeling at the missing fastenings at the neck of his overalls; perhaps he was cold. They saw he was not going to approach them and they swung slowly to the ground. They were tired by a day that had not been like other days. Their eyes were caught by the key of the house, lit by the dead sun, hanging from Jacobus's long first finger.

—I've told him. You're going to work here, now. I told him I'm taking you on.—

The other man had been squatting on the farm for many weeks, now. His family fed from everybody's cooking pots; Jacobus could not increase the amount of mealie-meal distributed without accounting for it when the supply did not last the allotted period of time.

The man was frowning. —And he said yes?—

—You didn't believe me, people always want everything to be done *now*. I told you, I know when it is the right time.—

—You'll give us a room? I want that end room, if—

—You've been living all right, haven't you? Your wife, your children—everybody. Just leave it a little while, I'll get you bricks from him. I'll get everything from him.—

The man moved his head in admiring disbelief. He suddenly came to himself: —Thank you, brother, yes, thank you.— —That's all right, brother.— —Thank you, brother.— —It's all right.— The comforting exchange wove back and forth between them. The man seemed to have forgotten Witbooi, forgotten the tractor, went off with head down concentratedly in the direction of the kraal.

Witbooi said—Two here now without a pass.—

Jacobus gestured towards the bulk of the machine; it ought to be in the shed by dark. —D'you think he's ever asked about *your* papers? He doesn't care if anyone's got papers or not, as long as you work. That's all he knows. And if the police catch you, he can just look in your face and say he doesn't know who you are, that's all, you're someone hiding with his boys on the farm. What has he got to worry about?— And he laughed: —I know him.—

Before Solomon recovered sufficiently to tell his story the legend had already grown that he was attacked in the night by a spirit: there was something down there at the third pasture. When he did give an account of what had happened it was a series of circum-

85

stances common to everyone among the farm people, and a cul-
mination familiar to their lives. His brother borrowed twenty
rands from someone, promising Solomon would return the money
for him. Solomon did not have it—a month's wages—and raised it
from someone else, leaving his bicycle as security. Solomon's
brother saw the bicycle and took it away, thinking it had been
stolen. The creditor to whom it had been pledged went to Solomon's brother's place and said that the brothers were both thieves,
demanding his loan back. In the meantime, only nine rands and
seventy cents had been paid to the first man; either Solomon or his
brother had used the remainder for some other need. There were
meetings, arguments, promises, back and forth across the veld,
beyond the reeds between farm and shanty town. The men to
whom money was owed sent henchmen to lure Solomon out at
night and beat him up. He did not know who they were—two
among thousands, over in the location and the shanty town,
ready to do at someone's bidding what they did to him; he knew
why it was done.

But the children did not go to the third pasture. They stopped
one another, hung back: There is something there. No one had
seen it; it had frightened one of the little ones. Which one? Who?
—Something there.—

They did not remember any more what there was there, down
under the reeds. What Solomon had found, months ago, in the
third pasture; still there.

'So,' said he, 'I awoke. When I had set out, my brother, Uman-kamane, followed me. He threw a stone and struck an aloe. I was frightened, and ran back to him and chided him, saying, why did you frighten me when I was about to lay hold on my antelope?'

I s this all that survives?
Is that all that is left?

The reeds are cropped by fire so that they present a surface like a badly-barbered crew-cut head. The whole vlei is seared off, jagged. —You can see that promised land the cows always want to get at; it's nothing but a flat bit of solid island in there.— Blackened, hacked: the whole thing exposed, brought down to less than eye-level, all around. And there's nothing. Nothing to be seen in those reeds, now that everything is bared and revealed. Not a trace. No place to be recognized from any other.

He could see before he ever got to the farm what has happened. Right from the Indian store. Same thing every year but one since he has had the farm; but this time the reeds are destroyed, never before. This time it must have started over at De Beer's place. A black map extends from below the gum plantation on De Beer's hill (the wind spared his trees by blowing the other way) down over the veld to the river, following the vlei about half a mile as if the invader were reconnoitring a place to cross—which eventually it did by leaping from reeds to reeds and burning down towards the hidden islands, establishing itself there and then snatching hold of the reeds once more to burn over the waters to Mehring's veld. The fire's territory: the invasion marked out with its inlets, promontories and beach-heads. Taken overnight.

The moment of first sight, from the store, roused an anguished revulsion, an actual physical reaction, as if the python of guts in which his large weekend breakfast was warming uncoiled against some inner wall of his body. The Mercedes meandered towards the side of the road, overtaken by its own dust. He may have spoken aloud to himself—cursed, the invocation of forgotten and (for him) non-existent gods. Then he put his foot down and drove very fast, feeling the tyres chuntering over the corrugations buried in the dust, conscious of swallowing, with a gulping movement of his adam's apple, conscious of taking in air and containing it, burst-

88

ingly, held in a tense lump at the base of his throat, needing to get there—what for?

It's all done. Smoking faintly. Quite cold. The whole farm stinks like a dirty ashtray. Worse than last year because the willows have caught it, too; but the lands are almost unharmed on his side. He walks along the new boundaries of black and finds at close quarters how inexplicably the fire has reaped a patch of tall grasses here, skirted one there, gutted itself greedily in a ditch, fanned a shrivelling heat over a clump of some tough marsh-plant without devouring it, leaked a trickle of black towards the fence. The picnic bank is in black territory; it's littered with twisted filaments of burned leaves and shapes of willow twigs that appear to have grown furry grey mould and fall to ashes at the touch of his boot. The stones of the pit, there, bear fire-marks like crude pottery.

He follows the black edge wherever it is possible to go on foot, along the river, both left and right of the point at which he approached it, coming down through the third pasture. Where black has made a promontory out into unburned veld, at first he skirts it all the way round, almost squeamishly, but later he strikes straight across these patches. His boots turn grey and he does not know whether he imagines a residual heat comes through the soles. A rat with head intact and eyes open is laid out. Not burned; overcome by fumes? Some coot swim clockwork circles on the river. They are black as everything except the glancing river, but alive, like it, where everything is dead. The river is extraordinarily strong, slithering and shining, already it seems to be making the new paths possible for it through the weakened foothold of destroyed reeds; it swells against its surface sheath and it is impossible to look at it in one place: he feels his eyes carried along. And it seems to have become silent; nothing opposes it. He pushes his way about through burned reeds and along fields the whole morning, trudging up to consult with Jacobus and then going off down again. Of course, Jacobus wants to take full credit for fighting the fire off the farm. It's a long story, like all their stories, and it has to be listened to with one ear. They go together to look at the calf that was thought to be caught by the blaze when it strayed. The man who is feeding the little beast its mash wears a woollen scarf tied round his face the way they do when they have a toothache or headache. —So what did those skelms do to you eh, Solomon?—

Jacobus says—That nice jersey the young baas he give it—you know that one? Very, very nice jersey—they's take it. Everything... You know that one jersey?—

He does not; he does not know how Terry chooses to dispose of his clothes.

—Trousers, shoes, that one jersey Terry give it—everything.— Jacobus is no beauty and when he makes dramatic emphasis he will draw back his cracked lips and show those filthy old teeth.

—It's all right again now, hey?—

The scarf is unwound with an obedience that wasn't called for. It's a pleasant enough black face, patient, with a half smile. There's a thick pair of puckered lips sewn together right across the forehead.

—Oh it'll still fade—get better—it takes time.— He doesn't know how much will be understood. He rarely has had occasion to talk directly to this one, before; Solomon usually has the talking done for him by Jacobus. But the man suddenly speaks:

—This stays by me up to the day when I'm die.—

The woollen scarf is carefully replaced.

—That jersey was very, very nice.—

Jacobus does not look while the white hand streaked with the soot of burned vegetation extracts the packet of cigarettes.

A moment's hesitation; four into the palms of Solomon.

—Here.— Two for Jacobus.

Someone neglected a cooking fire or De Beer's boys decided off their own bat they wanted to burn weeds or force the green through early in a patch of pasture. —Bad luck for us this winter, eh, Jacobus?—

Jacobus is showing with windmill sweeps of the arm, as they walk, how the fire was kept back from the lands. But the truth is it looks as if it reached its own limitation where it wasn't stopped by the existing firebreaks. The wind changed; something like that. Will the willows ever be the same again? They think if the lands are saved no damage has been done. They don't understand what

90

the vlei is, the way the vast sponge of earth held in place by the reeds in turn holds the run-off when the rains come, the way the reeds filter, shelter... What about the birds? Weavers? Bishop birds? Snipe? Piebald kingfisher that he sometimes sees? The duck? The guinea fowl nest in the drier sections, as well. There will have been no nests, though, at this time of year. But what else —insects, larvae, the hidden mesh in there of low forms that net life, beginning small as amoeba, as the dying, rotting, beginning again?

Burned off black. Back down there he moves, a lone piece of vermin through that convict's head of stubble manged with ash. Rags of black hang from the lower stumps of the willows. Perhaps it is not their substance but the remains of the feathery parts of the reeds. Up into some of the older trees fire has thrust a surgeon's red-gloved hand, cauterizing through a vaginal gap or knot-hole; the raised pattern on the trunks of all of them has been scorched into a velour of fine white ash.

His calves are aching. It's something to do with the way the circulation is affected: the doctor said smoke less. That's why he started to smoke cigars in place of cigarettes; except that he now smokes both, instead. But it's not possible to lie down here, not today, not in all this litter from the fire. No wonder they ache. Distress is a compulsion to examine minutely—this anguished restless necessity, when something can't be undone, when there's nothing to be done, to keep going over and over the same ground. He will enter the house today. Somewhere to put his feet up. He comes in as always, like a stranger; the living-room has its un- changing, familiar and impersonal components, as a motel room has when he travels—it does not matter that in this case the signs of a previous tenant, the old magazine, the tot left in the bottle, the remnants of the fruit-bowl, are his own. Even the scent of in- secticide disguised as a substitute for fresh air is there. Alina has been spraying against something although he keeps little for moths to feed on but a couple of pairs of boots; there are the few oddments of clothing his son wouldn't fit into any more if he were to come here now. They could be given away out of compassion as the jersey was. The house is a waste, nobody uses it. Of course the month of the school holidays when he might have been here is nearly over. Soon time for him to be hitching his way home now.

Inspecting the backs of hands as he lies on the sofa he can see the graining of the skin where black was washed in rather than off. Marks of fire: she showed him the clay pots, in her house. She puts out cigarettes by holding the stub down as if keeping the head of a drowning man under water while she talks. —Oh, compassion's like masturbation. Doesn't do anyone else any harm, and if it makes you feel better... —Maybe milord Terry'd agree with you, now, he'd find it adolescent to go down to the compound with his old clothes. One could tease him and tell him it was dangerous— for them to have possessions: a poor devil has his head split open for a few rands. You are right, you never know when you are going to do more harm than good, do you? I can bring porcelain from Japan, really beautiful stuff. But that's what you liked—something spoiled by the fire.

Now there is news to write to South West—the fire. If there happens to be any paper in the house. For the last few minutes he has known that Alina has come in and is on the other side of the inner wall, in the kitchen; he recognizes the slight sounds that follow the pattern of movements she makes in her idea of the preparation of a meal, as one can differentiate between the quiet presence of a cat, slipping into a room along the walls to jump on to a sunny window-sill, and a mouse scuttling and rummaging among food packets or papers. Keenness of hearing revives when one is alone. First the tap is turned on full blast so that it overruns the capacity of the kettle. The kettle touches down on the steel plate of the stove. The sound of the bread tin lid buckling as it is opened. Presently she must come into this room to get at the refrigerator; yes—and she does not knock because somehow the refrigerator makes of the room an extension of the kitchen, in a way. But she places her feet (in blue bootee slippers whose soles show the number 7 as they descend and lift) carefully and does not look at the sofa, as if someone were sleeping there whom attention might waken. —Is there a writing-pad?—

He speaks in Afrikaans, she doesn't seem to understand. She looks from the refrigerator to the kitchen and back. She opens the refrigerator reverently and is hidden by the door for a few long seconds, then emerges with a saucer with a shabby dollop of butter on it and a large milk jug which she hurriedly puts on the table, under the net. He wants to repeat what he has asked but she meets his look with that agitated yearn towards the kitchen again and hurries out. She returns with a tray covered by a plastic lace mat on which, since she holds out the tray low enough for him to inspect, before setting the contents upon the table, he sees a plate with sardines keeping the shape in which the tin confined them, a packet of sweet rusks, and the single tin-foil ingot of cheese remaining in a round cardboard box.

He forgot to tell anyone there are supplies to be brought in. —No—Alina—look in the car, you'll find meat there, and tomatoes. Bread.—

His hand burrows into the back of the section of the cupboard where Jacobus puts the invoices. Any blank sheet would do, but there's nothing, and tomorrow the urge will be gone. He usually dictates his letters, since he doesn't write personal ones. If there's a woman he's pursuing he would telephone; if he knew where she was. He has not written but he dictated a note to accompany a bank draft ten days or so ago. Old Emmy and Kurt will have known what to do with it, even if it has been scorned.

It is too late for letters, anyway. There has been only one from South West Africa and the present of the bank draft served as reply to it. It was headed 'Namibia'. That's all, above the date. Then a selection of suitable information. He has been out into the desert with Kurt and (name illegible or no longer attached to a re-membered face) some other old man from Swakopmund. They were wonderful, they knew everything about plants and animals, Kurt had tried to drive him where he wanted to go, but of course the uranium mine area was sealed off, you couldn't get nearer than Khan Canyon. The Damaras in the area have all been—the word was in quotes—'removed' and herded into a Reserve somewhere, the entire population. A figure was given; also the remark that it is much too cold to swim.

Why this sudden interest in uranium? Not because he wants to go into base metals, that's for sure. Damaras?—talking about the

Klip Kaffirs, in the stony hills around the dry ı ver bed. We used to come upon them when we were youngsters out hunting buck, though how a buck or a man survives in a place like that is a mystery. They are there like the stones—no, were there like stones, apparently they aren't any more. He hasn't ever seen one, but he tells me all about them. Not a very fascinating holiday for a boy of sixteen. Old people and some sort of study of Blue books or White papers (it seems) for company. He could come along to Tokyo or Canada. One of the times. What time would that be? When the school holidays coincided with a necessary trip. A time when there would be a father and son with a lot to say to each other, sitting side by side in the plane and making plans. The farm—who else is a farm for, but a son—doesn't interest him; the whole month of August could have been spent here. Could have planted trees together. One forgets that.

Although the fire was cold, he has come up to the house feeling and looking like an exhausted fire-fighter, and now the tension and weariness of the morning give way to hunger. He does not wait for Alina to bring the food but himself fetches the body-warm brown loaf he brought from town and cuts a rough slice in the meantime. Yes, one forgets; he really has not remembered until today, and the whole month has gone by. Too late for a letter. He is eating the bread without having quartered or buttered it, tearing the crust from the clinging, soft interior and stuffing it into his mouth; he eats slightly piggishly when he's alone here. There is a pleasure in it, even if there are no other pleasures in the house, the beds empty and that piano silent. He really ought to do something about fixing things up a bit; why must the refrigerator be in this room? Yet it is convenient, just to get up from the table and take what you want. Alina brings in a plate of tomatoes wet from the tap and the half-pound of delicatessen ham with slivers of red cellophane sticking to the fat. While he eats he does not look up to the window through which he could see the farm's burns, the beggared willows. He deliberately keeps his gaze the other way, towards the smaller window that gives on a peach-tree, a water-tank, and the utilitarian scrap—a car seat, the frame of an old electric stove—they won't ever throw away.

Chill around him, shadow over his head, wax-polished under-foot—the house is that part of the farm which matters least. What's appreciated is the value of the land. Inflation has contributed to that, but nevertheless it was not a foolish buy in the first place, and it's well cared-for. The land itself must be worth as much, now, as land-plus-house when he bought. There are other houses, other beds (he can never bring himself to lie down in the dingy bedroom, he doesn't mind if his boots smear ash on the sofa). She knew that, of course, though it is difficult with her kind to tell what is grand theory (what she thinks she ought to think) and what actuality. After all, *she* says 'Namibia' too, something that doesn't exist, an idea in the minds of certain people, as the name of a country where he was born and brought up and she had probably never been. Shoulders hunched, mouth clamped, show of a burst of laughter breaking forth: —And in what way, if you please, is your concept of the place any more than an idea? To the Ovambos and Hereros and Damaras? Can you tell me that? You who 'know' the country? Little white baas who ran barefoot with the little black sons of servants, now fathers of servants? A name on a map. A label stuck on them. 'South West Africa.' 'Mandatory territory.' You don't 'own' a country by signing a bit of paper the way you bought yourself the title deed to that farm.—

It is in opposition (the disputed territory of argument, the battle for self-definition that goes on beneath the words) that attraction lies, with a woman like that. It's there (in the divorce-court phrase) that intimacy takes place. Not that he has ever been mixed up in one of those affairs that end in court with detectives and accusing husbands; for a man in his position a scandal is out of the question. Her husband was safely more interested in his Bushmen than the activities of his wife.

She would talk about sex, too, as part of an ideology he couldn't share. Although she visited that territory with him a few times. He wants the boy to have a good time while he is a youngster—that was the way he put these things to her—get it out of his system, not miss anything, so that he'll see the whole business isn't all that important, when he is older.

—What bunk. A simplistic view of sex. As if you can get it over

95

and done with. If you haven't 'missed anything' when you're young, this doesn't mean you have no more to discover in your own sexuality. It's idiotic to ignore that sex is mixed up with emotional ideas that've grown round it and become part of it, from courtly love to undying passion and all that stuff, and these are not growing pains. They're as demanding at forty as at seventeen. More. The more you mature the greater and humbler the recognition of their importance.—

—I don't think about.—

—No, you just do it.—

—That's right.— With a particular smile that she took eagerly as evidence against him but that roused her to him in spite—or because?—of this.

—I remember you told me you rather liked to buy a woman now and then—to think, she's doing this because I've paid her; she has to. Sexual fascism. Pure and simple.—

Why not this house? There was not time; she had friends to stay and they would wonder at her lengthy absence. She laughs at the suggestion of the hairdresser. —Do I look as if I spend hours getting myself back-combed and tinted?— He had given himself away and she never left him unaware of such proof, to her, of what he was: the sort of women he was used to had nothing better to do than spend hours in beauty salons. And what was the corollary of that?—he could have trotted it out pat for her...'while blacks did all their work'. If such women wanted to make love, their alibi was in character.

Since she was such a free spirit, then: —Why do you have to account to your friends for where you go?—

—I have bonds with my friends that are more important than anything else.—

Of course. She didn't even allow herself to mention the friends' names. Some instruction to keep your mouth shut, keep your contacts isolated from one another, if I don't come back from my mission by twenty-one-O-five hours, alert everyone that I've been picked up, destroy documents...all that incompetent cloak-and-dagger romanticism she elevated to a moral code. Didn't it provide her, within its limits, with an alibi as good as that of any woman who goes to the hairdresser? Very convenient. After all, not telling anyone where you were going so that they couldn't reveal your whereabouts even under interrogation made it safe as houses for her to come to his flat those times, even if she had to be home before dark or whenever the countdown with her friends was.

—A duplex, isn't that what the estate agents call them?—Coming down stairs, she looks under her eyelids at her stomach; it is *her* moment of giving herself away. She watches herself. She flaunts early grey hairs but she fears, too—a slack belly. It is true that she is not flat, when you lie on her you do not feel, anymore, that ass's jawbone thrust forward down there. When you look down on her, there is no smooth concave pinned on either side by a hip-bone, that charming reminder of a nakedness beyond nakedness, a nakedness so complete it goes beyond flesh right to the bone, that some young girls show in a bikini, with cover over only the little padded beak that brings the female body to a point. She did not have a particularly beautiful body even then, five years ago, before she need really have begun to worry about what will happen to it, what happens to them all, around the waist.

—What, no sauna bath? No swimming-pool?—

—Communal. On the roof. You'll have to be satisfied with the bathrooms, pink with beige john, green with black john. Take your choice.—

—Oh very chic. Which does one use for what?—

If I had your money...

She came to the flat, like the others; it was in the flat, like the others. Only Terry has slept behind the wall of this room (not the wall behind which the kitchen lies, where Alina is talking to somebody); over behind the piano and the wall where a pair of china duck in flight hang up high. On the bed in his school sleeping-bag, Terry—that is certain—had no woman in there, only masturbation and compassion.

The dunes of the desert lie alongside the road between Swakopmund and Walvis Bay. Golden reclining nudes. Torso upon torso, hip sweeping from waist, smooth beyond smoothness, suggesting to the tactile imagining only the comparison, in relation to the hand, of the sensation of the tongue when some substance evanesces

97

on it. The sea is on the other side of the road. There among the rocks pelicans floated at rest like bath toys and those crayfish—lumps under mayonnaise in the sort of place he goes to—were caught by feeling with bare hands under the rock shelf. No fancy gloves and goggles and snorkels that old Kurt and Emmy demand nicely for their princeling visitor. There were old-timers who were friends of Kurt then, too, who knew nature lore and told stories. Could be the same old man. There's a quality in people like them that makes youngish men seem to have been old, in retrospect. The appellation 'old so-and-so' designates something other than age—benignity, perhaps? Some comfortable outgrown quality you don't see around. Goodness? Emmy and Kurt are good simple people—which means they have been left behind, they don't change, they are preserved by the desert back there in the past—as good for the boy as they were for himself when he was a boy. Childless women like Emmy are the ones who would have been the best mothers; old chaps like Kurt, who have no son, can do with any boy all those things the father doesn't have time or the knack for. That little house alone, with its back garden of desert sand raked into a pattern along the paths marked with seashells, and the dog's kennel Kurt made with the hinged roof so that, like Emmy's house, the dog's could be aired every morning. It's the sort of thing that makes children happy. One would think that for a boy of sixteen, a farm to mess around on would be a paradise; you could keep a horse to ride, if you wanted. If you took an interest.

—You must come out to the farm again, sometime.—

—Oh yes. That was a beautiful place... —

As if he had burned it down or something. Destroyed it by his touch. But it was all part of the sexual game with her, perhaps? He must try to entice her; she must seem to be capitulating. And then she bobs her backside up in his face, so to speak, and is off. —One of these days... —

—Take a picnic lunch. Just for an hour. I'd love to play hookie from the damned office.—

She looks insolently, thrusting her chin and waggling her head, making fun: —I know you would. Perhaps. Next week.—

Once or twice in the flat; that was nothing, really. She was not a woman who had an instinct for what you wanted, at particular moments, when in bed. No doubt she thought she was a remarkably 'intelligent' lover. In the flat, just like any other.

—Oh yes…sometimes I wish I had your farm…— She was the one who brought it up again.

He had not mentioned the subject. They had met at an hotel for a drink after he had not seen her for several weeks and did not know whether she would come somewhere—it would have to be his flat, he supposed—or whether they would have one more drink and part for the evening.

—Sometimes for such a small reason—any little thing—this afternoon I was rushing along the street to—I had to get somewhere in a hurry—and I saw a puppy outside one of those little houses with a polished stoep and ferns in a tin—you know. A spindly pup standing with its paws turned in and its silly tail hanging in the air. Then it sat down suddenly and watched everything going by. I wanted to have that puppy and that house and sit and play with it in the afternoons. For a few moments that's what I wanted. And I understood that by *that* I meant what it was to be 'good'. Can you imagine me?—

So you have moments when you want to submit to the 'system', keep out of 'trouble', be a housewife complacent in her white privilege. Just as you want to go and make love although you are ashamed of having lovers; again a man like him is quick to understand what is being said that can't be said.

—It presented itself as an awful temptation, honestly just for a flash. I must have been very tired today.—

To understand and to take the opportunity. —You don't look tired.— She would groan if you told her she was pretty, etc. but at the same time it was what she must hear, not in so many words. Time was measuring as it did when the half-candles were burning; —And if you had my farm?—

She tapped her foot a few moments, her thigh moving in her skirt; smiled, summing herself up in the way she prided. —Same sort of thing, I suppose.—

She looked at him.

—Grow chickens.—

—Raise chickens.—

—Well, whatever. Be a—a— She moved her head attractively, her lips, ready for the words, searching as if for a fruit being dangled at her mouth.

A brave revolutionary. Trouble, you said. You were proud, you had resisted all the temptations: oh *shame,* dear little puppy, dear little piccanins.

—I don't know why I tell you these things.— After making love it was always necessary to her ego to establish the difference, the vast gap between herself and a man like him, that might seem to have bridged itself in pleasure. And at the same time she was offering flattery: no ordinary pig-iron dealer, then? —I really don't know why I do. But don't you find the people it's most difficult to make confidences to are the ones who are closest to you? In fact confession is best made to complete strangers. Somebody who gets talking to you on a journey. It's easier with someone you don't know at all.—

The house has never been got into shape. He is closing the windows against the dust that is blowing up this afternoon (the burnt vegetation makes it worse) and everything inside is much the same as it must have been when he couldn't look in properly from the outside the first day. Seeing the black landscape out there, his fingers curl up into his palms, he's kneading his own flesh, he feels the nails biting and marking him, he can't help it—how many years have those willows been put back! Even if most survive; it is difficult to tell how dead or alive they are—those that he knows, from inspection close-up, have had the innards burned out of them have, from here, brown wisps blowing about on top, strands dragged over a pate of sky, that appear too high to be harmed. Even if it had been somewhere other than a couple of times at the flat, it would have worn itself out by now. It was wearing thin already. How many more times, before that day in the Greek café where she felt sure no one would recognize them? There are no letters of course. —I won't write. It might not be healthy for you to get letters from me.— That sort of thing; even when she was on the run as fast as she could scuttle, she still couldn't resist pulling frightening faces at herself in the mirror.

—Nobody opens my mail, I assure you. Except my secretary, when it isn't marked personal.—

—Ah yes, that's the trouble—you think you are inviolate, the Special Branch wouldn't dare take an interest in you, you're developing the economy, you're attracting foreign capital, you're making friends with the Japanese, you're helping to balance the balance of payments— She was amusing, all right, when she started with one of her dark political warnings and then took off on one of her flights of fancy into what she thought of—tongue-in-cheek—as his world. —Still, those wholly-owned subsidiaries. Tube Manipulations, what was it?—Hot-Dip-something—you have multiple identities and addresses, chairman of this and that, president of the other... She was reflecting now, envious, how she might have made use of these identities and addresses, coming to mind too late. He followed the thought across her olive-smooth face: You don't mind if a few letters come enclosed in envelopes addressed to the chairman? It won't be often. You can give them to me when we see each other.

She was the one to telephone, from the café, after weeks—was it? Months? Long before then he had forgotten about trying to get her out here. When she kissed him (in the car? Could it have been when he took her to the lawyer she wanted of him? No, he saw her again after that, but not in the flat, thank you, now that she'd really succeeded in getting herself into trouble and probably was being followed about)—she kissed him, he knew she would leave the country; there was no feeling to send his nails into his palms.

In spite of the wind that makes a loose-hinged window screech so that someone seems to be shaking at the house for entry—Jacobus must be told to wire it up until he remembers to bring out a new hinge from town—he gets on to legs that no longer ache but feel weakly cool in the calves for a moment, from having his feet up, until the blood comes back, and he goes out once more. Dust has the effect on his distant hills of a pencil sketch gone over by a soft rubber. Nearer, every object flashes, scoured by the wind in the three o'clock sun—cows' horns, new wire of a fence, the strap of his watch. Behind the house, looking up the lands towards the road, all is untouched. A field of polka rye cowers flat under the wind; it's ridiculous to have the irrigation jets going on it, the water's all being blown away. He struggles with the valve, where water keeps dribbling although he's turned it off. He likes to show he prefers to do things for himself when he's there, he doesn't believe in calling the boys all the time. The upper fields that have been ploughed are all right, of course, and—he has stopped, he has his hands on his belt, he is smiling and counting, eyes slitted against the wind—over there, over there, are twenty-three guinea fowl, some just the heads, others the leaden-blue oriental shapes in profile, something off the border of a piece of Indian cloth, stylized as the mango pattern on a paisley tie he's got. Twenty-three. He may have counted one or two twice, or missed a couple—they know he's there and they are moving. They seem to flow evenly, heads advancing over the clods as boats breast choppy water. But they're actually running like hell, just try and keep up with guinea fowl. Twenty-three, about. A flock of twenty-three on my place. Not bad. That's not bad at all. A small black sore on the landscape stays his pleasure—what's that, far from the river? But he knows at once what it is—that's up at a small road where one of their buses goes down to the industrial area opposite the location. The squatters who go out to work catch the bus there and it's cold, these mornings—must be—they just light themselves a bunch of dead grass to warm their hands while they wait ... It happened last year. That's how the whole thing began, last year, not on De Beer's side, but from the road. He will never know when the phone-call may be to tell him there's been another fire. There's a fire-break, all right; he saw to that early in the winter season, he had the boys up there. But what's to stop anyone going to the other side of the break to warm himself with a nice little blaze. Nothing to be done.

Passing under the glittering-scaled gum-trees with leaves blown back showing the undersides, it seems to him as if the fire from the vlei has gone through the kraal too. But no. The ground is marked by the heat of their braziers everywhere. An enormous ash-heap beside their rooms. The blackened sacks in the apertures are only curtains. Burned mealie-cobs lying about where they've been eating. It's just as usual, in winter, when there's no rain to clean the place. Their dogs lift shaky heads and bark at him, but they never come out; it's a bitch with puppies who's making all the fuss, and the puppies are starved, they ought to be taken to be put away at the S.P.C.A. It's no good talking to Jacobus, apparently. But the flock could have been fifty. If they increased too much, one could always cull a few, for the table.

From here, black desolation down there at the river is before his eyes again.

They are tramping past him on the road in their usual weekend peregrinations. He hears them at his back and they hesitate to overtake him, it's as if he's leading them in procession, ridiculously, for a few moments, and then they surround him at a polite distance briefly while gaining on him, two men on the one side, and one of their women on the other. The one man wears his farm gum-boots and the other has a balaclava enclosing him in a knight's visor against the dust—he can't take off his hat as his companion does while passing, but both intone, *Baas...Baas...* A bit tipsy already, he can hear, it's Saturday afternoon, the weekend's begun, for them. A disinfectant whiff of Lifebuoy soap where they pass; from the woman a smell of female (he supposes; he does not associate it with the intimacies of white female flesh) and wood-smoke. She wears a blanket pinned as a warm skirt over a dress and her strong shiny black calves and shiny black arms with elbows like pips in the flesh are bare. Children going towards the compound have not greeted him. There's a baby being carried among them that has light yellow-reddish hair—very ugly. He doesn't remember seeing it before; God knows how many people move into that compound.

No point in going down there again. Going over losses. There are no losses—none that can be measured to put down on the income tax forms—the polka rye is undamaged, no stock has been harmed. The fact is—his feet are carrying him over the frost-bitten lucerne stubble, anyway—he just had not remembered until today that the month of August is almost over, that—no, not a child who will play marbles in the schoolboys' winter season for the game, but the one with the long blond hair and incipient beard, has not been here.

103

An unnecessary presence. The fact is—he has reached the third pasture, he has opened the gate for himself and looped the wire over the post behind him—he would not have his gipsy back. He walks on and on, following the black, reading the topography of the new boundary, pacing it all out measuredly: what is it that he has? It is something they would never believe. It's not convenient for any to believe, it's contrary to all ideology; stop your ears, cover your eyes, then, if you don't like it. He is striding slowly. He hears his own tread, boot following boot, exploding faint puffs of brittle burned vegetable membrane, breaking traceries that are the memory of what is already consumed by fire. His thoughts space beautifully to the tread.

My—possessions—are—enough—for—me.

Who dares say that?

He has not spoken. There's no one to speak to, on the farm. He's aware that he's accountable to no one. There is no answer. You are not here, nor he. You are not here, nor she. The season is not suitable for picnic parties from town. The colleagues on the Board, the mining connections, the chairman who has a place of his own like this, the women who seat him beside them at dinner, the daughter who offers still the child's good-night kiss, they are not invited. A dead man, but he doesn't speak the same language. The coal-blue water's chapped by the wind. The dust has raised a second horizon, edged with mauve, all round the sky. Even in this wind, the burned reeds are silent, all strings broken.

He feels the stirring of the shameful curiosity, like imagining what goes on behind a bathroom door, about what happens under a covering of earth (however shallow; you can be sure it was done carelessly) when a fire like this one comes over. Is all somehow blackened leathery, hardened in baked clay, preserved, impossible to get rid of even by ordeal by fire? Or is it consumed as if in a furnace, your whole dirty, violent, threatened and threatening (surely), gangster's (most probably) savage life—poor black scum—cleansed, down there? Escaped from the earth in essence, in smoke?

When it rains again (if the rains are good this year; and every farmer must be an optimist, as he says with the professional pride of the amateur, in city luncheon talk) there will be smooth, olive-coloured tapers everywhere, coming out even from those trunks that may collapse and lie in the water, and the reeds will come up, too, high as a man, you won't be able to see in there. The damage is done. But it will seem as if nothing has ever happened. It will be as if nothing ever happened down here.

... That was the end of it, and he was not again told by anything to go and fetch the antelope. They went home, there being nothing there.

What had begun as their own passion to be let out had long since become a fierce passion to keep out others. The dogs held within their ring of savagery the Indians' store, house and family, and the blacks in the yard, surrounded together. It was the Indians' only form of tenure; and the Africans had papers that made them temporary sojourners where they were born.

Bismillah in shirtsleeves came from the chilly shelter of the shop and walked about in the sun for a few minutes and it was not to take the air. He saw at once where part of the fence was sagging or where another bit of old roofing was needed to reinforce the corrugated iron with which it was defended. No breach went unnoticed. And the black men who under his instructions hammered the iron into place or cobbled the barbed wire did so with satisfaction. Now no one could get in. They were safe against their own kind, all the others who had nothing of right and would take anything.

No marauder from the location could come near the store-room with the boarded-up windows where primuses, cooking pots and bicycle spares were kept. No terrorizing hand blew the door of the safe, with the coat-of-arms of the English makers faded on it, that was hidden behind a pink curtain in the passage of the house. No intruder's face frightened the gentle girls, or the beautiful children who clung to the drapings of maternal statues stationed at the kitchen stove. The tyres of the old Pontiac would never disappear overnight, nor the car radio and the batteries. And in the hovels where the blacks lived the bicycles would not be taken, nor the blankets, or Dorcas's sewing machine bought from Bismillah on instalments she agreed to have docked off her wages.

The dogs paced out the limit of this safety.

They were useless against the possibility—always present—of a visit from some official, investigator, inspector: many titles that all amounted to the same thing: a white man with the right to serve an eviction order. The dogs must be called in, chained helpless against the arrival of such a one; he was not an intruder or marauder, he came in the name of law, there was no defence to keep him out. He must not be antagonized: the only way was roundabout. A Group Areas order might be enforceable in six months, a year, two years? An extension might be granted. There was the question of designation of group area: Proclaimed White? White by Occupation? Bismillah was not an educated man—he'd seen to it that his sons were given a better start—but within this legal terminology he was as much at home as any lawyer. And although he was not a rich man (the family was large, the Pontiac they crammed into, secondhand) he had paid out and was paying out regularly as if *he* were buying something on the instalment plan, lawyer's fees to keep himself and his family one move ahead of the official visit. If the official came to warn that it would be six months, the lawyer must be ready to find the legal loophole that could make it a year. And when the year is up, another year. There was an old, old man in a country store like this one who simply refused to move when the evictors came, and went to prison, and fasted there to shame them in Gandhi's way by suffering in his own person, and died, at last, recognized as a kind of saint by the white newspapers. Bismillah's wife and old aunts welled tears when Nana Sita was recalled; but while everyone could be proud that he was a great man as only an Indian can be, most people had wife, children, and aunts etc. to think of. Not everyone was poor enough to afford greatness.

When Bismillah was satisfied that the fence was being put in order he went in through the store to the house, picking up on the way a bottle of cough syrup and a phial of pills that had stood, for the past few days, where they would be under his eye beside the till. The passage of the house was narrowed by things for which there was room nowhere else—the safe, a glass-fronted bookcase preserving the schoolbooks used by each child throughout his school life as well as a presentation copy of the Koran, Khalil Gibran, and *How to Teach Yourself Accountancy*, a folding crib propped against the wall, a tall rickety plant-stand with a vase of artificial chrysanthemums that shook over his footsteps.

The plant-stand had once stood in the room he now entered,

before it had had to be given over as the new home of the latest young couple the house had to accommodate. Into this one room was fitted all the proper provision made by her parents in Durban to set up in married life the bride of his second son, Dawood: the father-in-law was surrounded by white, gilt-scrolled furniture assembled almost as close as in the pantechnicon that had brought it from the coast. The mauve nylon curtains were draped across the lowered venetian blinds; the frilled lamps with their gilt chains were lit. At eleven in the morning, there was the intimacy of night. In the enormous bed, his face rosy-brown within pillows against the satin-padded gable of the bedhead, his son lay smiling. Two front teeth like those of the grandfather rested on his lower lip, but this lip was fresh and shiny. —Listen—she says I must get up now, I'm getting lazy— He spoke English, clutching the wrist of his young wife, who was struggling to her feet in embarrassment from where she had been lounging beside him. The sleeping bundle of baby was on the bed, too. Her trousseau *choli* was tight and Dawood pulled mimicking faces at the confusion with which she tried to lift the sides of the fashionable low square neck where her milk-bloated breasts bulged together under the gauze sari with the same heated, glistening look as the flesh of his face. There was a radiator warming a smell of new varnish, Vicks, and human milk. The whole tiny room with its furniture-store opulence seemed slightly feverish.

Bismillah said to the girl in Gujerati—Did you remember to take the temperature?— She put her hand over her mouth and drew in her breath.

—Just listen what she said—Dawood spread his legs under the covers and lifted his pelvis and laughed, wriggling lower in the bed. She snatched up the baby as he counted on her doing, as if he were about to kick it off. —Listen, man, listen— His huge black eyes held the enjoyment of attention of father and wife; he was exactly the way he had been when he was sick as a little boy, except for the stubble that shone strongly over his youthful double chin and round his red lips and white teeth. —But that stuff makes me cough worse!— Yes, with the beard, he was a gay little boy dressed up as a bandit, that's all. Bismillah had never trusted anyone but himself to administer medicine to his sons. He ignored the giggling young man's silly banter in English, and pushed the spoon at his mouth. Then came the antibiotic tablets, with the girl standing by ready with water in one of the cut-crystal wedding-present tumblers. Dawood made a fuss, eyeing himself; the whole scene was in the full-length mirror of the dressing-table that stood opposite the foot of the bed, with just room enough to pass between them.

—It makes me much worse, you see?— between bouts of coughing.

—No, the chest is looser. Let me tell you. I can hear it. Much looser. You must try and spit—give him something he can spit in. It should be here next to him all the time. Here—

—No—just a minute— But the girl was overcome by the audacity of her own objection.

—No, what are you doing!—not that, Bajee!— Dawood was gesturing and laughing at his father, which made him cough.

—This will do. Why not?—

—No, no, that's a precious thing to her—

Bismillah held up the bowl in challenge for it to manifest its special purpose.

—It doesn't matter. It isn't anything. But not to spit in—she doesn't want it.—

—What is the harm? It can be washed—

—But not to spit in it—

Bismillah put down the useless object, then, dismissing. They were all talking at once, in their own language, except that Dawood would always interject with his *Listen*, that's how the young ones were when they'd been to school in the city, they must mix English with everything to show how educated they are.

—Bring up the phlegm. You will never clear the chest—

—All right, all right—Ah no, d'you expect me to put my nose in that— And Dawood was thrashing around joyously, childishly in the bed again, fending off the small enamel basin his wife offered. —She cleans the baby in that. When he has messed himself, you know? That's the thing she put the bits of cotton wool in. No, no, man—

III

Bismillah stood for a while in the doorway. Dawood sank back into his pillows, teasing, complaining, showing the girl off as a pet unaccountably reluctant to do the tricks it knows perfectly well. She sat on the edge of the bed again and undid the bundle resting on her lap, wavering limb after limb. Her spread legs were ample support; alas, the boy had married one who would be enormous after a few more births. But at least she managed a foolish smile today, shut in the bedroom like this. She had not been very lively among the girls of the house for the year she had been living there, although the only complaint on her part that Bismillah had had reported to him (if the wives were dissatisfied how could they be good for his sons) was that she had not known it would be so cold here in winter. What did she think, standing looking out into the yard or across the burned veld—you could grow bananas, it would be warm and steamy and green, like the coast? If women started grumbling, hankering, there was usually no end to it. The next thing, she would be working on Dawood to let her go and stay for months at a time with her family in Durban. The infant's tangle of minute fingers caught in the gauze over the breasts that had outgrown the girl and were juggled as she moved, and Dawood drew attention to the incident delightedly, intervening with his own hand to disengage the baby's, half fended-off, half encouraged by the protests of the girl. The father-in-law suddenly decided she might want to nurse the baby—something of that nature. He left them.

—Get a dish from the kitchen, ay?—You must try to bring up.—

Yes, that was the short stage in life when a young man discovers his hands again, just the same as the baby, all over again, for a while. The boy will be happy anywhere where he can be touching the first woman he has all to himself. Anywhere. The room is paradise. The room is enough. Why should he ever want to get up and come back to the shop?

The old man sat there on his bentwood chair.

—With all this wind and dust how can the chest clear.—

His old father said nothing; that did not mean he was not listening.

—The medicine loosens, but I told him, he must spit.—

The old man cleared his throat; he came from a generation for which such an injunction was unnecessary, it must have seemed absurd to him.

Yinifuna? Yinifuna?

Some of the blacks would hang around in the shop for half an hour, fingering everything. Others didn't want to wait their turn to be served. Bismillah spoke the few necessary words of their language in the pidgin form that had evolved in the mines; he knew, as well, the pidgin Afrikaans and English used by blacks on the farms. A woman was asking the price of every bolt of cloth on the shelves behind William; when Bismillah had sold a man a bar of mottled soap he pointed at and measured a pound of dried beans for another, he called—What does she want?—

—She's look this stuff.— But the black man understood the semantics of the trade and told the woman in their own tongue that now she must make up her mind to buy. She took no notice, lingering, leaning across the counter to gaze at the rolls of crimped nylon removed from her reach, before drifting out of the shop with a weighing consideration for anything in her path and a remark or two that, rather than addressed to fellow customers, assumed a right to express unspoken thoughts shared with them.

Yinifuna? Yinifuna?

—Sugar—they said.

—Tea.—

—Matches.—

—Tin syrup.—

Some merely held out money and indicated. Sometimes the money was inadequate: —Fifteen cents.— Bismillah thrust the ten-cent piece back; often they would then expect time to consider if they could or would pay the price. They might grumble, or ask for a smaller quantity or another brand. —I want for ten cents.— —No ten cents, only fifteen.— Demand. Response. Counter-demand. Statement. No word was given away. Communication, narrowed down to its closest immediate confines, was complete. At the same time Bismillah continued with his old father the long conversation of their lives together in the shop, its rhythm marked but never broken by the pauses of ordinary daily absences and returns and the gradual fall, over the years, of the dominance of the old

113

man's voice to the corresponding rise of Bismillah's as the one lapsed into the silences of age and the other came into the loquacity of middle age. In a full shop, the privacy of this talk in Gujerati was as secure to the family as if the shop were empty. The language reached nobody else's understanding; in addition, contexts were so unvaringly established, grooved by time and sameness, in the minds of the old man and Bismillah, that no reference was puzzling or irrelevant.

—You can't be there to think for them forever. Do they realize? And what will happen then.—

Yinifuna? How much you want—twenty-five cent? This one thirty-five cent, this one twenty-five—

The black man's hand, permanently curled to the grip of spade or hoe, the nails opaque, thick, split as worn horn, did not presume to touch, but wavered from one to the other. He stank like an old hide. Children waiting their turn to be served after him rested soft lips on the counter edge, putting out their tongues now and then to stem the snot sliding down from their noses.

—It's all right to enjoy yourself while you're young. But can you talk to them. They don't realize.—

The small faces gluey with smeared mucus and dust stared at the old man sitting on his chair with ankles crossed, round white cap on his bearded head, hands clasped under his belly and first finger twitching to some beat of his being, and he stared back, not because he was seeing them but because that was the line and level of his daily gaze, as from a window, into the shop.

—Their minds are I don't know…somewhere—

Bismillah put out a quick palm, fingers impatiently signalling advance; a small black claw thrust a two-cent coin and got four fish-shaped sweets from the glass jar bleary with powdered sugar. —I can't discuss. You would think they would be concerned, but nobody shows any interest. An opinion, at least; they have got matric, they read the papers, don't they.—

He understood a question or demur in his father's silences. —Jalal, all right—but then with him it goes too far the other way, he would only get us all into trouble. I was drinking some tea at three o'clock this morning. She said to me what are you so restless for?

Nothing, I said to her, nothing, go and make some tea. What am I so restless for. How can I just lay my head on the pillow at night. Do they realize? What good does it do to lie awake, she says to me. Easy to say.—

The old man began to wheeze and clear his throat in the sign that he was about to speak.

Bismillah flourished the till closed and turned the red-stoned ring on his finger, working it with his thumb, talking excitedly as if he already had been interrupted. —Bulbulia says it will be very difficult this time. He's not at all sure what he can do. Don't count on it. He's a clever man, I trust him, never mind what Jalal says—but he can only do what he can do, we have to understand that. Where will it come from? Do the children realize? They only know how to spend. If I have to pay again, all right, I'll pay. He knows. But he says there's a new man in charge and he has to go carefully. Of course. He's a lawyer after all.—

The old man's voice came at last as a note sustained by the stiff and gasping bellows of an old organ. —We trust in God.—

—What? Yes, God. If God will help us.—

He and the old man watched each other; he had his back slumped to the counter and his maroon woollen waistcoat wrinkled under full pectorals.

—One who is not a Dutchman—the old man spoke again. —One from town. A businessman.—

Bismillah moved his head weavingly. After a moment he granted: —You're still thinking about the one with the Mercedes. But why should a man like that be willing? He doesn't need money. Why should he want to get mixed up. A wealthy white man like that comes out just, you know, for a Sunday. You can see it. To show his friends the country. He doesn't want the money. He doesn't want a general store in his name. With a Dutchman, that's different. These people around here always need money; all these farms are mortgaged. If you could know just the one that happens to need it badly enough—three hundred rands? five hundreds— perhaps you can come to an arrangement...—

The old man's finger shook faster in disbelief of the efficacy of the sum.

—A thousand. All right. They will get the last penny from us if you want something from them. There Jalal is right. But can he tell me what to do if we won't pay a white to get the licence in his name? Does he tell us where to go and make a living then?—

The old man said—Not a Dutchman. Perhaps...You never know. He's a businessman himself. He can only say no.—

—And go to hell, and who you bloody think you are— But Bismillah spoke to himself, in English, turned away already from his father and mumbling, out of the old man's hearing, his menace towards another who would not understand, one of the noisy kind who had come into the shop full of the courage of beer. —*Ufunani?* What's he want—ay? If he want something all right. Otherwise he must get out, no shouting. No shouting in this shop, you see?—

William said —He come speak to you.—

—You give him what he wants.—

The man wore a worker's uniform, overalls with gum-boots that had some sheen of red and rusty liquid dried on them.

—What's he want with me?— Bismillah addressed William although the man had planted himself where the storekeeper had come out from behind his counter.

—I want Dorcas' money.—

—What's he talking. I don't know what he's talking.—

—This the husband of Dorcas, the girl there.— A jerk of William's head to the back of the store, the house.

—I don't know anything about any money.—

—Dorcas is the girl for your house, yes? You pull back two rand when you pay this month. Why you pull back two rand?—

—I don't know who you are. I don't hear anything about money from you—do you work for me? That girl works for me, isn't it?—

—Why you pull back two rand?—

—This husband for Dorcas. He want talk you.—

—You tell Dorcas to talk to me. I don't know this man.—

—Tell me, why you pull back two rand?—

—You get out of my shop, I don't know what you want here.—

—He stay with Dorcas in the yard.—

—Now get out, I don't want to see you here or in the yard, you understand? You get out.—

116

All around inside they stood back detachedly. A squabble between hens or a dog-fight might have broken out between their feet. William's face became crooked with responsibility; in a seizure of self-control that took him more violently than any rage he low and urgently forced the man to back out, step by step before his hissing whispers. Their ranks closed again, waiting to buy; all owed money, were owed money, were in need of money, knew it was no good expecting to get anything from those other kinds of people, Indian or white, who always had money—there was nothing remarkable about what had just passed. Bismillah straightened his maroon woollen waistcoat as if he had been man-handled and went back calmly to put his counter between them and him.

But William went through his own people with the aura of some-thing dangerous standing away from his body like the rising of hair to static electricity. His eyes plunged into them blindly while his hands exchanged goods for the coins warmed in their clutch. His presence was a sensation, as the argument had not been. —She bought things and can't pay the shop, eh?— There was amaze-ment at the risk this casual speaker was taking. William stood breathing so that they could all hear. His voice struck—You talk about your own business, woman.— They bought what they wanted and went away.

The husband of Dorcas had joined the Three Bells Christmas Club in March and the receipts for his payments, with the em-blem of bells and a sprig of green with berries, tied together by a red ribbon, were folded small each month in his pass-book. No one else in the Indians' yard belonged to a Christmas Club. Nobody else there worked in town and knew that such things existed. No-body even knew what a Christmas Club was; he had spent the best part of a whole evening explaining, when he brought the member-ship card and first receipt home, and after that, other people had heard that he had joined something and come to hear about it, all over again. He also had the leaflet the club gave out at the abattoir, and this had been handed round. For the benefit of those who could not read English he had translated: here was what you must pay every week—30 cents for the Family Parcel No. 1, 35 cents for the Family Parcel No. 2, 45 cents for the Bumper Parcel. Then there was the list of what was in the parcel he would get, according to his weekly payments when Christmas came. He would be bringing home, on the 15th December, Family Parcel No. 1, which included in addition to flour, candles and matches, soap, jelly and custard powder, 1 Large Tin Peaches, 2 Tins Nestlé's Cream, 1 Tin Sausages, 1 tin Corned Beef, 1 Tin Fancy Biscuits, 1 lb Coffee, 1 lb Cooking Fat, and a Grand Surprise Packet of Sweets for The Children. Everyone recognized the bells, because of school and church, but several people asked what was the green sprig with white berries? Even Dorcas's husband had not been able to say from what bush it came.

He took out the receipts and unfolded them and spread them smooth with the hammering heel of his hand, one by one. He tore them up one by one and then swept the pieces from the packing-case table to the floor with a blow of the flat of his hand that went on pounding while he shouted. The wood caved and splintered. The candle in the saucer went over and an enamel plate with the remains of mealie-pap and gravy bowled off, ringing against whatever it struck. He kicked at the hens that rushed for the food. Dorcas was sobbing with regular energy, like a pump, her arms round the sewing machine. The rhythm changed to screams among the skittering, squawking fowls and people came in to interfere, argue and take sides. Someone carried the sewing machine to safety. William was there. —You want the police? I tell you he won't listen to me next time if you make trouble like this, I can't stop him—

Dorcas's husband put a hand at the neck of his overalls and tore down, ripping the buttons. —All thrown out, everywhere, all the Indias. No more taking our money. Kick them out. This is not India's country. You'll see, one day all Indias must get out. Let them get out.—

—And if the bloody shit is thrown out of this place?— The two words in English bubbled up in William's anger. —*Bloody shit*, where will *you* live, ay? You'll sleep in this yard if your wife doesn't work for him, you think? This's going to be your place if he is kicked out?— William's laughter pummelled savagely.

—Finish! No Christmas! No sewing machine! Everything finish and out. The government will throw them away. We are going to throw them away with the white people—

An old man who had heard out many fights said—They know how to speak with white people in the government. Very clever people, the India people, very clever.—

—Finish! No Christmas! Get!—

Rage sank to wrangling and became almost social. Dorcas, still weeping, took her youngest child and a cousin and went in the dark, on foot, to spend the night with Alina at the farm. Very late, her husband, who had not lain down in his blankets, whose feet felt tethered to the weight of the boots in which he worked in blood all day at the abattoir, took the keys from the nail in the room where William was sleeping. He sprang the padlocks on the gates and dragged them wide. The dogs were barking as he rode his bicycle without a light up the empty road but he did not look back.

In the morning, William found the gates open. Inside the dogs snarled and raced up and down before the gap, up and down, as if, for them, the pattern of closed gates was still barred across their eyes.

G olden reclining nudes of the desert.

Montego Bay. Sahara. Kalahari. Namib.

There are beaches of black sand where he has been to.

Wherever he has come from, there are hours on the way home over Africa when there is nothing down there. Sometimes it's at night and all you are aware of is perhaps a wave or two of turbulence, a heave from the day's heat, even at thirty thousand feet. Sometimes it's a day flight, clear, and even at thirty thousand feet you can squint down from the window-seat at long intervals and see it there, soft lap after lap of sand, stones, stones in sand, the infinite wreckage not of a city or a civilization but the home that is the earth itself. Sometimes there is a sandstorm down where you can't see, and even thirty thousand feet up the air is opaque. The plane is privately veiled, hidden in sand, buried in space. Nothing is disclosed.

Once this winter he had to take a tourist class booking because—such is the number of people like himself travelling about the world on expense account—first class was full. At least he had a vacant seat beside him, in the tourist cabin. But at Lisbon a Portuguese family came aboard and after sulky looks between the two daughters who both wanted to sit with mama, one of them had to take the seat. So that was the end of his intention to lift the dividing arm and spread himself for sleep. It was midnight. She was a subdued girl, not pretty, nor perfumed beside him when the cabin lights were lowered and conversations gave way to hen-house shufflings. She had not said good evening, just looked at him with cow-eyes, someone who never got her own way, resigned to any objections that might be made as she approached the seat. When the hostess offered rugs she opened her thin mouth in a soundless mew of thanks. He was aware that she twisted her body, several times, to look back where mama and sister were sitting some rows away but she couldn't have been able to see much. He could hear her swallow, and sigh, as if they were in bed together. He was not comfortable, although he had the advantage of the angle of window and seat to wedge the postage-stamp pillow against; of course she had settled her forearms along the armrests and he could not lean the other way without crowding her. She had the light soft rug drawn up to her chin and it touched against his left hand, lying on his thigh. Touched and drew almost away, touched and drew almost away, as she breathed, he supposed. He pushed it off and as he did so the side of his hand brushing a hand—hers, now lying, apparently, loosely against her thigh parallel with his— made of the movement a gesture of rejection: to excuse himself he corrected the movement into an impersonally polite one of re- placing slipping covering.

Who spoke first?

Was it at all sure that it was he? Here in the dark (only dim, if he opened his eyes; the centre panels of light were off and it was the tiny reading bulb, no bigger than the light in the tail of an insect, of someone a few seats back that gave shape to what was next to him) here in the dark a hand lies half curled against a thigh. The thigh is crossed (he guesses) over another, or its inner side swells laid against a second identical to it.

—*And if another hand should move over the thigh, from the outer side, near the knee somewhere* (her body takes up the narrative), *up and inwards at the same time, it will meet the parallel lines of the two thighs where, like two soft bolsters or rolls of warm dough, they feel the pressure of their own volume against each other.*—

They are covered with something—stockings, I suppose, I didn't see when she seated herself, I didn't bother to look.

—*The hand may be cool or it may feel warm. The thighs may freeze against it, tendons flexed rigid, or maybe they will lie help- less, two stupid chunks of meat, two sentient creatures wanting to be stroked.*—

The plane was a hospital ward where the patients had not entirely settled for the night yet, the attendant with her blonde chignon passed silently down the rows in surveillance and the exchange stopped until she had gone, the hand waiting quietly on the thigh. Then, despite the fact that there was still the occasional movement that showed others were still awake, and an old man strolled slowly by on his way to the lavatory, the hand took up the thread of communication as happens when interruption cannot really disturb the deep level of preoccupation at which it has been established. It was his left hand, which had been farthest away from him and closest to the other being, anyway, and he did not have to shift his position leaning against the angle of seat and window. Under the rug the hand found the edge of the very short skirt and there was a pause, quite delicate and patient, until the answer—she lifted her weight just enough to release the material so that he could glide his hand (yes, there were stockings) beneath it and push it up with his wrist as the hand rose.

An inquiry into what kind of flesh this was, to what milieu it belonged: as might have been expected, travelling well-chaperoned with a mother and sister, it was clothed in more than the usual garments for girls of the same age and more independent sophistication. A lining of some kind beneath the skirt, and beneath that, so surprising that they baffled him for a moment, at the top of the stockings those bumps of metal and rubber fasteners that lead by elastic straps somewhere up to the body. For years now women wore flimsy stockings and pants of a piece; there was something identifiably duenna'd about the suspenders and the belt they implied. His stranger's hand, man's hand, opened a forefinger and hooked it under the stocking-top and touched flesh.

In the cosy dark of other presences, in the intimacy like the loneliness of the crowd, the feel of flesh is experienced anew, as the taste of water is recognized anew in the desert. The finger went against the grain of fine down—yes, the flesh admits that it belongs to the Latin races, often hairy—and reached the warmth of the two legs pressed together. The skin was tacky, almost damp. It clung to his fingers with a message of excitement and pleasure. He felt how she kept her head absolutely still and knew he was forbidden to look at her face. Tucked, sucked in between the neatly parallel thighs his finger stirred only very slightly, just a murmur. He did not know its exact position in relation to the knees and the limits of the body; much higher than half-way, he guessed, because of the fullness of the thighs. The finger was in no hurry to broach the question; the thighs must be anticipating that it was coming. Even if they had never answered it before (neither she nor the sister looked more than sixteen or seventeen) they knew it had come now, whatever time this was—an hour between the hour of Europe and the hour of Africa, not registered on any watch glowing on passengers' wrists in the quiet dark—and whatever place this was: passengers are not disturbed by flight information while they sleep. It could have been the last of Europe or was Africa, already, they were unaware of passing over. She need not be afraid of wanting what was happening because it was happening nowhere. The other three fingers fluently joined the forefinger between the thighs and then unexpectedly (it must have been, for her) lost coherence and freeing themselves all the fingers trailed back and forth over the mound of one thigh, under the stocking but without unfastening the suspender, because the hand liked its confinement beneath a web. Then the fingers curled—she must have felt the tips if not the nails drawing in—and found, of course, another ridge of material that gave easily, in fact care had to be taken not to let it snap back against the skin—a crinkly edging round the leg of panties of some tight stretchy weave. If she had been sitting more upright, this was where the crease of juncture of thigh and body would have been. But she was lying as fully stretched under her rug as the seat on its reclining ratchet would allow, and his fingers recognized the juncture only by the different texture of the skin, a sudden grainless smoothness, silky and hot.

This time the question was differently phrased, that's all, but it must have been understood all the same: there was no rejoinder of change of position. The thighs, he could feel where the heel of his palm rested a moment on them, continued to clasp excitedly against nothing. His finger, just the one forefinger again (an appreciative monologue) roamed amid the curly hair in no hurry, delicately burrowed beneath this soft second rug as it was already concealed by the first and—suddenly—found itself tongued by a grateful dog. That was exactly what it felt like—delightful, fluttering, as innocent as the licking of a puppy; although it was he who was stroking movement along this wet and silky lining of her body, he had the impression it was his finger that was being caressed, not the finger that was doing the caressing. Now and then, quite naturally, he encountered the soundless O of the little mouth that made no refusal. As the night wore on—oh God knows how long it went on—the finger was able to enter, many times. At first he himself was magnificently tense, not only his sex but his whole body and legs, arms, neck, huge in the seat, swollen into un-usual awareness of the bounds of himself, but later there were even moments when he must have been so fatigued he dozed, his finger inside her. He woke with amazement: in the tunnel of seat-backs, the dim curving walls, the very faint creaking that was all there was to indicate that the sensation of motionlessness was in fact the nest of extreme speed—just as the extreme intimacy, his hand, finger still inside the body beside him, laved with it, was the extreme of detachment.

The gradual coming into the light of a morning somewhere did not bring an end. He could not leave her and she could not let him go. The only thing he could not get her to do was touch him; her rather plump and quite womanly hand went limp and stiff-wristed when he tried to carry it over to himself; she would not. Soon it was light, anyway, the lights went up brutally on the sleepers as prisoners are forced awake, and he took his weary hand back in good time before the trays of synthetic fruit juice arrived. The hand smelled of the body it had just left. The girl waited for him to take a plastic cup of juice and then took hers, with the same soundless thank you to the hostess. They did not speak; she emptied the cup thirstily (yes, my girl, lust dries the mouth), put the soft rug aside and went up the aisle. When she returned, she had to stand a moment before taking her seat because someone was blocking the aisle, and he looked up and met her gaze, her pale, thick-skinned face with heavy eyebrows arched, hopeless, accept-ingly. A stranger's face as the face of a woman with whom one has lived so long one doesn't see it anymore, becomes once again closed, a stranger's.

She carefully put back the rug over herself.

He had pushed up the eyelid of blind in his oval porthole. The reluctantly-awakened plane drifted to half-sleep again. Orange searchlights of rising sun pierced from window across to window in the prostrate humming silence. It all began again, uncanny in the daylight. Down there below reddish eddyings of the upper air and the glint of wing flashing monotonously at him, sand was an infinite progression of petrified sound-waves. It flowed on and on, echoing itself since there was no organic renewal by which life could be measured. On and on, shimmering, fading, paling, deepening nothing. His gaze was carried on it while he continued to stroke, fondle, dabble, on and on, all the way, caressing her all the way. The desert became forests, savannah, mine-dumps. At Johannesburg when he handed down a pink coat and a package of something that looked like a plant laced up in plastic, he spoke: —You are on holiday?— She answered that she and her mother and sister were coming to live with her uncle. Her English was strongly accented but quite intelligible. He said—Oh you'll like it there, in Durban. At the sea.— Her mother, moving with the other daughter along the queue in the aisle, nodded a faint and humble acknowledgment of the help he had given with hand-luggage.

He had washed his hands; used his electric razor; her hair was combed. The same clerk always came along with the driver to fetch him from the airport; he saw waiting at the barrier the respectfully alert, cocky young face, the sideburns and striped shirt advertised as correct wear for budding executives. An immigration official recognized him and waved him through ahead of the other sheep. The plant was being taken out of its wrapping at customs—of course, you can't bring in live plants from other countries. There was the usual making of conversation with the clerk in the car. —Good trip, this time, sir? Everything all right?—

—My knees need a week to straighten out, that's all. I had to travel tourist. Cramped as all hell.—

Her fluid on his hand as one says a man has blood on his hands. She screamed, or got up and told her mother. What an insane risk. A prosecution for 'interfering' with a young girl; yes, *crimen injuria*. That was the name; the girl had no name. A TAP mohair rug. Who would have thought it. Not without tenderness, but who is ever to know that is part of the scandal—perhaps even of rape

125

and murder?—sometimes the only tenderness possible. A man in his position would never be free of tittering disgrace. Never. Silence in the boardroom, change of conversation at the dinner-table when his name came up, and the young daughter of the house not told the reason, because she had known him as a family friend since she was a child along with his son. An insane risk. Nothing will ever be disclosed. It was so easy, and god knows who the stranger was and where, in these streets or those, this town or that, she may anytime be quite near, with the mother and sister and whole clan those people have, guarding young girls.

L inking brazier to brazier, darkness to darkness and smoke to
smoke, the calls of winter evenings are not addressed to him.
On his way home his headlights hold out of the dark—foun-
tain jets balancing objects aloft—the shrouded shapes of the queue
waiting for a bus outside the location. The blur of frost: a cold bloom
formed on the outside of a glass. A sheet of plastic he's annoyed
to see left lying at the windmill tap turns out, when he strides
over in the warm sun of ten in the morning, to be a valance
of icicles fallen from where they formed overnight on the water
tank.

But already at the centre of the wind that blows from ten until
sunset, there is a hot breath, some days. It happens literally from
one to the next. He was out here, say Wednesday or Thursday,
looking at the extent of the damage that reveals itself.in decay as
the weeks go by: the vlei is the quilled back of a porcupine, striped
black and white where the reeds have paled and died off beneath
their burned tops. He thought he saw a yellow weaver fly up and
down a couple of times. And only two days later (the vlei looks the
same), a single green nest: newly woven, or perhaps an old one
repaired. That weaver was reconnoitring; they're back.

And now today he sees what he didn't before—probably because
it wasn't there yet—on the damp verges there is sufficient new
grass to make a nest. It's very thin and pale-bright, almost transparent. It looks bluish, perhaps only in contrast to the grave of
black from which it has grown. He begins to find all the signs that
were not revealed to him before (is it possible they really have
appeared so quickly, were not there two days ago; last week?);
things come to life under his eyes as the syntax of a foreign language
suddenly begins to yield meaning. Along the strands of willow,
nibs of glossy brown; catch them in his nail and they break back,
green. Some spread small green leaves as hard-backed beetles will
unfold thin gauzy wings from beneath a carapace. On the irrigation
canals there is a scum of bubbly livid, in places velvety. Break it

with a stick—the stagnant broth has swirls of emerald and bottle-green slime like the markings petrified in a semi-precious stone.

The tongue-tips of new reeds are forcing through sodden burned clumps.

It could have been worse.

—Oh yes.—

—It could have been worse, I suppose—

Words to that effect. But were they referring to the same things when they talked together? There was time to drive him out at least to have a look at the place again, because one of the secretaries had been instructed to book a seat on a plane instead of the usual school train.

—Thirteen thousand Ovambos on strike, that time, and the police didn't dare touch them because of United Nations. That's something. But the settlement was a sell-out. Nobody knows what's going on in Ovamboland. We had a chance to talk to some Ovambos in the fisheries at Walvis—

He doesn't look at his father while he speaks, it is a profile that presents itself beside the driver's seat. The soft little downy beard is coming on; the eyelashes are arrogant and curved as a girl's and the expression in the eyes cannot be seen.

—What in God's name d'you find to do in Walvis! One street and a couple of beer *stuben*. At least in my day.—

He went there with some university student who picked him up. One of those who stick their noses into everything. No good blaming Kurt and Emmy; there was nothing they could do to stop it. But he does not seem to want to pursue the subject; he seems to keep resisting the urge to talk about what preoccupies him: what? The blacks in 'Namibia'? The prospect of army service next year?

—Not my idea of a place for a good time!—

The incredibly long and slender creature so newly emerged into maleness; does it realize its capacity, diaphragm drawn in slimly tentative in the seat, back slightly bent, as if sheltering itself, from the broad shoulders and muscular breast towards the long legs. The hard blade-shaped thighs are exactly the width of the narrow breadth between hip-bones where the belt rests. There's no belly at all, all grossness burned up, at this age, into the powers of muscle and sex. The whole encased in skimpy covering that looks as if it is peeling from the extremities of wrists and ankles; the jeans are so frayed that the tatters curl, now. Out of the androgynous square feet of the little boy have pushed these tense, hammer-toed, prehensile things that belong on some dangling Christ. —You'll find the going rough on your bare soles. Everything's burned.—

—It's okay. I'm used to this.—

—How's old Emmy these days. Her English better than ever? Still *aber* every second word?—

He has turned, this brings him full-on, smiling, in love, the sunburned skin round the eyes actually pinkening with response. It would be possible to put out a hand and even touch him, now, it would not raise the alarm within. The ribs of long fingers with an oxidized snake ring (the kind seen so often set out on the London pavement in the vicinity of the statue of Eros; he would never have thought to bring back a present of one—there you are) are spread to indicate the impossibility of describing the perfection of this old German lady who will always look, to both father and son, like an inquiring, sceptical schoolgirl with eyes as amber-freckled as her face.

They talk about Emmy for a few hundred yards; he is dawdling the Mercedes in order to fall behind the dust raised by some vehicle ahead that it hides. —I should go up and see them sometime. It's years since I was in South West. Time, time… I've only been back ten days. Brazil, Jamaica—

He never asks any questions about his father's work. I might as well be running the Mafia. —What was it she found me guilty of, again? Collusion, 'industry-wide collusion', a lovely term, why should a good-looking bitch like you know all the dirty words? And what's it mean, anyway?—

—So what d'you suggest we call it? Your pig-iron ore—the mine gets its blacks from the mines' combined recruiting organization, mmh? That cuts out competition for labour and competitive wages for the labourers.—

And while you talk like this you take my hand and put it on your breast, your hard (brown gipsy) nipple is a dog's nose at my palm. Always promising what you can't give, your kind. You waved to them from the newspaper picture, leaving, leaving them to it.

The dust is no more than a pollen in the air and the Mercedes could regain speed without catching up with whatever's ahead but they are level with the Indians' at this moment and his passenger says he'll run in to buy cigarettes. It's not a defiance because smoking is not an issue, although he's only sixteen and it might well be, with another parent. The request is made casually, as of right, not concession, and without the gratitude or the least pleasure that such a concession might be expected to win. An obstinate indifference: the implication that there's munificence only over what he doesn't want, doesn't care much about one way or the other. The measure of generosity taken by the recipient, not the donor. You'll decide. I'm not to judge. Kaffir pots or genuine porcelain from the Far East.

—I'll pull up a little way along. It's embarrassing, they've got some idea in their heads I might let them put their shop in my name! The last time I was in there for a whole five cents' worth of something, the one who's in charge of the show, not the old man, of course, the other one, got hold of me.—

Immediately those dogs are bouncing themselves at the fence where the car comes to rest, hooking their claws through the mesh and snatching at thin air with jaws that snap like shears. Apart from the racket, it's not pleasant to be only just out of reach of such a passion to get at him. He engages the gear and slides on a few yards past the blacks' outbuildings that mark the limit of the Indians' property. It won't be possible to use the place any longer for odd necessities he sometimes forgets in his haste to be shot of town; a nuisance.

Blond locks flying, careering on bare feet, there he comes, even skittering in the dust for the fun of it—that's how he must be, in the company of others, then? Yet drumming up some young company for the occasional weekends out of school didn't work. Brought together again—the two who used to play with one another as children—the only reaction to that lovely girl with a waist the length of a swan's neck was a remark that she couldn't help it but she was a typical spoilt Johannesburg girl. At sixteen (going on seventeen), has he no eyes? No dreams burrowing the bedclothes into flesh all night—good God, what that matters can be 'spoilt' in a girl, at sixteen, for any boy: teeth sweet and clean as fresh-peeled almonds, a tongue that's only just stopped being used to lick ice-creams, breasts larger than expected, delightfully heavy-looking in contrast to the rest of her, at her mother's swimming-pool. At that age—oh but what is the use of saying 'at that age', the gipsy is right, it goes on forever, for all one knows, need outlasting performance, in the end, a Churchill with an unlit cigar.

He's got something in a bit of white paper in one hand. He's eating. —Look. Have some.—

—What'd you find to buy?—

Instead of getting straight into the car, he has come round to the driver's window, holding out the plate of his hand, very friendly. —They gave me some. Samoosas.—

Breaking bread together. He puts the neat, crisp, greasy triangle whole into his mouth in order not to dirty the steering-wheel while he drives. It's not exactly the sort of thing to eat just after a late breakfast. —Thanks, no more. Very good, ay?—

—Are you going to do anything about it?— The jaw moves with the last mouthful of one little geometrical pastry parcel while the hand has already taken up the next: the appetites are there, all right.

—You mean they knew who you were? They asked you? Nerve enough for anything.—

—Of course not.— He has crumpled the bit of paper, transparent with grease, he wipes his fingers on it as best he can, and now he winds down his window.

—No. Stick it in the ashtray. Or on the floor.—

The window is wound up again without a word.

What does he want me to say, about what? On what subject?

—Some wangle. They're experts. These Indians run rings round anybody when it comes to palm-greasing. They know how to survive. Well! They'll find some Van der Merwe who won't turn his nose up at coolie money, no matter what he says about them to his Boer pals. Anyway, I'll just give the shop a wide berth, that's all.—

Of course; sitting there picking (he sees out of the corner of his eye) at a dirty thumbnail, you are made moody by the simple generosity of kind people. As if they didn't recognize perfectly well who you are. Probably saw it was my car although I drove past, and they're no fools, they understand tact in the service of their own interest, clever as Jews—not a word, only goodies to please the child of the father!

Why do you call it 'Namibia'?

Driving along, that is the subject on which he himself wants to ask the question, will get the urge to ask all day, meaning something different every time. He never asked *her*, although she was using the name already, then. He would have phrased it slightly differently, with her—Why call it Namibia?—i.e. why that and not another invention expressive of a certain attitude towards the place. Why a geographical, descriptive root to the chosen name? It's not all desert. But she would have been too clever to fall for that, she knows when questions to which the answers are already known are asked, merely because the questioner thinks the answers are going to cause the adversary to give himself away. Then she snatches the advantage by exhibiting that unlike his kind, hers has the honesty to admit their evasions. —The Namib doesn't conjure up jealousy in anybody. So it doesn't suggest the country belongs any more to Ovambos than Damaras, Hereros than Basters. It's demographically neutral. A desert. It's nobody's in particular.—

—And your husband's Bushmen? They won't press their claim?—

—Oh, the Bushmen... —

—You're not interested in minority rights, then?—

She's irritated to get her own sort of phrase thrown back at her. —What's it got to do with minority rights? They'll have the same rights as anyone else; but they're not likely to claim the country belongs more to them than the others because it's named for the Namib desert. It'll be everybody's except the whites who occupied it unlawfully.—

But 'why *do you*' is the substance of the question, here today; what has made *you* take up these causes with your sixth-form athlete's arms? What does your adolescent brain think the name means?

Perhaps again the answer is there before the question.

I know what you think. I know what you say when you don't speak, sitting there with your body in its penitent's rags for all the sins of the fathers.

You are too green to try her trick; but I should be able to—I could—make you roll over, nothing but a wretched little puppy under attack, trickling a few drops of pee to show it's culpable only of youth.

What's our subject?

The pleasures of travel. All right. You've crossed, thirty years after me, thirty years ahead in time, the plain of *Welwitchia mirabilis*; those great vegetable octopuses, living fossils beached out of evolution seven hundred years ago. One of the old chaps, Kurt's cronies who know it all like the brown age-blots on the backs of their hands and have no claim at all, neither a share in Rio Tinto nor a hearing at UNO, takes tourists to the plain to see these ancient monstrosities of plant life. —He's bought an old Land-Rover.— —Oh really?— All the desert is the same but he knows where the very biggest Welwitchia is to be found, the one that will be photographed and projected in colour slides and movies on walls in Munich and New York (the plant is actually a conifer—but you know that, the old ones will have told you everything they know). Specially in Munich and Berlin and Bonn and Frankfurt-am-Main the pictures will be shown; there's your story about the German tourist you met who remarked, We Germans have very much interest for this country, young man. Our fathers have been here. Did he think you were too young to know, not knowing that you have just learnt too, from your Blue books and White papers, what he has forgotten—the how-many-thousand Hereros the fathers killed? Nineteen thousand. —You know the exact figure, of course. Everything was ready for you, up there, and you for it; it has 'taken', finding a host entirely innocent of any immunity.

You came to Khan Canyon and saw the peaks, thorns of rock hooked and crooked against the sky; you stood under one of the camel-thorn trees down there and looked up at the mountains where the uranium lay hidden, something the world didn't know it wanted, thirty years ago when I was there and for millennia before.

—You can't see anything?—

—Nothing. You aren't even allowed on the approach road, where it turns off from the Swakopmund road.—

—A tremendously valuable installation. Probably the biggest single find in the world. Millions sunk in it.— Driving over the soft dust, avoiding the crown where the bald corrugations are, it is possible to talk of this subject as a normal exercise in security. —Swakopmund must have gone ahead?—

If that's what interests you, the tone implies: —There's a whole new part of the town. I don't know how many houses, for the whites who work on the mine.—

—I should go up and have a look sometime. How d'you like our new sign?— He has slowed, at the left turn into the property itself, not only for safety but also to let his passenger see. His passenger gives his attention, smiling slightly with pursed lips as if he's sucking on his tongue, taking his time—is he simply looking at the thing, a yellow board with black lettering, baked enamel on steel, clamped to two iron poles painted shiny black and sunk in concrete, or is he reading the message three times over, in English, Afrikaans and Zulu. NO THOROUGHFARE GEEN TOEGANG AKUNANDLELA LAPHA.

—As if anything'll keep them out. It's a constant parade, all weekend especially, cutting up through the farm to that shanty town over beyond the vlei. And old De Beer and Nienaber, too—a short cut for their damned milk trucks. It's the fire-risk that bothers me.—

You nod; and to what are you assenting? The signboard's absurd, a hopeful claim that can never be recognized? Or that it's not a sense of possession but concern for the land that has set it up? What do you mean, *Namibia*? With that bloody affected laugh of hers: You can't own it by signing a bit of paper, the way you buy a farm, you know.

—At least it'll never burn down. I made sure, no wooden posts.—

—It all looks all right— He's gazing round almost shyly as the car pitches smoothly over the bumps (it should be possible to keep the surface in better repair once the milk trucks take the longer way round).

134

—Ah well, now—the willows are almost out, and you're looking at the rye—that wasn't touched. But the vlei!—

Sure enough, there are Sunday visitors tramping along the private road. They have some touches of fancy dress about them. They stop; in daylight, stand like hares caught in headlights. It is an admittance that these can read, they have surely read the sign because no one ever stopped at the sight of the farmer, before. But (almost like one of Kurt's old cronies not missing out any points of interest on a tour—it really is a long time since the boy was on the farm) he pulls up and, arm on the window, accepts their obeisant greeting. One calls him 'master', the other 'sir'—a city type. This one wears the jacket of the employees of a bus company, khaki with initials that make up the name of the firm PUTCO embroidered in red, on the top pocket. With it goes a sort of string necklace with small beaded pouches pendant. Both men carry ceremonial staffs or canes encased in coloured beadwork—really quite an art. (Of interest. —Look at that, Terry.—)

—Is there a dance?—

And all the to-and-fro, comfortable, assenting noises come with the affirmation, Yes, there's a dance. They smile shinily, greased by excitement or effort. God knows how far they've walked.

Perhaps there's some ceremony, initiation or something, that would provide entertainment. —What's the dance for?—

—Someone he was sick and now he's all right. Yes, master.—

—To say thanks because he is better?—

The two of them laugh, flexing their knees to applaud the farmer's quickness; their unexpected welcome to the farm. —Yes, sir— —Yes, yes, he's coming better. Yes.—

—And plenty beer?—

More laughter. The one flourishes his stick and peers jokingly into the car. —If you got beer for us we can be very pleased, master.—

Everyone is laughing, except the boy, he doesn't manage more than a distant grin.

—D'you like to go along and have a look at this 'dance'?—

—No, no, it's embarrassing.—

He means to avoid using this tone for the few hours he's going to be spending with him, but—For God's sake—why embarrassing?—

The face goes through the contortions of taking a breath, looking for where to begin, beginning again. —Because it is, that's why. It's a private thing. Nothing to do with us.—

—Nonsense. They'd love an audience. Why shouldn't dancers love an audience.— But he lets the subject sink down under silence between them as they drive slowly, as he always does once he's on his own property, almost as if he were already strolling on foot, looking alertly about to see how things are. Some young bullocks being let out of a paddock buck and frolic, and they are both amused. The little boy of a few years ago says—Gee, I wonder how long you'd be able to stick on when they come out like that.—

—Well try, if you don't mind risking a broken bone or two. But you wouldn't have far to fall.— The bullocks are only half-grown and his legs are so long now.

—And here we are.— He recognizes old landmarks, returned from the pilgrimage with begging bowl, thirty years off, down in the Swakop river bed in an ancient jeep breaking through tamarisk and wild tobacco with yellow flowers.

Here we are. Along with the main farm buildings which are grouped around, this remains the centre of the farm's existence, empty as the house is, shut up as usual. It's here that people tend to hang about on one piece of business or another. There are two ugly ones with stocky greased legs stuck out before them in the sun against the workshop wall. They wear black berets drawn down straight to their ears. They have the stolidity of women sitting for many hours. There's a group of four or five others, more of them come for the dance, and they're standing around, a man in a white, high-collared jacket (doctor's? waiter's?) and various females draped in blankets. And there's Jacobus— Jacobus's going through the whole unavoidable ritual of seeing you at last, after so long, not since the Easter holidays... ?

—I was here at half-term in May—

—Were you?—

So you were, but time-changes, Japan, South America, Jamaica, lost hours in planes, they make it much longer. Jacobus first stood up straight from whatever he's tinkering with, he received the sun of your presence full in the face, he exposed himself in a broken, stinking-toothed smile and lifted a hailing palm that he's holding up still, a standard, as he approaches. You cannot escape Jacobus, you can't disappear under the seat or look the other way out the window or pick at your dirty thumbnail. He greets you, he thinks the world of you, he's crowning you with a laurel of thorns whether you accept it or not.

—I'm happy for this day. This day! Why you don't come long, long time, Terry? Terry.— The name is handled lovingly, admiringly, since it's conjured up in the flesh, there in the car. —I think I'm never see you, my young baas—he's very very good, this young baas, you know?—

—I know. I know, Jacobus, you like him— Smiling, Jacobus and I; kidding the old devil.

—And he's growing too strong! Coming big man now! Yes, I'm very very please.—

Out of the car, looking down over himself under this regard, this praise, smiling, snickering with shame under it, staring at the bare Namib-burned feet with gingerish hairs shining on the big toes, at the ragged jeans, the sweat-shirt washed colourless, the big hands with the snake ring, as if this—*self*—is something he picked up somewhere, any old thing.

Not for Jacobus. For Jacobus you are my son. You go to school. You will learn everything. You will have everything. A car. A house. A farm to come to on Sundays. Everything I have.

—From pig-iron, she says (yes) enviously. If I had your money—

You will have my money. There is nothing you can do about it: —He's grown up, now, ay, Jacobus.—

—Yes. Yes. Very good. I'm happy for see.— The welling of enthusiasm settles at high watermark; Jacobus, looking down from it, always vigilant in his own interest no matter what a loyal old devil he seems to be, turns his attention—Those peoples they want ask they can come today—

—A big party on, ay?—

Jacobus can't stop grinning fondly, distractedly, at the long

137

blond hair and the quite respectable beginnings of the beard. —Yes. The wife of Phineas she's want to be witch-doctor— He giggles with what he anticipates will be white amusement at this. —She's learn, and today is come big witch-doctor from there-there, in other side town. You know? He must see this and this, if she's know how to do.— He has sidled right up close to his young baas, he puts his arm on his shoulder conspiratorially, he lowers his head, grimaces on those teeth with the effort of extreme secrecy, and draws his little group in with a whisper: —You—you mustn't go in the barn there. Not in the barn. There's—(he looks down under his dropped eyelids so that the visitors, a little way off, will not be able to learn anything from his expression)—there's the goat inside there.—

Hunching your shoulders and looking at me, mouth pulled up at one corner, smiling, not wanting to offend, not knowing what he's talking about. A goat?

—No, no. I'm tell you. Sshh. The witch-doctor he's tell the people they must buy the goat. Then he's put that goat away somewhere, somewhere, she don't know where. Nobody must say her. Since three day she mustn't go out, nobody must talk to her in her room there. She don't see nothing. Then lateron, she going to throw bones, everything, you know, and she must tell where is that goat.—

—And the dance?—

—Yes, sometime five or half-past. Everything's coming ready.

The three have turned gradually to regard the visitors standing by, Jacobus casting a watchful eye over them as he does when taking a white man to inspect some particular group of cows in one of his paddocks. He certainly has a sense of attachment to the place; one could do a lot worse, although it's business-lunch exaggeration to say (he sometimes hears himself) his old boy does better than any white manager. What this really means is that they're more honest than any white you're likely to get in a menial yet responsible position. He may filch a bag of mealie-meal for perks but why the hell not, who wouldn't—but he hasn't the craft to crook you. There is laughter when—frankly confidential—there comes the observation that you can always trust a man who can't

138

write not to keep a double set of books. The chief accountant appreciates that one most.

The man in the white coat (yes, now that we've heard the witch-doctor story it definitely looks surgical, ay, Terry) holds his arms respectfully down across his body in a V whose base is the hat he removed as soon as the car drove into the yard. He bows: —'Nkos', 'Nkos'.—

Jacobus makes a sweeping gesture, and says, now loudly—They want to go to the compound, they asking—

The man's greeting is acknowledged; the women neither greet nor expect to be greeted, they do not see themselves at all in the eyes of the white man and white boy. —All right. Tell them all right.—

It's true those feet are so toughened he trails along (just like one of them) without any apparent discomfort while Jacobus presents his usual weekly crop of problems; he's smoking, not possible to say if he's taking any notice of what's going on, until Jacobus demonstrates what has gone wrong with the disc-plough. Then he jack-knifes down on his haunches and the blond, not-too-clean hair hides his face: —But look at this. It's bust off here, something's missing.—

Jacobus never stops his running commentary of explanation and the two of them seem to understand each other. Rising at last, even the black face shows the darkening of the blood that suffuses both heads. The veins on his black forehead above that prominent frontal bone they have give him the appearance of frowning while he admires, encourages. —You too clever, Terry. Why you don't come this time, holiday time? What is wrong you don't want help us?—

You laugh. Laughing to please Jacobus.

—He went away, far away, to see my old home Jacobus.—

—But he's coming Christmas time, yes. You come help us Christmas when the school is finish. Yes!—

—I want to plant another hundred trees along here this summer.—

139

He has his thumbs hooked in the diagonal front pockets of the jeans and he picks his way easily through puddles made in the road by the irrigation jets. —What kind?—

Tsk-tsk-tsk-tsk-tsk: the long, wavering squirts jerk round, changing direction under their own pressure; tsk-tsk-tsk-tsk-tsk.

A decision is made. The answer's going to be unexpected, with the shadow of the fast-growing eucalyptus ahead. —Oaks.—

You don't plant oaks for yourself but for those who come after.

But that is not our subject, apparently. The response that comes is a question. —You're not going to Plet?—

Arms, staggering flailing arms, flowing sleeves of water; one trails suddenly over their faces, so that they smile at one another under the caress. Forced by irrigation the lucerne is green and thick, it's as if summer were already here.

—I am not. I'm going to plant trees. Let the others catch the big fish and booze at the Christmas parties.—

What is it you want me to say now?

A-hah—you were thinking of going to the cottage at the sea, maybe, you could have had a good time this year, that's true, soon seventeen, all those daughters of friends grown up just your age. But that means in January you'll go into the army, that's where you'll be when the party's over. What is it you want me to say? If you're waiting for me to broach that subject, you're mistaken— yet he doesn't say anything, he speaks but he doesn't say anything, he won't bring it up himself.

At the compound sleeping women lie on the ground beside the ash-heap rolled like corpses in new blankets, right over their heads, brightly checked and fringed. There's no child to be seen and their dogs seem to be shut away for once. —Looks more like the morning after, to me. But they probably walked all night to get here.—

He's jogged ahead a bit; he turns —Oh the picnic place was burnt!—

—It's all recovering now, you should've seen it a couple of weeks ago.—

There's just time to go down there; it'll take the best part of an hour to get to the airport. He's fallen behind again. Down to the third pasture through the gate, and he closes it after them, struggling to get the hoop of wire back over the ant-eaten post with the goaded air of an action performed too many times without question. Why Namibia? The great thing was once Spain. You are not the first. It's always been like that. Yes, it's all been thought, what you're thinking, a thousand times before. They went to fight in Greece, club-footed poet and the well-meaning romantic muddlers or freaks. They went off to Spain and lost the good cause and as a result today, despite the great loss to the country because a gipsy and her professor wouldn't dream of going there any more than they'd consider enjoying themselves in what she calls the Colonels' Greece (—But of course if you ever should have to get off your farm, the next thing'll be a villa in Malaga, eh. Isn't that the latest for rich South Africans—), yes the people are all better off today than they ever were. They have work and they eat. They wear shoes. A uranium deposit on that scale can raise the gross national product to a level where development—viability—becomes a reality, not a dream that depends on 'justice', wherever you're expecting to find that. He pads behind on those bare feet, he's nothing to say for himself but he's there. They want shoes for their feet. They'll have the Germans and French and Italians and South Africans to thank for that, whatever name you use for the place.

The swift flight of single birds laces across vision. They're building. The urge is on them; they might almost skim blindingly into your face. Those feet are very strong and supple. He's standing on the blackened stones that he helped carry to line the pit for the spit last year—long skinny toes grapple the stone—as if this provides an elevation for survey. Out of a black sedge or bog that is waterlogged burnt reeds, the new reeds are brilliant silk, sugar-cane green, the colour of the bits of new grass moistened with saliva he shows between his teeth.

—There's nothing. I always wanted to see what was in the middle of the vlei.—

—Just vlei.— There's the proof: to someone who was away at school at the time and was never told, it looks as if there never was anything. Come to think of it all the earth is a graveyard, you never know when you're walking over heads—particularly this continent, cradle of man, prehistoric bones and the bits of shaped stone (sometimes a plough has actually turned one up) that were weapons and utensils. It's all the same. Their ancestors. No one knows who they were, either. No way of making known: the mouth stopped with mud. Doesn't exist unless one happens to know—always knows, down here—that it's there, all right. Already the new growth of reeds must be eight inches high.

—I remember when I was little I used to think if I could get in there I'd build myself a secret hideout on that bit of land. I tried to roll boulders into the river to make stepping-stones, but it's too deep, they disappeared.—

—We could have built a foot-bridge. I suppose all you need are some decent logs. A couple of cement piles—

The feet wobble on the stones, take a leap that at once regains balance and lands him free of the pit. —And that ring that woman lost, your friend?—

A couple of hours before the plane leaves is not enough. There is no point in beginning a discussion about anything; why 'Namibia' of all places. He will have to get on with it, go through with it like every other boy of his age. It was here that the letter was torn up and, for a moment, the bits of paper were about to be stuck under those stones which have been slightly dislodged by the weight they have just borne. A crust of earth-line shows on one that has been tipped free of the ground.

What is it you want of me? There is no need to go into the house at all today; it is better to allow time to give him a decent lunch at the airport before he takes off. —I hope the damned goat doesn't eat its way through the last of my hay before she gets her bones thrown.—

But the barn, as it is passed, holds nothing for him; whatever is hidden lies where his mind is—elsewhere.

They are still standing around the yard and those women haven't moved from the wall of the workshop. Jacobus must be said good-bye to; it is necessary to listen all over again to everything said before. Little white baas running barefoot in 'Namibia', black sons of servants now fathers of servants—you can't escape it, you can't hurt old Jacobus's feelings. It all belongs to you. It will all belong to you. No need at all for either of us to go into the house; but as the Mercedes is turning in the yard, in good time for lunch and airport, he suddenly says he's remembered there was something he meant to take along. What is there in that house? A few old clothes? You'd never get them near you, now, miles too small.

—No—something I think I left... I promised a friend at school— He's evasive, he doesn't want to be precise, probably because it's not worth hanging about for, one could buy whatever it is, a new one, and not bother.

Jacobus is there the moment the car stops again. Pleased, used to delays, he is usually the one who lopes up with a request just as you're leaving. Jacobus takes him to wherever it is the house keys are concealed. He stoops, blond strands falling over his face so that one never sees what the expression is, to run a hand over one of the cats at the kitchen door—those cats have gone wild, they don't understand a hand may not be a threat. —And what does your kid do for love?— Tremendously concerned about love, your kind, although they hate so many and despise so much—governments, exploiters of cheap labour to extract ore, the people whose job it is to interrogate the loving activities of those who have right on their side (no doubt) to blow up trains, hijack planes and send letter bombs. —And your husband? What does he do for love while you are making love in there behind the locked-up windows in an empty house, a perfect place, with cologne in the bathroom and whisky by the bed.

Although the kitchen door is standing open the house is empty as if there were no one inside going silently over the polished floors barefoot, rummaging in the cupboards and pulling out a cache of remembered boxes from beneath the unmade beds. The interior of the car is as personal as a room; it is the habitation between habitations, hardly less than they. It even has its own sounds as a house has its creaks: a tick or faint tapping as metal cools or expands. He presses the keys of one radio station after another, running down the scale of snatches of music and voices back to silence. That stained rucksack adorned with the peace sign in red ink is all the luggage there is; it lies on the seat, the one strap is broken, the outside pocket is torn and scarcely holds a book sticking out of it. God knows what he's doing in there; five-past twelve. The visitors, moving in the manner of people fettered by a long discussion that is not being concluded but merely made clumsily portable, are beginning to move in the direction of the kraal. He's taken the book out of the rucksack to glance at for a moment—what sort of thing does he read. EROS HIMSELF overprinted on a picture of the god, bow and arrow, wings, everything between his legs, the lot. A nice sexy love story, just what at that age— A little sticker on the inside of the cover, with the name and address of a Cape Town bookshop. Borrowed. Handed from boy to boy at school. But why no girl on the jacket? EROS HIMSELF AN ANTHOLOGY COMPILED AND PUBLISHED BY THE CAMPAIGN FOR HOMOSEXUAL EQUALITY

As if—indeed, at that age again—he had suddenly got his hands on one of those copies of Lady Chatterley that, pirated and ill-printed in Egypt for sale to English-speaking soldiers, had found their way down from one desert country to another, he opens the book here, there, anywhere. The hands are deft and hasty. The sunglasses trap the warmth in his face—he takes them off roughly. It's not a story—articles, essays, with bits of poetry in between, an extract from the famous trial (Oscar Wilde). *Homosexual Marriage: The Case for Sanction by Church and State. Sexual Pathology—or Love? The Healthy Norm: Law of the Jungle.* An index means nothing. His eyes remember how to skim with intense concentration, tossing aside. *...the old equation of Darwinian selection with the healthy norm is an argument which, carried to its logical conclusion, must equate civilization with the jungle...residual disabilities...in any case, given the change in the law, why is not the homosexual campaign for equality, even if this involves attempting to change public opinion, as decent as, for example, the highly decent campaign of women who demand...if strong feelings are consistent with a wide range of pathological activity...gay marriages are 'repugnant' to... inasmuch as heterosexual marriage as the basis for family life...*

What does he find here? In books like this? If *this* is all, text-book mumbo-jumbo, legal jargon to make it sound dully respectable and normal—if this is what he wants.

144

Is this the subject?

Hidden away like the goat; you have to find your way to it. There is not much left to shock a man who knows the world.

—Ah yes, inviolate, you. You have multiple addresses and identities. That's what you mean—you know how to hide and protect what you are.—

—In pig-iron, that's what.—

—If it were as simple as that!—

—Well isn't that how you see me by candlelight? Isn't it your perversion to dirty yourself with what you call a tycoon?—

What instinct has led him to look at the book? Instinct? Sometimes his are what he thinks of as bestial, but different from this. A lover of women may have many inclinations in a lifetime, he remains a lover of women. His heart is actually beating audibly in his ears, hard and slow. For years he hasn't been in communication with that other woman, his ex-wife, except through divorce lawyers, but he is writing rapidly now, Your son's a pansy-boy. A bugger. She will understand; she will remember and take as an insult, perfect family woman that she is, these days, the reminder that she didn't object to being made love to like that, herself. It must come from someone.

Could this be the subject?

Published by the Campaign For Homosexual Equality.

He belongs to some club, then. Already. Or did the university student give it to him. He got it all from some university student. That's it, that's more likely. That could be it. In Japan they would have arranged things better. By now, going on seventeen, some suitably worldly uncle would have taken him off to a suitable house with experienced girls. Or was that the French. Someone explained (talking late in a hotel bar, a night-cap after a conference) Latins never leave an adolescent to find his own way in these matters. Very sensible. Because unless you are lucky. It's pure chance you meet what you need, just put out a hand...

He has materialized in the dark empty kitchen doorway of the house. There he is. That hair hangs in his eyes and makes him frown, he always looks as if he's frowning or puzzled, even when he smiles. His gaze is concentrated by the vertical line between his brows; he dips gracefully, sideways, to touch, once again, a cat that glides away before contact.

The book is in the hand resting on the steering wheel. It's as if the father has been discovered rather than the son.

—What makes you read this?— There is no use temporizing. Anyway, the words come out as involuntary exclamation, the book might be a ball that has landed in the car.

—I'm curious. Curious to know.— He smiles. He's pushed back his hair as if to show his face, he's hesitated, just a moment, giving account of himself, standing there, before opening the door. He heaves the rucksack onto the floor, then gets in.

—Why not on the back seat.—

—It's okay, doesn't bother me. This car's so big in front. You should have seen us squashed into the Von Falkenbergs' Land-Rover!—

He holds out his hand to relieve the driver of the book that encumbers him and it is given over.

—Doesn't look very interesting.—

His eyes can't be seen. The blond head—from the back and side views like the head of a woman, although he isn't effeminate at all, in face or body—gives the impatient gesture of freeing itself of some trace or ornament. —Quite interesting— He's leaning awkwardly over the rucksack, trying to find a place for the book more secure than the torn pocket. No—he has been searching, while the car turns out of the yard, the angle pitching him forward towards the instrument panel, he delves, even displacing and repacking a pair of dirty socks that release the sourness of his desert sweat: he produces something.

—I bought it in Windhoek. I thought, for Mummy.—

In the palm of the long hand with the three strands of the snake ring round the third finger (head and tail meet on the other side) is an egg. A semi-precious stone in the shape of an egg.

He will go straight to town once the plane has gone. Which means once he has delivered the passenger to the departure lounge on a full belly of T-bone steak and mushrooms, strawberries and cream, with a newspaper and a ten-rand note (prohibited; school pocket money is restricted to half that) for the journey. He never waits to see take-off; today the observation balconies are filled with families who have come to do so as a Sunday entertainment, watching planes that bring in or carry away no one known to them. He traverses yet again the murmurous reverberating concourse with communicants clutching talismans and holy relics—the bunch of proteas or lapel orchid for exit, the duty-free bottles borne home—and the liturgical announcement of arrivals and departures punctuated by the note of a musical gong, almost as in the similar concourse of one of the great cathedrals of the old world, to which stopover privileges give access, stages of the service are marked by the tinkle of a bell. Past the baggage claim area where this time a party of Indians returned from Mecca are grouped like a theatrical troupe in tinselled regalia, being embraced by weeping relatives. Habitually a face looking out for him, and the conversational ritual that is the ultimate sum of all journeys. —Good trip, sir? Everything all right?— —My knees need to straighten out, I had to take tourist class, cramped as all hell— He's quickly free of the place and racing the engine unnecessarily as he reverses out of his slot in an echelon of cars.

He will be back in town within half-an-hour on the expressway but where the overhanging signs of different exits present him with an alternative he simply glides off, maintaining speed without hesitation, as if that were his intention all along, to the lower lane on the right. That road dives under the highway he has left, literally dodges—it is overhead a moment—the road to town. He's on the way back to the farm, that's where he is. The car is making for the farm. It's done now. These great new roads have no provision for the retracing of steps. Once you're on course, you're on; that's it. So he drives without let or hindrance (as the phrase goes) as one can only on an expressway, without distraction or interruption, a mechanical hare set streaking along its appointed lane of track.

There is the usual sort of Sunday gathering he was expected at—people would begin to turn up only in an hour or so from now, but he remembers the invitation or rather obligation as if it were something he has already missed. Not missed much: the drinks set out beside the swimming-pool in the hope it isn't really still too chilly in the evenings for a braai, the host (Consolidated Steel Mills and twenty-eight per cent of the reopened platinum mines at Rustenberg) in his 'Smile' T-shirt—and who would not, at the sight. Pretty women laugh and hug him, his witty wife explains drily that he stole it out of their teenage son's drawer, while the hoarse yelling exhortation of rock records provides exciting castigation from another generation, as if some mad prophet were being allowed to carry on raving somewhere in the beautiful garden. The expressway has dumped him in Sunday joy-riding traffic, but soon he is past the location, past the buses and the overloaded taxis swaying about on their rumps, and set down sweetly on the dust of his own road, the farm road. The dust rises, he is lost in it, it's kicked up behind him like covers drawn up to the ears. He's driven straight back to the farm and to hell with it all.

It is still early enough for him to have come out for the first time on a Sunday. The sun's still high—dropped from its zenith but hung flashing there like a smashed mirror, the last moments of the full of the afternoon. Sometimes when there has been a lunch-party to go to he hasn't got out until around this time. He might never have been there already, today. The wait, outside the Indian shop, outside the house—the blond head, the toenails, from which the dust shakes off, standing out like eyes in a dirtied face: might never have been at all. A day last half-term—in May, he says it was.

He has the farm to himself. They ignore him, not even Jacobus is to be seen this afternoon. Over at the compound, a kind of swarming in the air, a thickening of sound and activity. It's in full swing. Every now and then a reek of burning meat, burning offal—not the goat? Already? He goes into the barn; no sign there ever was a goat. Old goat Jacobus. Old devil. One story about a witch-doctor; another story about a sick man. Anyway, they are all at the compound and they ignore him, he can believe what he chooses.

Little dark birds are like snapped fingers in the air. The farm is striped—green of lucerne, blond of old dry grass where it was saved, green of new reeds—even the black of the burning is part

148

of the pleasing composition. He should get someone out to paint it. —And what's this? One of your country seats?—walking around the flat sizing up; even for one who despises coquetry there has to be some sort of delay before the taking off of clothes.

—A cottage we've had for years at Plettenberg Bay. Doesn't look much like that any more; that whole mountainside's built up now.—

—All your friends followed you.— Judgment or sympathetic observation? That's your form of coquetry. But it palls, it's just like every other novel form of arousal, it would no longer work after a time, my girl, because it's easy to plot a graph of the reactions of your kind.

I know what you're thinking.

Yes I know—kill the thing you love, that old saw. But d'you mean my kind does it, or both our kinds—is it a sneer or acknow-ledgment? Are you like me, or giving me a dig?

You are like me in some ways, or you wouldn't have been stand-ing there showing amused interest before a picture (*naturally*, a house at the sea as well as a farm) while I was behind you pressed up against you and moving your hair aside from your neck with my tongue.

The jets ejaculate tirelessly over the lucerne, there is a heavy bloom of droplets, of the fecundity of summer on that field. They have forgotten to turn off the irrigation but he will not look for Jacobus and he will leave the flow of water to continue for a while before stemming it himself. Even their neglect is something he can afford to allow himself; they are not about, any of them, he is free of them all. Let them smell out their goats wherever they believe them to exist. Down there, the river is perpetually-flowing. He has it all to himself, thank God. A big disc-plough has been used here: he stands in the company of the round backs of a field of sleeping beasts of earth.

He returns to the house without anyone padding along behind him (even a dog is a hindrance, always having to be called off the scent of birds) and sits, this once, like a real farmer on the stoep, although he has not bothered to unlock the place but simply has gone round and climbed the front steps. He is not watching the

149

sunset; the stoep faces east. The house grows dark as closed, empty houses quickly do at sundown. Drumming has been going on quite a while; it started so vaguely and sporadically he's not sure when it really began—there were those odd thumps, the sound of a carpet being beaten, it often seems—and then some sort of rhythm emerged. Ordinary Castrol drums they use, so there isn't that thundery resonance you get from the real thing. They don't know how to make the real thing any longer.

Unwinding, relaxing, getting quite away, is what is described by business associates who also have farms. Moving from the covert of reeds and darkening fields, losing a fugitive's defiant heartbeat in the steady muffled drums, the dark shape on the stoep could be some creature holed up in the shelter of the doorstep of a deserted habitation. The red eye of a cigar opens and closes. No one will ever find him here, this evening, in their minds; he is placed as they dub him, as they've decided what he is. Up at the compound they'll be so full of beer they didn't even hear the car, and they know that on Sunday nights he is back in town. The gathering round the underwater-lit pool knows he's a man with an active social life—he's at someone else's party, or perhaps he has a woman somewhere, he's discreet, he doesn't flaunt these things. Back at the school (if the plane was on time, if he is prefigured there at all) he is seen at the party in town which was mentioned to fill a silence over lunch at the airport.

Time to let go, as the saying has it. It's agreed that's what a place like this is for. What will she do with the egg? It will lie on a table in New York in a bowl with those old-fashioned china decoys—once put in nests to encourage hens to lay at home and not at large—she used to rummage for in antique shops.

—And this? What's this thing?—

—That's an old silver butter-stamp. My wife somehow missed it when she packed up, I suppose; I don't know why I've kept it. She used to collect. All kinds of junk.—

—Of course. It's what the wives of men who're getting rich are expected to do. You don't imagine I thought she made butter?—

—And you collect pots.— His turn for the ambiguous statement-or-accusation.

Not at all slow for a pig-iron dealer! She's always ready to acknowledge with a laugh that she wasn't wrong when she thought there was something else to him, something that explains his attractiveness.

—Well of course. In me you see expressed the guilty yearning for the artifacts of the culture we've destroyed. The same thing as young Americans wearing redskin fringed jackets and head-bands.—

But those with whom you make common cause of bare feet want to wear shoes. They'll have on the rubber boots I supply, I'll bet, while they're cutting the poor bloody throat of their goat. There's no one to blame—not really, no matter the irritation in the heat of the moment—neither Emmy and Kurt for letting him associate with hippy students nor the mother to whose nest he's threatening to return (perhaps?). No, no, he's on his own. He'll flounder along, pad along on those skinny feet till he's had enough. Curious. Curious to know. You will know everything I know, you little idiot. You can have everything I've had. That's all there is. Only sixteen, in that same Swakopmund, during the war, I managed it all for myself. I found myself a woman of thirty-five and a great favourite of Emmy's believe it or not. Emmychen was a friend of her mother, and she had come to stay with the mother because her husband was fighting in Egypt. She was beautiful the way they used to get themselves up then, with hair in a curly ruff on the shoulders, and a very red-painted big mouth. She took no notice of me and then sometimes when she was eating with us would turn to me at table—What are you day-dreaming about? What's he thinking, that one, Tante Emmy? Does he tell you?— I started to answer back even though she was a married woman; I learned how to talk to women, to sense she liked it although I was still only a kid. We made Emmy and Kurt laugh—they thought I was so clever. She used to linger on at the house until it was dark and as there was petrol rationing Kurt couldn't drive her, so I was told to walk her home for safety—there were plenty of black men around—your Ovambos. I used to take my bicycle along for the ride back, pushing it between us as we walked. She asked me about school and whether I didn't want to run away and join the army? She said she wanted to see if she still remembered

how to ride and she mounted, giggling and wobbling; I had to
steady the steering and she kept losing balance and landing
heavily against me. I suddenly understood—there is no explaining
how you recognize it—she was feeling something when she
lurched against my chest. She was no longer a married lady, a
grown-up friend of Emmy who teased me at the table—she was
what I was looking for. She was what I wanted when I was in bed
at night. I held her tightly on the bicycle—good God, it was I who
was suffocating, I remember it because it was the first time and it
happens many times, you never know when it will happen. The
more she laughed and protested the more she seemed to swell up
against me, she was tumescence itself, externalized for the first
time. There is no need to be curious; it happens of itself and can't
be stopped. She liked the business of the bicycle, but I don't
think she thought she ought to go so far as to go to bed with a boy
of sixteen. I had a hell of a time with her, I can tell you. She
agreed to let me come to her mother's house one night when her
mother would be out. But she wouldn't take off her slacks. I
remember distinctly she took off her blouse. Then she said the
reason was the house wasn't a safe place and she would get the key
of another house, an empty beach-house. It was one of those old
wooden places from the German time, with a fancy turret and a
name—*Haus Wüsten Ruh*, I think it was, something like that—
you've seen them, there must be a few left. Perhaps it's still there.
The sand from the desert and the sea-sand had piled up all round it.
The key wouldn't turn in the lock and we couldn't get in; we
looked through the windows in the dark but there was no way in.
She wouldn't let me force a window. Christ almighty! She wouldn't
lie down in the sand, I suppose at thirty-five that was beneath the
lady's dignity. We went back again another night with a can of
Kurt's Three-in-One oil and got the lock to yield, and we climbed
under the German feather quilt on a bed and—all of sixteen
years old—I was confident as a man of thirty. But the silly bitch
kept saying I was too young, she mustn't, she really shouldn't,
and it was only about the third or fourth time we went to that
house that she let me in, at last I got her to let me in, I got in,
after peering through the dark closed windows like that, shut out,

imagining what it would be like inside, with her, in that house.

The wind has gone down with the sun. There are even crickets; the first time this season.

Banging away.

Lulling, every now and then, into silence.

G-dump. Long pause. G-dump. Hesitation. G-dump. G-DUM-DUM-DUM G-DUM-DUM-DUM Gi-Gi-DUM Gi-Gi-DUM Gi-Gi-DUM Gi-Gi-DUM Gi-Gi-DUM Gi-Gi-DUM

The fullness of the night is stepping up all round him, the fullness of the night's possession over his land. Their old Castrol drums exhale and inhale it regularly, G-DUM G-DUM, the crickets sing it. There isn't anything I haven't had. To want for nothing; to sit here and want for nothing. You stare at your dirty toes and know only what you don't want. Poor devil, give you a year or two. It may not be pig-iron. You'll be in—something.

If I had your money. A night bought and secured. The price of an air ticket has put him on a plane, and the fee of a good lawyer has you safely six thousand miles from this house. He might telephone, why not, after all this time, at this distance, if he knew where she was. He had the impulse once, from Montreal. No danger of tapping-devices there to alarm you: —*Trouble*, you said, loving it. All you do love. The international exchange found the nomad in the London directory, but someone else answered and said you were away, would the professor do instead? The hotel clerk supplied a slip with the time and cost of the call as a record for expenses—that sort of impulse costs nothing, you're right, it's thrown in, like the sauna baths.

What more could you ask? Four hundred acres of arable land. Perpetually-flowing water, a perfectly sound dwelling-house that only needs a bit of fixing up—

You stood with your sallow, sunburned hands with the silver rings on your thighs in tight trousers, you weren't much interested in the house. You didn't even notice the joke of the estate agent's lingo. —How long's it going to last? How long before they need more land to house the blacks that work for your subsidiary companies?—

—I haven't any interests in this area, you might care to know.—

—Ah, you think of everything. But what does it matter—other people's companies, then. The location'll have to be extended, you'll need to let your land go—

—I've thought of that, yes. At a very good price. I'll buy something somewhere else, farther out.—

—Your peace will have to go for the sake of growth and expansion, ay? But isn't that what you believe in? Development? Isn't that the deal?— Walking round the house together, you not so much as looking at it with the eye of a woman; your kind curls up and beds down anywhere, but has no home-making, Emmychen instincts, only theories about the disruption of family life by the system of migratory labour in mines etc., oh God. You run on: —You'll opt yourself out of existence, Mehring.—

Yes, that's the deal, the hopeful reasoning of the impotence of your kind, of those who are powerless to establish their millennium. The only way to shut you up is to establish the other, the only millennium, of the body, invade you with the easy paradise that truly knows no distinction of colour, creed and what-not—she's still talking, somewhere, but for me her mouth is stopped.

—You'll deal once too often, Mehring.—

Oh for God's sake. Leave me alone. Touch me.

The unexpected warmth of the spring evening, a premonition of summer (is it possible the irrigation creates a local humidity, just in this valley of his farm) reaches up his shirtsleeves and down from the neck of his half-buttoned shirt to the navel. He has been sitting so still he has the fanciful feeling that so long as he does not move the farm is as it is when he's not there. He's at one with it as an ancestor at one with his own earth. He is there and not there.

—What's the final and ultimate price of pig-iron?—

The Amatongo, they who are beneath. Some natives say, so called, because they have been buried beneath the earth. But we cannot avoid believing that we have an intimation of an old faith in a Hades or Tartarus, which has become lost and is no longer understood.

There was not enough meat on a goat; most who came got only beer.

Solomon had dreamt of a young bull with a white face and a copper ring in its pink nose. He was not troubled by dreams, but it had come up. Phineas with whom he was ploughing this spring was plagued by dreams—those of his wife; she had begun to see, both asleep and awake, the form of some wild animal. She described two lights, the eyes of the animal, now on the ash-heap and in the fowl run, now in the eucalyptus trees; but nobody else could make out anything. She said when she went about alone the eyes accompanied her.

She was a woman people laughed at privately; used to drink a lot, coming home singing to herself and even trotting a few dance steps, across the veld from the shanty town behind De Beers' farm, and when the farmer first bought this place she would go up to his car and ask him for work in the house, pointing a finger down her open mouth, shaking her head hard, and saying in the pidgin white people understand, *Ikona puza*. All the time, Alina had the job of course. But the woman knew about plants. If she didn't always do her share of work in the compound, she was very useful at collecting wild spinach and other leaves people liked, also roots for purgatives. She had no living children even though for the last birth—and women said among themselves it was in fact the last, she must be somewhere around the end of the childbearing age —she had gone to the hospital in the location. Since she had begun to dream she had stopped drinking; she went about with a cloth tied low on her forehead like a mourner. She would shake hands with no one except very old people. At times she held her shoulders like someone whose back has been burned by hot water and winced if anything touched it. She wore a strand of large-holed white beads from the Indian shop threaded on string round each ankle.

She wouldn't eat what she saw in a dream she must not eat.

She dreamt she was going to turn into a snake. Everyone heard about it. Then she said it was a lizard she was afraid she would become, and she used the name *isalukazana*, the lizard that is a little old woman.

—She is certainly becoming an old woman.—

Solomon could think of nothing to say in answer to Phineas. Ever since he had known the woman nearly all her front teeth had been missing and now that she was so thin the cheeks sucked the empty space and her skin was grainy and dark round the eyes. He had heard she was not really Zulu at all, but came from Pondoland.

He remarked to Jacobus—I don't know those people.—

He was crowded into the room against the wall along with others when she had the desire to dance and confess her dreams to them. There was no getting out of it. With her cloth hanging in her eyes she stood in what little space there was and gave the time that was to be clapped and the phrase they were to chant. Somebody had to beat a folded ox-hide. It was awkward to move elbows and clap in such a pressure of people. Izak's radio was playing outside. When the chant and the beat of clapping was steady in counter-rhythm to it, she began to lift those ankles with the white beads, lift her feet, first one then the other, coming down lightly on the toes. She began to stamp her heels and quiver the muscles of her body like a young girl, right up to her cheeks, flapping the loose skin. The claps fell faster, the chant was drawn from deeper and deeper places in the men's chests and higher and higher behind the women's noses. The ox-hide gave off dust and hairs. The radio was pressed out under a far greater volume. Then she stopped; hands were in mid-air, some spattered claps completed themselves. Panting like a skinny dog chasing a rat in the vlei, she was after those dreams of hers, rambling, pursuing, speaking of leopards and chameleons—creatures the children in the doorway had never seen—speaking of snakes she had dreamt she was going to turn into, Umthlwazi, Ubulube, Inwakwa, Umzingandhlu; of imamba and inyandezulu, the snakes that are men and if killed will come to life again; speaking of the spirits, amatongo; describing how she had seen the ugly and rough-skinned lizard that is the itongo of an old woman, and how in her sleep there were also elephants and hyenas and lions and full rivers, all coming near to kill her, how they followed her, how there was not a single place in the whole country that she did not know because she went over it all, farther than Johannesburg and Durban, all by night, in her sleep. She started to pray then as people do in church and broke off, saying that when she tried to pray this desire carried all kinds of death to come and kill her at once. Now and then her words became songs she said she heard in her head without ever having learnt; and the songs became words again, telling dreams. She was so exhausted that sometimes her voice was lost; Izak's radio took up with an advertising jingle about washing powder that the children knew by heart. But the sweat that had filled the room with the smell of her (as if she were leaving her body like smoke) while she danced, continued to pour and trickle while she talked, started and oozed continually, as if her whole body were weeping, as if every pore were a puncture from which life were running out. There was no point at which this gathering of hers broke up. Released from the binding rhythm of clapping, people got restless and began to shift and talk. They simply found their way out to go about other things. Afterwards Solomon suddenly saw her, washing her hands in a tin basin in the yard like a woman who has just finished plucking a fowl or some other ordinary work.

He did not speak to this woman about her dreams. That was her husband's trouble, not his. But he was told she said if she had dreamed of cattle instead of a wild animal, she would have known what she must do. She would kill a beast and then she would be well again.

It was too warm for the woollen scarf but he wore a knitted cap. He pushed it up from the pursed lips that were like the raised imprint of some strange kiss on his forehead. He had not let the sun get at it yet. It did not hurt but felt tender to hands that touched it. He smiled at the thought of the poor creature, Phineas's wife. —I'm not ill.—

The woman who lived with him said—But you were nearly dead. You were dead there in the veld.—

Jacobus was always talking. He waited and waited for the right time to ask him. But the only thing to do if you wanted to ask something was just to say it, even if it had nothing to do with what Jacobus was busy telling you. —Was I dead when you found me?—

They were washing the old bull after he had been out to stud.

—Well how could you be dead, you are here now.— Jacobus grinning; or grimacing with his enthusiastic scrubbing among the curly suds of the bull's flank: the old rake had shat himself, he stood wearily on his stumpy legs, a drooping mustachio at the end of his retracted penis, while Solomon played the hose onto him under Jacobus's direction.

—But did you think I was dead.—

Jacobus looked up dramatically. He was ready to tell the story again. Spray from the hose sprinkled his woolly beard with tinsel.

—Would you have said, he is dead.—

—Of course you were like a dead man! Didn't speak, didn't move, didn't snore the way people do when they're dead-drunk—

A sensation of terrible cold and darkness—that must have been when he was left lying there naked—and the cold, cold edges, the freezing-edged pain over which another, warm darkness flowed— his wound and the blood flooding it. And then he died, alone in the third pasture with the one who was already dead there. As if he died—because he knew nothing, remembered nothing, he did not know he was found, he did not know he was being carried, he did not know Jacobus and the others were weeping over him, trying to get him to open his eyes, leave the other one and come back to them.

The dark, the freezing ragged edges—they did exist, as the other one did, outside himself and the moment before he died: he knew where. In the sky when a great storm was coming and a thick darkness was suspended from the hills over their heads on the farm, at the edge of a precipice of dark, terribly high up where the frozen rain, the hail, came from, out of the heat of summer, the black ledge of the storm was torn and ragged. That was where it seemed to him he was, that was what he had had knowledge of when he wasn't there in the veld to answer Jacobus, or to know himself travelling in the pick-up and lying in bed in the hospital.

*   *   *

Phineas's wife was a nuisance to everyone. The business of wanting to dance and confess was not something done once, over and done with. She wanted people to come and clap for her again. But they all had better things to do when work was finished. It was not as if she ever had any beer to put people in the mood for singing and clapping. Izak laughed and laughed, softly, and would not come near, even the first time. —Why?— But he wouldn't answer anyone. —It's not his religion.— —When did he say that?— —I'm telling you, I know why.— Izak let them go on talking about him; he smiled in their attention. Dorcas came once but was forbidden by her husband, now known behind his back as 'Christmas Club', to do so again.

—He's right. There was enough trouble already.—

—What trouble?—

All very well for Alina to take that tone; but between Jacobus and Alina there was the special circumstance of their accountability to the farmer, which the others did not share.

—She's bringing people from over the hill there. And also from the location.—

—Tsa! man! He doesn't know who is living here and who isn't.—

—He'll tell me, why do I let everybody walk around on his farm, they will steal cattle, there will be fights, look how Solomon was attacked...that other business down there...this, that—I don't like her sickness, myself.—

Alina was authoritative with the speculations and evidence of her long talks with the other women who lived up at the compound with Phineas's wife. It was even said that the woman would not sleep with her husband any more.—You know what's supposed to be wrong with her, don't you?—

—I don't like that woman. I never liked her. First always drunk, so that he complains there's too much beer on this farm. Now this. If Phineas was not such a good man with the cattle, I would say let them go. But poor Phineas—

—You know, don't you? She feels the amatongo in her shoulders. It's the disease that means you're going to get the power.—

Jacobus drew snot through the back of his nose into his throat, tasting something unpleasant. He circled his forefinger, pointing it stiffly at his right temple. Alina's face wanted to laugh, but she was afraid to. —She says she's not surprised—they tell me. It's true she always knew about plants for medicines.—

—I will buy my Epsom from the India.—

And now she could laugh.

Solomon told his brother he had dreamt of the bull with the white face, that young one whose nose-ring was still new. They had never found out who the men were who had lured Solomon out at night and left him for dead in the veld. They could only roughly calculate how long he must have lain in the third pasture. Solomon would have liked to have known how long he lay there. It was a miracle that he was alive now. Although he was the younger, his brother had treated him with a special respect, ever since he had recovered. He listened carefully to everything he said; he listened while Solomon told him that the woman who was making a nuisance of herself had said if she had dreamt of a beast instead of wild animals she would have known what to do. He said —There is no pain?—

The cap was being worn, the stitched lips were not to be seen.

—Sometimes a headache.—

Solomon did not tell his brother the thought that he had lain in the veld (how long?) with that other one down there who had never been taken away, never been buried by his own people. For—how many hours?—there had been two of them dead there instead of one.

Jacobus said: —That's his bull, the young one, you dream about, you know.—

They owned no cattle: not a single beast between the lot of them. That woman who thought she was going to be a diviner, she was dreaming back somewhere in the old days, somewhere in the Reserves, where you killed a beast from your herd for a wedding, a funeral, a thanksgiving, or to put things right—cleanse the kraal, they used to call it.

If a beast died of some illness that did not make it dangerous to

161

eat, Jacobus was always given permission by the farmer to cut it up and distribute it to the farm workers. Sometimes it was possible to buy from some other farm meat from an ox that had died in this way. Solomon's dream had been of a young Hereford bull like the farmer's, but even a live slaughter ox would have cost the money he earned in six months. He paid five rands for the goat. Goats were unobtainable from the farms round about because the farmers didn't allow them to be kept; it came from a man in the location who grazed it on waste land near his house. It turned out to be a goat with a white face, although Solomon had not asked for anything special.

Everybody seemed to have a hand in the arrangements. The goat arrived led by a child the day before and was tethered in the barn on Jacobus's insistence—If he sees anything eating his grass or anyone even picking up a bird's egg on his farm, you know there is big trouble.— Jacobus was not pleased about the whole thing; the farmer always came out at weekends.

But they all knew Jacobus ate meat at least once a week. The farmer brought a brown paper parcel for him that was put in the refrigerator in the locked house. Many of them had not had any since a calf had broken a leg and been slaughtered two months before. —Well if you want, we can have meat and beer instead of working on Monday or Tuesday?—

Jacobus ignored the joke. —You never know when he comes these days.—

People started arriving on Saturday night. The old women from the location who came to the farm for weeding in summer must have heard about it, and they walked over on Sunday morning. There were Solomon's brother's people, from across the vlei. That crazy woman seemed to have asked some people of her own; they behaved almost as if it were her goat that was going to be killed. Anyway, they brought a lot of beer. The goat was led into the yard where everyone was already gathered except her followers, who were still at their singing and clapping in Phineas's room. It was happy to be out of the dark of the barn and pulled determinedly towards the cabbage leaves some woman had left from her cooking, breaking a chain of droppings like a broken string of shiny black

162

beads. In the instant of straining for the leaves it was thrown on its right side by many hands. Solomon's brother stabbed it over the aorta. It took quite a few minutes to die; the noise it made seemed to be muffled out gradually, as if some invisible weight were descending on the creature. At last—quite soon—it made no sound.

Solomon heard what there was to hear but did not see. He stood as he had been instructed by people there who knew about these things, facing away, with a friend who worked with his brother for the bus company. The friend spoke conversationally to the air —Here is your beast, Bengu, father of Solomon, Nomsa, mother of Solomon. It is to say we give thanks that you have cared for him. May God protect his child—

No one among the crowd was paying any attention; already the men were gathered over the dying goat, everyone was animated by the thought of meat and wanted to get on with the skinning and cutting up so that cooking could begin. The butchering was done expertly under advice and argument from onlookers. Some parts were given to the women, others reserved for the men; the gall was poured over the entrails to make them tasty. Somebody remembered to collect the blood in a tin and put it at the back of the room where Solomon slept, where it was to be left overnight. Among the older people, a clay pot of beer circulated from mouth to mouth as they squatted; the others filled jam-tins and mugs of their own from the milk-buckets and plastic petrol containers of beer. Even Phineas's wife drank again, darting eagerly as the goat towards good things after her days of incarceration in a room. Dancing and clapping and singing were fired by meat and drink and the two oil-drums covered with hide sometimes beat so strongly they vied with the shouting and laughter, sometimes lazily dropped to a panting mark-time, but never ceased, never broke the tempo of pleasure, of excess, that regulated everyone's blood. The sound of a party drew comers across the vlei. It went on all through the afternoon and almost through the night; people came and people went, long after the meat was finished, people slept and people woke. Jacobus was there like everybody else, as drunk as everybody else. There was nothing to worry about; the farmer and the young one had been and gone early in the day. Once or twice Jacobus remembered the irrigation but could not remember whether it was turned off or not; then he no longer remembered what it was that bothered him. The evening was nearly as warm as a summer night; later, when the cold rose from the river, beer had given them all a skin thick to it. They sweated and sang. There was no one to come up complaining to their rooms built of reject breeze-blocks, their lean-tos of tin and sacking, their fowl-runs made of scrap and filched fencing, that jigged up and down, appeared and disappeared in the light of their braziers blotted out and released by the movement of their bodies. The farmhouse was locked; Jacobus kept the key on a nail hidden from everyone: Jacobus kept them safe, he was hostage among them, hidden among them like the key, there was no one to come and find him. All the farm was dark except for where they gathered the life of the place together for themselves. He and his son with woman's hair came and went away, leaving nothing, taking nothing; the farmhouse was empty. Stamping slowly, swaying from one foot to another, dancing conferred a balance of its own that drunkenness could not fell, and those who felt blows gathering in their fists mostly could not find their target. The night stood back from them; their voices, their treading feet and thumping drums spouted from it in plenty. The sleeping cattle, the barn, the sheds, the fanged and clawed machines the colour of football jerseys and smelling of oil, the pick-up and the caterpillar tractor, the water obediently flowing forever down there in the reeds—all—all might have been theirs.

On Monday Jacobus was relieved to see that he must have remembered to turn off the irrigation. The compound stank of fermented maize in various avatars—spilt beer, vomit, urine. And the few bones feasting dogs and flies were testimony to the inadequacy of a goat. Someone—who else but that woman?—had hung the horns above the sack that covered the doorway of Solomon's room. He threw them on the ash-heap.

You should just see it. A pity you can't see it. It was getting on for autumn that first time I came to look over the place—wasn't that the year the drought had already begun, anyway? You couldn't imagine, looking at it then, it could be like this.

It is true any woman would go crazy over the multiple-headed lilies that are suddenly blooming out of these untidy streamers of leaf. Some were burned, in the fire; he remembers kicking at the exposed apexes of the bulbs, thinking they were done for. But no, with the early rain, they are out all over the veld: they don't look like wild flowers, at all, they are something you'd pay through the nose for, from a florist's, stems rising two-foot tall with a great bunch of five or six blooms at the top, white striped with red. He has counted seventeen over on the island that the fire made visible; the new reeds aren't thick enough to hide it completely, yet. And where the river is narrower and the banks are clear of the reeds, red-hot pokers are flowering right out of the water. Down here at the third pasture the place looks like a water-garden on some millionaire's estate.

You wouldn't believe it was natural. If you could show it to Kurt and his old cronies! Genus: *Amaryllidaceae*; species: *Crinum bulbispermum*. One of the secretaries at the office has been sent out to buy the best book available on veld flowers and from it he's identified the lilies as the Orange River Lily, *Crinum bulbispermum*, spring-blooming, favouring swampy ground. It belongs to the amaryllis family, most of whose members are distinguished by the arrangement of the flowers in an umbel subtended by two or more bracts.

—Look—a perfect mandala— Showing off, or flirting by pretending to assume he would know what she was talking about, she gestured with her foot at some bedraggled plant. But in that courtship dance that led over pasture and donga, he had seen the foot rather than the plant: chipped red shield of a big toenail that protruded from the sandal like an imperious finger.

165

—A what?—

—The shape of these leaves—you know—it's that whorl you see inside a marble. A symbol of the universe.—

—What sort of word is that?—

—Now you have me. Sanskrit, I think.— Crawling through a fence while he held the barbed wires apart for her, a strand of her hair caught and remained there. A pause; part of the fine old chase. She laughed while he jerked the hairs loose and wound them round his finger to present to her. He often saw tufts of coarse blond hair from the cows' tails left like that, on the fences.

Crinum bulbispermum. The bulbs of many species contain alkaloids and some have medicinal value. (He keeps the book now on the sideboard in the house.) Perhaps that's why the boys seem to have gone round clumps of the plants instead of ploughing them in, over here, and in other places where they occur on the edges of the mealie fields. Fortunately the piccanins don't pick flowers (they're not interested in such things) but he does remember last year seeing some woman from the compound digging up roots. Jacobus ought to be told that medicine or no medicine, these bulbs mustn't be taken.

—What *is* pig-iron? No, I'm serious—

Pig-iron really doesn't interest me that much any more, you know—but since pig-iron's what you conveniently associated me with, since that's my label—I've sold enough of it and all the other things, sold and bought, known when to buy and sell enough for several lifetimes. Oh I've had my fun among the big boys. Now there are possible new markets in Brazil; enormous potential. I've been over to have a look (a weekend in Jamaica on the way back—ever seen a black beach?), but I don't get excited about such things. Was there ever a transformation like the one brought about by the early rain on this place? Could there be anything finer? And it all happens in its own time, nothing can force it up, corner or rig it, and when it's ready, nothing can hold it back. Did you know that when there is drought, hippos abort? And now with the early rain the lilies and red-hot pokers were in full bloom in October, and by November the lucerne—he suddenly noticed as he came to that high ground near the eucalyptus trees, this morning—is turning blue in flower. You'd never know the vlei had burned. More birds than ever. You'd never know anything had happened there. The ploughing was early because of that good rain and half an hour ago I stood within thirty yards of a dozen Hadedas feeding among the young mealies. Several Sacred Ibis, too. The plants are up to my knees already.

—Now that you've bought that place, I can just see you in a few years time, falling into its bosom. When all *this* is finished for you—

Was it so great a bounty, naked clairvoyant, that you read in your body? The Hadedas looked around from time to time but went on sticking their beaks into the earth as if I weren't there.

—Mother it and husband it and lover it—

There's some sort of wild clover, with a yellow flower, that's come up among that special mixture of pasture grasses I got from the agricultural research people, and I can tell you, it has a scent like fermented honey, it blows across all the time, makes you breathe deeply, makes you want to lie down and sleep...

—You'll wallow in it.—

That wasn't one of our more successful get-togethers, I suppose. Something a bit pathetic about the way the two bodies separate with a little sucking noise like two halves of a juicy fruit being pulled apart from the pip. Women expect something then—a caress, an endearment—they often don't seem to know what. You were like the others, although you were going on about my 'historical destiny'. I don't have anyone hanging around here, thank God, if you walk about this place on your own, I can tell you, you see things you'd never see otherwise. Birds and animals—everything accepts you. But if you have people tramping all over the place—

—All to yourself. You've bought what's not for sale: the final big deal. The rains that will come in their own time, etcetera. The passing seasons. It's so corny, Mehring. I thought you had more to you than that. I'll bet you'll end up wanting to be buried there, won't you? Down there under your willow trees, very simply, sleeping forever with your birds singing to you and Swart Gevaar tending your grave. O Mehring!—hiking herself up from the bed on one elbow, the way she did, so that her brown breasts swung like weights in a sling—O Mehring—her laugh—you are a hundred years too late for that end! That four hundred acres isn't going to be handed down to your kids, and your children's children—

—Come on—I've only got one—

—Well, his children's children. That bit of paper you bought yourself from the deeds office isn't going to be valid for as long as another generation. It'll be worth about as much as those our grandfathers gave the blacks when they took the land from them. The blacks will tear up your bit of paper. No one'll remember where you're buried.—

—Asleep down there at the river, what will I care.—

—You think you've discovered the joy of simple tastes, I know, but it's just that you've made enough money.—

—If you had my money…it offends you to think I've got what I want, through it. Free soul that you are: you've never forgotten your Sunday school dictum that money is wicked. And your psychologizing—doesn't Freud say money is shit? But even shit is good—if you could just see this good thick carpet of ordure the cows have laid down in their paddock. It's dry and friable, and when Jacobus spreads it on the fields and the irrigation jets wet it, there's the smell of the sea here, a wonderful freshness, salt and sensual.—

—You think you've found peace but it's just that no one as intelligent as you are—basically—(always a reservation, from her) could go on forever seeing those awful people you mix with, and eating those awful expensive meals in those ghastly hotels, and meeting those bloody awful charity-dispensing wives of other businessmen—

The young ones aren't so bad. There are some lovely girls among the daughters. If one were to have long blond hair oneself, almost as long as theirs (from the back you can hardly tell the difference) and go about barefoot, it might make sense. Otherwise not.

—I can hear it. 'He's in love with his farm,' they'll say. But you don't want them to come out and play at milkmaids. Perhaps you'll really believe it's love. A new kind. A superior kind, without people. You'll even think in time there's something between you and the blacks, mmh? Those 'simple' blacks you don't have to talk to. The little kids we saw pulling a toy car they'd made of wire in the image of one like yours.—

Jacobus respects me. Perhaps. Old devil. They respect the people they know they can't fool. They know where they are with me. I'm the one who feeds them. I wanted to buy you the toy—you raved over it so much as a great work of art. Could have put it with your collection of pots. They would've been thrilled to get a nice big fifty-cent piece and go off and pinch another bit of wire to make another car. But no. Your face: there was some dreadful blue I'd made by such a suggestion. You know the tactics: your expression saying, well, if you can't see why not, it's something that can't be explained. What are you rich people made of, anyway—pig-iron? But I'm serious. What exactly *is* pig-iron? I really ought to know. I do know it's used in the manufacture of steel—

I really don't care a bloody damn about pig-iron. I leave most of that to my partners these days. You were always so transparent. After a little while I could see your bright little female brain working as one can see the innards in the bodies of those pale ghekos that run on the ceilings in Central Africa. Who knows when it might be useful to spout a few technical terms relevant to the base metal industry? Perhaps in London now, six thousand miles away, thank God, from this mealie-field where the Hadedas, having flown up shouting, have circled and settled once again, you are adding your knowledgeable background comment to a discussion of the labour crisis in the country you left so heroically. Now let's look at one of the biggest employers of exploited black labour, the steel and engineering industry. SEIFSA—?—oh ask the professor's wife, she's the expert on the inner workings of South African capitalist exploitation; she infiltrated the bed of a prominent industrialist—the Steel and Engineering Industries Federation of South Africa has not only maintained but in most cases accelerated the substantial improvement reflected in its half-yearly figures. Pig-iron production showed the biggest increase, and production of non-ferrous alloys the biggest decrease. In September the pig-iron industry produced 435,600 tons, compared with 340,000 tons in August. This brought the production of pig-iron for the period January to September to 3,296,200 tons, an increase of 12.7 per cent over the 2,924,400 tons produced in the same period last year. Now there are hundreds of thousands of blacks in the steel industry, more than 80 per cent of the labour force is black, and from a little research I once did I happen to know that in the pig-iron industry alone... She's as well-informed as she's good looking; and tough, too—a brave smile from the doorway of the plane before she turned tail and disappeared.

That long-suffering professor of yours whom I never met—You regard him as an honest man, then?—

Lying in my bed, you answered the question as if it were another: —I respect him.—

Just as I said—Jacobus respects me.

—Why do you laugh? I do. He's devoted to his work and he doesn't live off anybody's back. Not directly. I suppose if one looks into where the money for those research grants comes from—

A bore in the end, just as much as any of those women whom you despised as being nothing more than a body. It would have become a bore. Ingesting, digesting and excreting moral problems clearly as a see-through gheko.

Fuckers, not lovers.

Once you were waiting for a phone-call from a lover late at night. It didn't come. You slept, and were awakened at three in the morning, the phone already in your hand, by a voice abusing you with filthy words. One of those anonymous 'nuisance calls' one is supposed to report to the police. You told me it was the worst thing that had ever happened to you; but that was before you got yourself interrogated at John Vorster Square.

Lovers write letters and say things that the others feel obliged to trot out only in bed. One piece of flesh of all flesh remains opaque with mystery for them; it must be returned to again and again. And even when it has become too familiar, it is invested with something of what it once was. There is the obsession with which that yellow weaver thrusts worms and grubs and whatever it can find, down the gullets of those ugly fledglings—and there are thousands upon thousands of weavers, this year, and hundreds of the young must fall from the nests or be destroyed in other ways— you find them in the veld, ant-eaten already, the night after any heavy rain. Nourishment. Lovers take presents from each other they would not choose for themselves (what will his mother do with that agate egg when he gives it to her for Christmas?—every knick-knack shop in Madison Avenue is full of such things). They want something of each other; doesn't matter what it is—a horse to ride? A bridge that could so easily have been built, just a matter of getting the boys to mix a bit of cement and carry over some posts and logs on the tractor? A dog kennel with an ingenious roof that lifts like a lid?— They find out. There is always a subject between them, my dear gipsy, always, always, they know what it is even if they are being shown round a farm that doesn't interest them much, even if they don't speak much, sitting side by side in a car. Look at that funnel of web some spider's spread leading to its hole, and the beetle that's struggling there, caught. If you come back to the same spot this afternoon, if it were possible ever to find it again, on this farm, you might see the beetle there still, maybe still alive, bound with filaments of shroud the spider will wind it in; sometimes it will be there for days until the spider drags it down into the hole—everything takes its own time out here, whatever you do. Listen to the frogs. The great rough rachet at which the throat of the first one of the evening engages at the same time every day. You are bored? I'm not. The frogs cease suddenly, later, just as they begin. This place is a quiet sleeper. Is he facing without eyes up through a sky of earth or is he lying here as they found him, turned away. There are languages and cultural difficulties. It isn't possible to follow, from where he is one can't imagine someone speaking as they speak: yes, master, the skelms from the location got me, just like the policeman said. Those blacks hit me on the head, they stuck a knife in my heart, they threw me away— No moon. You could lie out, down here. A quiet sleeper. Turn to her and without making contact with any part of her receive from her open lips, warm breath. Breathe her in as the kiss of life given a dying man.

He's spent the night in the house quite a few times this summer. There are no sheets but a cushion from the sofa does as a pillow and there is the kaross he once bought in Botswana when there was first talk of a consortium to prospect for nickel deposits, and he flew up for a day. It's nicely made, well-matched skins of Black-back jackal; but one buys these things when one goes about the world and then doesn't know what the hell to do with them, or whom to give them to. It didn't look right in the flat. The mosquitoes are bad in that bedroom. Spraying stinks but doesn't help much. Yet shaving in the dark little bathroom an hour or more earlier than he would be if he were in town, he is feeling as fresh as if he has had a particularly good night's sleep. Through the eye-level window that opens upwards like a fanlight he watches the arrival of women and old men who have been taken on by Jacobus to come from the location to weed. Thirty cents a day, Jacobus says he can get them for; but if you see how they're taking it easy, how they're strolling up and having a good old gas with Alina, and sitting about against the workshop wall—probably not worth more. He is shaving by feel, not looking into the small foxed mirror at all—good God, what's going on? Now they're leisurely unwrapping their babies and their bundles, apparently they bring their bread or mealie-pap along, and now young Izak arrives with a can of milk. So it's a picnic, before the day's work begins. Everybody's squatting on the grass in the yard and being sociable. Some of these old girls are quite characters; one crone with nothing but a big safety pin to hold her rag of a blouse together over her huge old tits, now that she's shed her blankets, catches him out watching through the window and calls a loud and jaunty greeting, one word in Afrikaans and one in their language: Môre, 'Nkos'. The borehole water is soft; one gets an exceptionally good shave. Those women are giving Jacobus hell over something but it's all banter; barefoot, his hands hooked in the braces of new bibbed overalls that stand away from his waist like Chaplin's trousers, he's arguing theatrically, but there's laughter, they shout him down, behind their din there is the hurrying tripping skelter of cattle being driven out of the paddock by Solomon and Phineas—a sound queerly equivalent to that of thousands of feet coming up out of the railway stations, away from the buses, far off in the city. Jacobus pretends to threaten a woman with a fist. So that's how work gets going on the place. Everyone

172

takes his time, nobody's developing ulcers out here, you've got to grant them that.

At the stove Alina is stirring something that already smells burnt. She looks half asleep and moves reluctantly; spoilt—she's not used to being required in the house in the mornings. Anyway, he doesn't want breakfast. He flings up the screeching steel fly-screens on the windows in that airless, lifeless bedroom—the moment he's gone she'll close everything again—and emerges through the kitchen door, an apparition (sees himself as) in that light grey summer suit with the back vent, Roman coin cuff-links and red silk tie. The guise or disguise of the city; he was here straight from the office yesterday—the old pair of corduroy jeans he keeps to get into at the farm is lying with the heap of the kaross. As he walks through scattering cats (they've been attracted from the roof by dregs of mealie-pap dirtily thrown about the yard) to his car, he comes face to face with the weeding contingent, who have been down to the barn to collect their implements and are now on their way to the fields. He is surrounded by the passage of a ragged army advancing on him with hoes, the grinning, know-ing faces of the old women, the younger ones not meeting his eyes, their babies' heads lolling above their backsides as they pass, the old men in scarecrow coats blindly not seeming to know what they are making for. It is only a few moments: they have him in their midst, so that he cannot go forward. It would be absurd to back away—they are all round him.

Jacobus has a bucket and mop and is sloshing water over the windscreen but he waves him off. He must get into town. —What about the lucerne?—

—That far one, there by the pump? I'm going cut today. Is very good day.—

There could be other opinions on that. The weather report on the radio has predicted thunder storms in the afternoon. How big is that field?—it could be cut and then drenched before it's dry enough to bale—say, two hundred bales lost. Instead of driving towards the farm gate, which is open for the day (the night-watchman is drinking tea out of a syrup tin in the yard, and has touched his hand to his red-and-white tea-cosy cap in respectful greeting) he'll take a quick look at that lucerne first. The road is really bad; there's not time to see to everything. Children run ahead of the car to open the camp gates but they don't follow him as he heaves through the last one.

Oh my God. What a crime to wake up morning after morning in that flat. Never mind the huge firm bed and the good coffee. The car door shuts under the slow swing of its own weight behind him. The mechanical two-syllable sound disappears instantly as the substance of the morning closes over it, heavy and clear as the sea. Oh my God. The field dips away before it rises again towards the river. It has drifted into flower since the sun rose two hours ago— yesterday afternoon it was still green, with only a hint of sage to show the bloom was coming. Just touching, floating over its contours, is a nap of blue that brushes across the grain to mauve. There is no wind but the air itself is a constant welling. It is the element of this lush summer. He has plunged down past the pump-house where a big pipe makes a hidden foot-bridge buried in bowed grasses and bulrushes over an irrigation furrow. His shoes and the pale grey pants are wiped by wet muzzles of grasses, his hands, that he lets hang at his sides, are trailed over by the tips of a million delicate tongues. Look at the willows. The height of the grass. Look at the reeds. Everything bends, blends, folds. Everything is continually swaying, flowing rippling waving surging streaming fingering. He is standing there with his damn shoes all wet with the dew and he feels he himself is swaying, the pulsation of his blood is moving him on his own axis (that's the sensation) as it seems to do to accommodate the human body to the movement of a ship. A high earth running beneath his feet. All this softness of grasses is the susurration of a slight dizziness, hissing in the head.

Fair and lovely place. From where does the phrase come to him? It comes back, tum-te-tum-te-tum, as only something learned by rote survives. It's not his vocabulary. Fair and lovely. A place in a child's primer where nothing ugly could possibly be imagined to happen: as if such places exist. No wound to be seen; and simply shovelled under. He looks out over this domain almost with fascination, to think that, somewhere, that particular spot exists, overgrown. No one'll remember where you are buried.

174

The shoes are a mess.

There ought to be a yellow duster on the glove shelf—but an old company report serves. He smears off the wet and scraps of grass. There are some early grass-seeds, too. Once on the main road, there's heavy traffic at this time in the morning. Truck-loads of builders' supplies, road-making equipment mounted on huge, slow trailers marked 'Abnormal Load', haulage of all kinds, although he calculated that factory workers would have gone to work already and the office and shop people would be going a little later. Overtaking and being overtaken, the tread of these vehicles and his Mercedes criss-cross again and again the experience he has just left behind him (half an hour he wandered, stood in the field, or maybe not more than ten minutes): quickly it is covered by a kind of grid. On its tracks are laid down many automatic re- sponses to everyday situations of no importance and one of these is that he does not see people who thumb lifts; he would certainly not have been aware of the pair (even though the old man was dressed so peculiarly) who take courage to come right to the car while he is held up behind two crawling trailers just before the entrance to the freeway. An elderly man in commissionaire's uniform and a girl or young woman. Difficult to say no, when you can't drive off, and there's a whole great empty car. He has told them, shortly, to get in, then. They have both scrambled humbly into the back, just time to bang the door too hard behind them the way people do who are not used to these big cars that respond to the lightest touch, while he suddenly sees the opportunity to get past the trailers, in a fast manœuvre, and work his way into his lane again.

He is up front alone like a chauffeur and would be content to leave it at that. But a face under a gold-braided cap, cut off by the lower limits of the rear view mirror where thin pink wattles are caught into an even more elaborately-braided stand-up collar, determinedly catches his eye, although it must be impossible to tell, from the back of his head, whether this sociable move has been successful or not. The old chap must be sitting forward on the edge of the seat. —No, I was just saying, as a matter of interest, weren't you at the late show, *Trinity Is Still My Name*, on Friday?—

175

—You're talking about a cinema?—

—That's right. The Elite 300, Starland City.—

—No, no, I wasn't at any cinema.—

—Now that's funny, you know I've got an eye for faces, and when I come up just now I said to myself—I've seen that one recently. Not Saturday night, then? There was a gentleman with a party of four, nice-looking people, a blonde lady one of them—I could have sworn it was you. Well, I'm not so young as I used to be, old soldiers never die, they say, but I reckon I see three to four thousand people a week going past me, and often I'll say to one of them, Good evening, sir, and did you enjoy the show *last week*— giving the name of the picture, whatever it might happen to've been, you see, and who was starring—and by George you should see their faces then! What a memory, they'll say to me! See a face once, in all those thousands, and pick it out again just like that! Not that every face's a face you'll remember, you know. There's some you don't want to lay eyes on again, I can tell you that.—

—I'm sure.—

—It takes all kinds. You'll get them that push the tickets under your nose like it was a bone for a dog and you'd think you're expected to have four hands at once, they can't stand a moment. A person must take their turn, one man's as good as the next, and what's the rush, you're going in for an evening's pleasure aren't you? You want to relax, take it easy, isn't it so?—

The old face in the mirror is smiling in the bounty of its philosophy. He nods vociferously enough for this to appear, from the back of his head, adequately appreciative.

—But most of the time you meet a nice class of people coming to the shows at Elite 300. Lots of them know me by sight. They've got a smile and a good evening for you. You don't get these young hippies you get in the big cinemas, putting their feet up on the seats and burning the carpets. Some people've got no respect for anything. It's the parents I blame. I'm not prejudiced, I don't say that every kid with long hair's a loafer, mind. I've had youngsters of my own, and I've got grandsons. But what would I do with myself sitting around at home? Dad, my daughter tells me, you've done your bit. All through Delville Wood in '14–'18, yes. But I'd go out of my mind sitting doing nothing. I was five years at the old Metro before they pulled it down. But you can't compare the comfort with a small exclusive cinema like the Elite, no question about it. You've been there, of course. Once you get down into one of those seats you're like in a beautiful armchair in your own home. Just as good.—

There is an anxious silence for the last few minutes of the journey; the old fellow seems to feel guilty that he has run through his conversational repertoire. Anyway, at the first robot towards the centre of town both passengers alight, with sounds of heaving and pushing as the veteran slides along the seat and gets himself out (perhaps he has some disablement). The girl has never uttered a word during the ride; the old man, after profuse thanks, suddenly signals as the car is about to pull away. Of course they've left something.

—It's still on. Trinity, I mean. It's a good Western, I think you'd enjoy it, you know— The light's green, everyone is nosing and blaring at the stationary car, the old man is carried in a momentum of people let loose from where they were damned up at the crossing, and some impatient bastard even shouts abuse whose sarcastic twang catches at the car window as he whips by.

All right. All right. The Mercedes sinks into the entrance of the underground garage where the attendant Zulu with disc ear-rings stoppering his lobes, and a cap less grand than a commissionaire's, has recognized it instantly, and drawn aside, cere-monially as a curtain, the loop of chain that bars unauthorized entry.

He felt that he really must have a strong cup of coffee. Doing without breakfast when he slept at the farm was a good thing, almost a virtue he liked to enjoy, but there was an arch of emptiness under his diaphragm that only decent coffee and a first cigar could support. One of the little girls at the office would bring him a cup of instant if he waited a few minutes for them to come in, but he was earlier than the lowliest messenger on days when he came from the farm, and he didn't want to wait even ten minutes. Not that that muck was coffee. He went up to the foyer and out into the street. There must be a place nearby. Business lunches simply meant driving from one underground parking bay to another; the only time he walked through the streets was when he went to get his hair cut.

The coffee bar was packed. Apparently young people crowded in to meet their friends before work in the mornings, clustered along the counter like birds on a telephone wire. It was an Italian place, smelt deliciously of what he'd come for, and was noisy as the street. He got a double espresso and stood where he could find room for himself, at a ledge that formed a table of sorts for the cup, at elbow height, round a pillar. How they talked, little typists and students—whatever they were—predominantly girls, although a few young men fooled here and there, a few moony couples were holding hands between the stools and absently caressing. How they could talk! Confidential, animated, fresh from the toothbrush, their eyes circled with colour, butterflies on their trousers, hieroglyphs on their satchels, almost skirtless bottoms almost bare on stools—they could have been his daughters. Any of them. The coffee seized upon his tongue. He concentrated on sipping it round the edges of the cup, it went down slow, thick and fiery as dark molten metal poured into the ingot and as soon as it was comfortable to drink he was already at the dregs, and ordered another. To get the fresh cup off the conveyor band that moved along the main counter, carrying orders to customers one way and dirty cups the other, he had to lean his long arm in the pale grey sleeve with the half-inch of striped shirt cuff and the Roman coin cuff-link, between blonde and dark heads: a strange intrusion. The two whose conversation it parted slowed talk momentarily and looked at it as something disembodied, out of their world. He caught a whiff of scent—not perfume, something they washed their hair with or sprayed under their arms. This cup he could take more temperately; he could wait until it was possible to hold a mouthful, hot and strong. He had lit a cheroot. But one was smiling at him— one of the dozens of girls—twiddling the fingers of a hand in a childish wave. He looked away as when, in a crowded room, a glance intercepts the greeting intended for another. When he looked up again the girl was laughing, shaking her head a little as if to say: it's me.

He put down the cup. He was not sitting—no chairs in a place like that—but he stood away from the ledge, the pillar, he took a step, drawn up, as if he rose from a table.

She had slid round and off her stool in one easy movement and was coming to him.

—Hul-*lo*. We haven't seen you for such a long time. Mummy was saying only yesterday. And someone said you were in Japan or Brazil or somewhere.—

—No. Not at the moment. As you see—

They laughed, and without meaning to he actually opened his hands as if to display—one of the half-dozen well-cut summer suits, the edges of the trousers giving him away by just a hairline of grass-stained wet where they hung at the right length over his shoes.

—What're you doing here?— So early, in our coffee bar, the smile suggested, not unwelcomingly.

—Thirsty. And what about you? Why aren't you at school? Or am I being insulting—you've left school, that's it? You're a lady of leisure.—

—Oh ho. Am I! Slaving away. I'm at art school. I have to get up at quarter-to-six to catch the bus every morning.—

—Why doesn't Dad buy you a car—

—I know. It's mean.— She was laughing as if this were the wittiest conversation of her life.

179

—I'll have to talk to him about that.—

—I just wish you would. You tell him.—

—A nice little sports car. What would you like? A Jag? A Triumph? Something with wire wheels?—

She pulled a face that made white dents in her firm pink-brown flesh. —I'll take *anything*. Any old jalopy. And what's Terry doing? I suppose he's got a car, lucky thing.—

—Not so lucky. Writing matric at the moment. Still incarcerated at school.—

—Good. Good—she said, vaguely.

There was a pause; the espresso machine made a gargling, hawking racket at which he raised his eyebrows and she laughed again, the *habituée*.

—But this coffee's wonderful. My second round. Will you have one with me?—

—I know. It's great. I've just got mine. Wait I'll fetch it.— With a turn of the long waist, she was off and back again, pushing through her friends or at least contemporaries. He had guarded the ledge against the intrusion of anyone else who might approach with wobbling cup. The two of them leant over their coffee a moment, breathing it in. —You don't smoke, do you? I don't have to incur parental wrath by offering you one of these?—

She shook her head. —You've always smoked that kind. I used to know you'd come when I smelt that smell in the house.—

He blew away the cloud that in the close atmosphere made a curly nimbus round her hair. He was obliged to ask: —And how's your mother? I've been away such a lot—

—Oh fine. We had a bit of a hassle over my flunking out before matric. You can imagine. Dad was all right but she was difficult. She wanted me to go to a finishing school in Switzerland...no *thanks*—

—If you go to Switzerland it'll be to ski.—

—Exactly.—

—You're enjoying this art school of yours? Have you any talent?—

—I don't know. I don't suppose I'll ever do anything inspired. But it's fun.—

—Specially the part that's spent in places like this, mmh?—

—If I'd still been in that bloody school, do you know where I'd be now? At prayers!—

—So it's gossip and romances and slipping off to drink espresso and go to the pictures?—

—Of course. You know it all!—

—Lucky thing.—

She smiled debunkingly at his use of her idiom. —What stops you? You can just walk out of your office and go to a movie if you feel like it? Why not? Daddy always groans as if he were in chains in that big plush office of his—I think you people make it all up. Why can't you just say, I'm going to a movie this afternoon? If you feel like it?—

—Will you play hookey with me? What about something called *Trinity—Trinity Was Here*—

—Oh you mean *Trinity Is Still My Name*—

—I hear it's a good blood-and-thunder Western—

—I've seen it. Not bad.—

—How many cinemas have you been to this week, mmh?—

She lowered her voice to her mother's pitch. —I don't think there's a show in town I haven't seen. Isn't that awful. And some are such trash. It's just a game, to us. We'll get sick of it in time. I suppose so. —You don't really feel like it, or you would just walk out.—

—That's so.—

—There're other things though, I mean that you really want to do, perhaps...?—

—Sometimes.—

A thin blonde with hunched shoulders attracted her attention and pointed at a huge wristwatch.

She was still so young she did not know how to take leave. She hitched her bag like a navvy. —Well, are we going to see you and Terry at Plettenberg Bay? We're going down next week—Daddy'll follow, he's got a meeting or something.—

—Terry's off to America to see his mum.—

—But you?—

He put money down beside the cup and the three walked out

together. They had to make their way through people entering, jostling; she didn't introduce her friend, didn't remember she had had no answer. —Fine. I'll tell Mummy—

His smiling gesture of correction, protest, uncommitted denial she—already a few yards off, accustomed to the easy uncertainty of her own plans—took laughing, miming the business of not having quite heard or understood. —What? *What*? You'll be around, then —okay—lovely—

The newspaper that was placed folded on his desk each morning usually went straight into the basket. Today he had not already read it in bed in his flat. Iron ore and manganese were steady; copper down a few points. He started near the back, at the financial pages, and worked his way to the front, where there was a report of yet another scandal in the business world—this time a big construction firm in trouble. No one he knew personally seemed directly involved, but he made a note to speak to his broker about some stock he held in a company subsidiary to the firm. He had bought because he'd been tipped off the company was in line for government contracts for the Sishen-Saldanha railway, if that ever came to anything.

He had lunch with someone out from Bethlehem Steel and an old friend, now busy negotiating royalties for Platinum Holdings with the native chiefs in whose Bantustan the mine was, on the one hand, and the General Motors people who wanted the platinum for anti-pollution exhaust devices, on the other. Quite a story.

They had scarcely parted—he was hardly at his desk—when the friend he had left phoned to say that someone with whom they'd both been associated for years had just been found gassed in his car near the Country Club. It was the girl's father. He was chairman of a bank, an investment trust, and connected with half a dozen other concerns, including perhaps (even those who knew him best would not be familiar with all his interests) the bankrupt construction company.

Thus it is with black men; they did not come into being when it was said, 'There are no Amatongo.' They came into being when it was already said, 'There are Amatongo.' But we do not know why the man which first came into being said, 'There are Amatongo.'

... since the white men came and the missionaries, we have heard it said that there is God.

I t's me.

Drawn up, he has been seized, he is going to be confronted, at last, at last. Here it is. This is it. It is true that he did not recognize her because he doesn't know that he has been expecting anyone—anything. Yet it's as if he must be eternally waiting, eternally expecting, eternally dreading. The excitation is suffocating; men have died in the act.

No one'll even remember where you're buried.

He is not the sort of person given to morbid reconstruction of how it must be when these people are waiting for the carbon monoxide to take effect. Before you actually pass out or however it comes: do they arrange themselves head in hands, registering despair etc. Just keep eyes fixed on the instrument panel: speedometer, oil gauge, engine heat. Grit in the mouth, face-down.

No one'll even remember where

Stood up, stood back—or was it a step forward he took, dreadfully—good god, one immigrant girl in a city full of girls, she can hardly make herself understood, she is there somewhere all the time. Or you—it would be typical of you to appear just like that, stirring up *trouble*, enjoying the sensation: They've graciously allowed me back in again, of course they're following me everywhere—

It's me: don't you know me? (Her mother would have corrected the grammar, she takes care not to speak like a colonial.) Don't you know me? Even Japan isn't far enough, even getting away to your own four hundred acres, disappearing in the grass (almost could, now in certain places) isn't far enough.

He gave a name to what was there only when he saw the wide belt that pressed down where that long waist stemmed or ended at the ledge of hip-bone (couldn't call those hips). More medieval cuirass or Elizabethan stomacher than what one understands by a woman's belt. The great round medallion dipped in front, slightly convex to follow exactly and flatly the slight curve where there would be a belly if she had one. He admired the belt; oh yes, somebody had just brought it back from Paris, mummy or daddy, everyone in Paris was wearing them. It's a suggestive piece of rubbishy embellishment behind which her body approaches (across the coffee bar) and is guarded, she perhaps knows this. As she leans over the pungence of the coffee, elbows on the ledge (tall, the top of her head would come up to his eyes) the medallion holds her under there like a cupped hand. Don't you recognize

What a bloody fool, burn to remember how you rose to it, think you'd never seen a woman before. If it'd been all the women ever had, suddenly there in one body, as it seems to be with the first one when you finally get the door open and at last, at last—this little schoolgirl. If it were some sort of seizure or attack for which one goes to the doctor. Or makes up one's mind to ignore. Except for the excessive smoking, there's been nothing wrong.

The degree of hotness, the sweetness, and the bitter consistency of the coffee is something he is precisely aware of; he's not avuncular, he's never had any special way of talking to young people because there's not much to say to them, anyway, but while he chides her easily, nice kid, about her lazy life and she pretends to be complaining to her father's friend about not having a car, she too is feeling some precise process taking place, as specifically as the progress of some hot sweet liquid tracing a passage of the body of which one is normally not consciously aware. He's sure of it.

Thank God I have no daughters.

His gullet retains the burning trail. Like a kind of heartburn, but recalled at will. Some of them take poison. A dose of cyanide, it's quicker. But that's for spies and brave revolutionaries—ay? Not the tycoon's way. Cyanide is the stuff that is used in the most effective and cheapest process for extracting gold from the auriferous reef. It is what saved the industry in the early 1900s. It is what makes yellow the waste that is piled up in giant sandcastles and crenellated geometrically-stepped hills where the road first leaves the city. The freeway gives a balcony view of them and of the stumped and straggling eucalyptus plantations between which used to provide timber for these old mines. He drives past so often, approaching from this side on the way out, and that on the way back, that he doesn't see them any more than he sees people thumbing for lifts.

He has escaped his colleague's funeral by sending, in addition to one of his junior directors to represent him, and a large donation in lieu of wreath to the black charity appointed by the widow, a huge bouquet to convey his sympathy to mother and daughter. They are all such old friends. The only way to get out of it was to be un-available—most unfortunately out of town on business. Out of the country. A sudden call to Japan. Australia. They won't know the difference.

He and a few other colleagues may have to set up some kind of fund for the two women if it turns out that there is nothing left. But it will take months for that financial tangle to be sorted out.

There is always an autopsy in a case like this, and by the time—as the front page of the newspaper puts it—the verdict of suicide and no foul play suspected is confirmed medically, it is Thursday before the funeral is fixed, and he invariably spends most of the weekend on the farm anyway. Just as well be Melbourne. No one will ever know. She stood silently with her mother and sister in line at customs waiting only to declare the plant tied up in newspaper and plastic.

A narrow escape.

Probably they will still go to Plettenburg Bay, after all they have that nice house there, and friends will rally round and persuade them to get away; for the girl's sake, if nothing else, the women friends will urge: she's so young, life must go on. (And the widow herself not old; soon they will be looking for a suitable partner for her at dinners.) *You* could at least write the girl a line from your beloved mother's apartment in New York—after all, you grew up together. But there's no contact; the only person who even mentions your name is the native on the farm. Every time I go there since the schools closed for the Christmas holidays: Terry he's not coming to help us? Terry he's not in Jo'burg? Why Terry he isn't here?—

Let the telephone recording device answer when the telephone rings in the flat. We phoned repeatedly over the holidays but you

were just *never* home. We'd like to have seen something of you—
Flung down hidden in the grasses, no one would know there is
anyone lying there. Walls of soft silvery-beige lean over him. The
grasses are just breaking into their kind of fruition. They are
tipped with water-colour brushes, feathers, and beaded with fine-
whiskered seeds. He is open only to the sky and that huge jet
mouthing its roar high up in space couldn't pick him out any more
than a grain of sand can be singled out while flying over the deserts.
The reeds have pennants of bladed leaf. They seethe softly. On
their thin masts that would bend under the weight of a moth,
plush red Bishop birds cling, dandled and danced. He is alone
down at the third pasture, so sure to be undisturbed. Alone and
not alone. In the heat of the day flies and midges fly into the eyes
and nose as if one were a corpse.

Without the services of the Girl Friday (his office is watched
over by her in his absences abroad as a kind of disused parlour, the
rolled financial journals put aside on his desk, the air-conditioner
kept going and the ashtrays kept empty) *bonsellas* for the boys are
not bought, ready for him, this Christmas. He has remembered
just in time, and there is the Indians'—he can stop a minute and
find something that will do. Months have gone by, they must have
found some solution to their troubles long ago—anyway it's just
too bad, he has no intention of driving back to town to shop.

A figure of purpose enters past rusty wire stands of wilted
vegetables and blackening bananas and among the blacks who
block the doorway drinking cans of sweet drinks or waiting
dreamily to buy. The middle-aged Indian and his son have
noticed at once, he produces a kind of alert; but perhaps that is
only because he is such a large man, white, a head above every
head; a sticky piccanin is staring in fascination at the level of his
knee. They are affable as only shop-keeping Jews and Indians are.
It's as if they expected him. They've forgiven him; he made some
social blunder that nobody's going to mention. They knew he
would come back some time; they can't be dispensed with.

—I got something very nice. This is what all the boys buy. They
like. You'll see.—

The denim trousers are so stiff the garments could stand alone.

187

They have 'Lone Ranger' or 'Deputy Sheriff', a choice of legend, embroidered between two star-shaped studs on a back pocket. But he can't see Jacobus as a movie hero. —Now something for the older boys.—

—This's the right thing. First quality polyester, no-iron. Nice colours, very nice colours. That's what they like. Let me tell you.—

—How much?—

—Oh it's cheap. It's not expensive.—

—How much? And the pants?—

—Don't worry, we give you a good price, you know that—

The purchase is a large one, and the plump son with the liquid eyes heavy with good-nature or laughter or last night's sex has dropped what he was doing and father and son are energetically folding and stacking garments to make a neat parcel. The father hustles spectacularly—No, no man, that's no good, get one of the big sheets from inside there—no, put that shirt here, look what you do to the collar! —There you are. Try that, sir. Is that okay? You sure? Just don't carry on the string, eh, I don't want the paper to tear and everything falls—wait—Dawood! What about one of those shirt boxes, man—

—No, that'll do fine.—

—He'll take it to the car for you. Dawood—

—Give here, it's perfect.—

They are beaming at him. Except the old man who sits as always, not dead yet, and looks through him and the blacks as if all are the same to him, or are not there at all. His gaze meets the old man's and nobody sees; a chink in the eye of a blind man.

—Compliments of the season to you. If you need anything, we open right through to seven tonight. I suppose we be greeting the young gentleman over the holidays. Oh that's a nice boy. And he like the Indian foods, you know! Tell him he must come—

Yes, yes, he'll tell him, thank you, thank you.

They beat a dog at the compound on Christmas Day. He lies down there and hears it. He's given them their pair of trousers or shirt each (ten per cent discount from the Indians') and the beer and hunk of meat Jacobus was deputed to buy; probably that's what the dog's got at: the meat. The bellowing howls die to squeals and

188

whimpers and then it's started again. He cannot *not* hear it. They've got no bloody feeling for animals. Well, if the cur had had any sense; they'd murder for meat. There is no such thing as a continuous cry of pain, eh; interesting. Man or beast, there has to be a stop for breath although the pain doesn't cease. Unless it is that pain is transmitted in waves or pulsations or whatever you call it—back to the brain from the spot where it's being inflicted, back from the brain to the place where the sjambok's cut or the boot's landing. They should be stopped. They shouldn't keep those dogs. But you can't get through over things like that. —What dogs? Is only one small dogs, he doesn't know to chase the birds—grinning on brown-necked teeth. You can't get through. You are right, reading the cards on the table; charity's a waste of time, towards man or beast, it only patches up a little bit of pain here and there. If it were as easy as that! If I stop them hitting it now that won't stop them doing it again when I'm not here. Everything needs changing. Don't you realize, if you were here these days they wouldn't want to have you on their side, they'd want you to be a white bitch. It makes things clearer all round. If you had any sense in that intelligent head of yours, you'd know that's how you had to end up. There isn't anything else they need from you.

The howls have throbbed themselves out and sunk away into the peace. This place absorbs everything, takes everything to itself and loses everything in itself. It's innocent. The pulse, the rhythm now is a coming and going of flights of birds just after sunset. The oceanic swaying of layers of boughs and swathes has stopped; the force of gravity sinks everything that is of the earth to the earth, chained to a ball of molten ore that has rolled over the dark side. All the weight of his life is taken by the tree at his back. Swallows are a flick of dark flying droplets. From the far curve of the sky, finches: they spring up and down in and out of the line of their formation as they go. Darts of doves aim at some objective of their own. Like showers of sparks, birds explode into his sky, and—a change of focus—close to his eyes gnats are raised and lowered, stately, as they hover in their swarm on strings of air. He feels (see him in her crystal ball and have a good laugh if she likes) almost some kind of companionship in the atmosphere. You predicted it—right—you are so clever, your kind, you always know the phrase: —The famous indifference of nature really sends people like you, doesn't it—it's the romanticism of your *realpolitik*, the sentimentalism of cut-throat competitors—

But for all the brown-titted warmth and revolutionary humanity you exude, you fastened the seat-belt and left them all behind.

Tracing his consciousness as an ant's progress is alive from point to point where it is clambering over the hairs of his forearm, he knows he is not the only one down at the reeds. He doesn't think of *him*, one of them lying somewhere here, any more than one thinks consciously of anyone who is always in one's presence about the house, breathing in the same rooms. Sometimes there arises the need to speak; sometimes there are long silences. He feels at this particular moment a kind of curiosity that is in itself a question: from one who has nothing to say to one to whom there is nothing to say. Falling asleep there he was not alone face-down in the grass. There are kinds of companionship unsought. With nature. Nature accepts everything. Bones, hair, teeth, fingernails and the beaks of birds—the ants carry away the last fragment of flesh, small as a fibre of meat stuck in a back tooth, nothing is wasted.

In the harbour of the summer night the city rides lit-up at anchor across the veld. The telephone answering device waits to provide his only conversation. It's Barbara, darling. Where on earth are you hiding yourself? Seton and I want to have some people over for New Year's Eve, just a small thing, not a great lush-up. But we can't imagine it without *you*. I mean, we really do want to know if you're going to come? I've phoned umpteen times.

This is Mr André Boyars' secretary speaking. Mr Boyars would like Mr Mehring to come to Sunday brunch to meet Mr and Mrs David Lindley-Brown, of

Does this thing really work, Mehring, or am I shouting down the wind...look, Caroline and I want to make up a foursome to sail with Blakey Thompson to the Comores early in January. How does that strike you? He's refitted his yacht and he's got all the info, but we both feel, good chap though Blakey is, we couldn't take him unadulterated all the way across the Indian Ocean—Caroline's interrupting, she says it's up the Moçambique Channel, to be precise...

I'm getting a coloured band Jan's dug up. The girl at your office said she didn't think you'd be back in time, but it'd be so lovely if you could just make it...it's going to be enormous, keep thinking of more people I can't do without—you know how I am—

Someone told me you've gone off skiing in Austria?—René and I want to have a civilized New Year away from the mob, and I said to him, d'you know, there's only one person I'd be happy to have with us...truly. You've never been to our game lodge on the Olifants River, have you? Well, we'll take lots of good drink and food and watch the hippos. We've built a sort of little tower... René's got a cousin out from Belgium, a charming girl, I know you'll get on famously, we'd be cosy.

Some people are intimidated by the machine and couch their messages in telegraphese, as if paying so much a word. Others are cut off just when they are getting into conversational stride—they forget or do not know the span of the recording does not take into consideration how much you may still have left to say. The machine simply stops listening.

Just as he gives no answer. He takes no part in the conversation. He sits with his head tipped back in a long chair, but not negligently. If it were not for the drink in his hand, anyone looking in on the closed-up flat where the owner is away on holiday would take the attitude to be one of a doctor or other disinterested confidant, reliably impersonal.

On Christmas Day they beat a dog and on the last night of the year their radio is turning out *boere musiek*, the sawing, thumping concertina-stuff that Afrikaners love. The monotonous rhythms must have come originally from the chants of tribal blacks, anyway. Listen to one of the farm boys singing the same phrase over and over to himself while he walks, or hear them singing when they're drunk.—As they soon will be.

He takes a walk along the road past the compound and in the adjoining paddock the beasts are all lying down. It's said that cows like music. They breathe in deep animal sighs.

No one shows a sign of life from the compound though he knows they're all there. The L-shape of their shacks hides them and their mess and fowls and cooking-fires from the road. Some year the whole thing will have to be pulled down and decently rebuilt where it ought always to have been—up behind the house, near the public road, clear of the river frontage. There'll be dissatisfaction because they were here when he came, they were squatting God knows how long before he bought the place and they'll expect to have their grandchildren squatting long after he's gone. Everyone pretends he's not there, at the compound, but when he comes back to the house where his car, clearly as any flag run up, signifies his presence, Jacobus is hanging about obviously waiting for him, although his trouser legs are rolled and he's carrying soap and a piece of towel as if he's simply about to wash his feet at the yard tap. He doesn't like an arrival in his absence or any wanderings about without his knowledge; that's an old story. God knows what goes on when they're left to themselves. Clever as a wagon-load of monkeys. He's only got to see a cloud of dust to know from the shape the Mercedes's coming, and he's got the word out, it's telepathic or witchcraft, they understand each other, they back each other up so well. Today Jacobus is expansive and reckless—had something to drink; well, hell, why not.

—Baas, I'm going wake you up twelve o'clock. Knock on the door.—

—Yes! then we drink whisky— He happens to be taking a bottle, sheathed in the twist of thin white paper in which they are packed by the case, out of the car.

—What, whisky…!— The laughter is turned towards a marginal presence; the night-watchman. It beckons him like an encouraging hand. The offer—or joke—is explained in their language.

He has not thought about which party to go to until it is too late to make up one's mind. Lightning in a soaring cave of black cloud on his right, and on the left a huge orange moon is turning yellow, as the skin of a bright balloon thins and lightens as it is blown up. An extraordinary sight; an extraordinary night. There are times when exactly the particular combination of degree of warmth, humidity, direction or absence of wind, occurring at exactly the right time of evening on precisely the right date after the vernal equinox, will bring winged ants floating out of the ground. Or (a completely different combination: high temperature in an early, dry spring) fireflies, running lines of burning thread through the reeds. They were captured in a school cap and put in an empty chocolate carton with cellophane windows, to make a lantern—a great success with a small boy. It happened only once. No one knows the formula. If the phenomenon should recur it would be too late, now. The air tonight is of the temperature and softness that will bring out women in flimsy dresses. They'll all swim in the nude at midnight among the moths that have been attracted by the underwater pool-lights and fallen in. Those guests who have jumped clothes and all will have cloth pasted sodden against them like the water-logged wings. It is impossible to put any kind of shelter between oneself and such a night. He has moved away from the house, the neck of the whisky bottle still in his hand; he goes back to the house for a moment—the kitchen door is open, Alina is back and forth for those endless buckets of hot water they seem to draw—and he takes one of the thick cheap tumblers and a plastic bottle of water from the refrigerator.

With the glass resting capped over the water bottle in one hand, and the whisky swinging from the other he makes his track across a great field of lucerne. Behind him the moonlit pile is now cleaved diagonally by a narrow darkness where the pressure of his feet and the volume of his two legs at calf-height have furrowed through the tender plants. The sheet lightning dances and softly capers before him; it seems to touch about his body, to run over him. He does not know where he is making for but he too, on a night like this, will know exactly, when he reaches it—where all the qualities of such a night may be present to him in perfection. He has taken lately to sitting in the evenings on the roofless stoep of a stone outhouse where bags of fertilizer are conveniently stored, since it is in the middle of the lands. No one has ever lived there—who can say, people will squat anywhere—no one has used it to live in since he bought the place and he has not yet decided what use might be made of it. With a new roof, it would be a better house than any of them has at the compound, but that's out of the question because he has discovered, coming there in the evenings, it has the best view of any spot on the whole farm. A guest cottage?—if one wanted such a thing.

There's a metal folding chair whose plastic thongs are not all broken. That's how he came to sit down here, the first time, in the first place. He has no idea how it got there; a ring never turns up again, but something no one remembers they've left will never be claimed: many months ago some guest afraid he might be expected to sit on the grass must have brought his own comfort along to one of the picnics down at the river. And he himself must have forgotten to fold the chair and throw it behind the fertilizer bags the last time he used it; it is placed at an angle just to the left of a stunted and much-hacked mulberry tree that has survived (somebody must have lived here at one time). It is strange to see a chair there as if it had been appointed. It is rather like being disembodied and seeing himself sitting there.

He inhabits—by filling—the place prepared for him. The whisky and water is delicious. Although one may eat like a pig when alone, drinking becomes a more careful and conscious pleasure when it's not fuel for social intercourse. Every few seconds the whole night undulates with sheet lightning and now and then the pitchy sky on the left cracks like a teacup from top to bottom in a blinding scribble whose running instant (complex as a capillary vein or the topography of a river) is branded upon the dark of eyelids blinked in reaction. But there's no thunder. The fading call of his guinea fowl in the mealies comes quite clearly and all around— or the firing seems so, because the hills on the horizon throw a retort swiftly from one to another—De Beer and his kind are amusing their kids by letting off fireworks. All occasions are family ones for them. No thunder: that tremendous storm is miles away and it's possible, just once, on a night like this, to sit at the point where its element ends and the absolutely calm, full-moon-lit element begins. It is really two nights at once; just as midnight will bisect two years.

He is fully aware that he's feeling what he's drinking but it certainly isn't enough to do more than heighten a little his perception of this miraculous night. At any of their parties he would have drunk much more by now, as much as they will be drinking, until they all sway together, clutch each other's hands and hold on, as if they could help each other, as if some rug is about to be pulled from under their feet.

He feels what can only be a sense of superiority. Not because he is not among them any more, not this year—Someone of your (basic) intelligence, Mehring, even you had to get shot of that lot eventually— No, not because of what they may or may not be, drinking Veuve Cliquot while the coloured band plays, watching that little green rocket ejaculate weakly over the vlei while the children cling to their mother's pink close-together thighs, or taking over anyone's festival, any excuse to begin beer-drinking before the weekend—but because no one is watching this night the way he is. No one is seeing it but him. That's the feeling. You produced tears when you left the country but do you know about this?

And you don't know that he and I sat together, just the two of us, out here in front of a house that isn't a house and a tree that at this moment doesn't seem to be a tree but a paper shuffle in the sudden breeze, a blot shifting dark against the light. We two men sit here where you can keep the whole stretch of reeds and river before you, not so much as a bat can move down there without making a shadow in the moonlight, and we kill the rest of the bottle. From what direction he comes won't be sure, not more than a shadow among shadows, a rustle in the night-secret movement of harmless creatures in the grass—but he said he would come: loping up, with a hop on to the old roofless stoep, where he squats comfortably enough. He must be grinning on those filthy teeth, if the moonlight behind him didn't make the face a dark blank. —Good, Jacobus! Now we have our drink, eh? Come!— There's no second chair, so any awkwardness about taking it wouldn't arise. Rather the way it used to be in the old days in the desert, when the Damara boys would squat with us round the fire and tell us tall stories about their hunting.

—You like it? Very good stuff. Very good. It's nice, eh? Warm inside the stomach?—

He has perhaps never tasted it before. But of course he has, like the *boere musiek*, they develop a taste for everything, they want to wear shoes all right, just give them a chance.

—Here.— (And at once he's holding out his glass as if he did so every day.) —I'll give you some more. You're happy tonight, eh? Everyone's happy tonight. Music, drinking, pretty fireworks in the sky…you too, eh? How long you been here?—

No, not how long he's worked for me; how many years on this place is what I mean. Jacobus was in residence when I bought; he had worked for the previous owner, or perhaps it was only on some neighbouring farm: boundaries mean little to them, when they say 'here'. —How old are you?—

He laughs, of course. —Not old—he always says—not yet old.—

Probably doesn't know. —Happy-happy. Tomorrow another New Year, eh, Jacobus. Long time, long time now.— Yes, it doesn't stand still for any of us; his children (which are his children?) must be growing up. He has daughters I know—sons?— I ought to know. Which of them is his? They have probably gone away. He'll never leave this place. Where would he go? —We're going to finish the bottle, Jacobus, you and I, just this once. You think we're strong enough to finish the bottle?—

And of course he laughs. Everyone knows how much of their own brew they can put away. It's a feast or a famine with them; they gorge themselves when they can and starve when they have to, that's their strength. —Everyone's happy. It's a good farm, a good place to work, mmh? And the cattle are looking fine, this summer.

We're building up a nice little herd. Except for that young bull—I'm not so sure I made the right buy, with that one. I was taken for a ride. Wha'd'you think? You must know as much as the next man about cattle stock by now, you and Phineas and Solomon, you mayn't know the jargon, but you know the feel of a chunk of good beef-flesh under your hand, I'll bet—

Just this once.

They can talk together about cattle, there's that much in common. The old devil's no fool when he doesn't want to be and it doesn't suit him to be. He was quite sharp about the bull the other day; one would almost say needling, pretending innocence.

—That bull, that young one, it's all right. But what it is wrong with the legs in front—the legs are little bit weak.—

Yes, yes, I can see that for myself. —But he's young still, the legs will get stronger.—

—No, he's coming big, here—like this—but the legs is staying little bit weak.—

Yes, yes, I know. —But when the beast is fully mature...—

—Why the other bull, that old one, he is not weak like that when he is young?—

—Oh Nandi, he's the one Terry named after the Hindu god he saw on the temple in Durban, oh Nandi, now you're talking—that's a bull. But where d'you have the luck to find that sort of quality again—

—No, when you buy bull, you look long time, eh? Then why you don't look at the legs they must be strong like Nandi? Nandi is coming old, but the legs is strong.—

—Yes, and why not garland the beast with frangipani as Terry wanted to. ...I know what you're getting at, if it were your bull, you'd make sure you didn't buy one with rheumatic legs that wouldn't be able to mount a cow properly, you'd see to it, if you had a thousand rand to buy a bull—

But we are getting along fine. We're laughing a lot; I would always recognize him by his laugh, even if his face is hidden by darkness. —D'you remember at all what he looked like? That time, Jacobus? You must have turned him over, seen the face, surely? When you took the sunglasses and the watch, all that stuff.

Would you know it if you saw him again—were shown a photograph, the way the police should have done, for identification?—

He holds his liquor well; he bears his head as a man deeply considering.

He says what he said, before, in another time. The tree splashes back and forth across the moon; we are talking unhurriedly, sometimes with closed eyes. —Nobody can know for this man. Nothing for this man.—

Well, he's welcome. Harmless. Let him stay. What does it matter. We would give him drink if he were to be here now, poor bastard. We wouldn't ask any questions, eh? Just this once. No harm done.

We drink the whisky and we talk and laugh, he's having the night of his life. Despite the language difficulty. That would give you something to think about, if you ever knew.

All around, on the periphery of the night, not touching upon it, are the pathetic distant sounds of human festivity. It's difficult to distinguish them one from the other; a kind of far-off wail from which now and then a single note, that could just as easily be laughter as pain, wavers higher. You can not imagine what it sounds like, so long as you are part of it. He has tipped back the chair and feels the moonlight on his left cheek as if tanning in some strange sun; but perhaps that is only because of his consciousness of the darkness of the storm which the right side of his face receives. The moon is so bright he can read the dial of his watch. On an impulse, he drags down from the house a sleeping-bag and canvas and metal stretcher (folding, like the guest's forgotten chair) and one or two other necessities. If anyone looked out—Alina's room's in darkness, the *boere musiek*-drugged cattle do not so much as turn their pale gleaming horns—they would see him going burdened back to the outhouse over the path he has already set for himself through the lucerne, guided along it as if he were already being drawn through his own dreams. He has brought a mosquito coil as well as a fresh box of cheroots. The night has run down very still if certainly not silent and there will be mosquitoes out here, all right, on the stoep among the fertilizer bags. These coils are supposed to be used indoors but they may help. He lights the taper several times before it takes and begins, very slowly, to touch with tiny red the coil that is a skinny cobra with an upright head erect from the centre. Now slow smoke trails from its live mouth. In the sleeping bag he feels gleefully cosy and can see everything, like a hare (there must be a few, if they haven't eaten them all) or a jackal (De Beer says there were still a few around until about ten years ago) putting its head out of its hole. He has thought he would smoke a final cheroot lying there but his eyes close. There is a strong human presence in the sleeping bag, other than his own. He presses his nose into the thin parachute silk stuffed with down. It's the smell of the blond hair of a schoolboy, none-too-clean hair, although it wasn't so long then, that has rubbed against the cowl through many restless adolescent nights.

Jacobus has not come.

A touch of the cold metal tag of a sleeping-bag zipper is what awakens him. It is already light. But perhaps very early. Morning comes at a different time when the curtains keep it out. A sun as pale as last night's—last year's—moon was orangey, is stiffening the topmost leaves of that tree. In metal silhouette against the sky the truncated limbs for which twiggy and leafy growth has provided flimsy cover are solidly revealed as maimed stumps. He knows in some layer of consciousness that there were new wails, louder, calling what he has heard at that hour on that particular night of each year as long as he can remember, Ha-ppee, Ha-ppee. Ha-ppee...ha-ppeee...it's a cry, not a toast, and it does not attempt to define further the quality, state or desire expressed. Happee happee. At midnight they yell it in suburban backyards and in the streets and they produce their own kind of carrillon. Yes. They hit the telephone poles with dustbin lids and garden spades, wailing, happee, ha-ppee. They must have been doing it with their hoes up on the road where you can hear the telephone wires hum if you're alone, they must have been clanging outside the Indians' store. The Boers were sleeping, the Indians were sleeping. And he himself never rose out of that level of his consciousness. It's all over. A narrow escape.

199

Of course—stupid not to remember! If he did come it was to the *house*. He knocked on the kitchen door perhaps, a long time, and went away. He realized it was said jokingly. Will you play hookey and come with me to *Trinitywhatsisname*? —It was a joke, of course. She took it as a joke. Christ almighty. Last year's joke.

Everywhere he stood down the lucerne last night is bruised dark green where the sweet damp juicy leaves are crushed and wadded. Apart from a path between his two points of destination, here and the house, no purpose can be read from these scattered tramplings in a field broken out, pristine and crystalline, in a heavy dew. What on earth was he doing, stamping round and round himself, a dog making a place to lie, or a game bird flattening a nest with its breast. Only the cows are awake and sounding their long affirmative noises: mmmmmmM-Mh! Up at the compound not even a thread of smoke. Still in the arms of their women. Widow-birds— idiotic popular name, what could be more male, in nature, than that assumption of an exaggerated tail of plumage—trail themselves low over the mealies, which are turning fields from green to curds as their tops flower all at exactly the same height. Not a whiff of the soapy bad breath of the river. There is absolutely no one. It's his own place. No eyes keep watch on him. Like any healthy creature still in its prime, he squats privately in the sweet wet lucerne and has produced, with ease and not without pleasure (the cheroot unlit last night smoking past his nose) a steaming turd. The faint warm smell, out here in the open, is inoffensive as cow-dung. He kicks loose some earth and lucerne and buries this evidence of himself.

So we came out possessed of what sufficed us, we thinking that we possessed all things, that we were wise, that there was nothing we did not know. ...We saw that, in fact, we black men came out without a single thing; we came out naked; we left everything behind, because we came out first. But as for white men...we saw that we came out in a hurry; but they waited for all things, that they might not leave any behind.

Riding his bicycle without any particular destination, Izak stopped to see what the Indians were doing. It was one of the sons from the shop who was climbing the struts that supported their rainwater tank. They didn't have a windmill like those at the farm, but there was that old well in the yard where the people used a hand-pump to get water. The Indian was going to paint the struts; a tin of paint was wedged in the angle formed by a couple of bars that formed an X on the way up, and he hung easily, when he'd chosen where to begin, feet balanced wide apart on a cross-piece, left hand round an upright while with the right he drew long strokes of red-brown down the bars. He was dressed like a white boy from town on a Sunday—Izak saw them when they came heading along the main road on their motorbikes—with rubber sandals held by a thong between the toes and tight cropped shorts of the kind that have a little metal buckle and built-in belt. He was naked above the waist and as he moved so did the chain with something gilt hanging from it that he wore on his breast. A little girl from the Indians' house stood, immediately below, gazing up and asking questions and wouldn't go away. They argued in their language until her brother or whatever he was pretended to hold out the brush to dribble paint on her, and she ran screaming and kicking her legs in long white socks. Izak could see him press up the muscles round his shoulder-blades and get on with the job. It was tricky to stub round the angles of the iron but he was doing quite well; Izak did not know why he should suddenly stop and climb down, feeling for his footholds and not missing one, and then walk all round the whole edifice, looking up at it.

Izak spoke, in Afrikaans—It's high, ay.— The Indian was the young one, not one of the schoolboys but the youngest grown one, about the same age as himself. Jacobus and even Solomon did not know exactly when they were born, but Izak knew he was born on the 21st April, 1956; he had it written down on a piece of paper.

The Indian turned dark glasses upon him. That shiny curly

hair they have dangled over the metal rims and he was showing teeth, his face screwed up against the sun. —It's all full of rust. Going to fall soon if a person doesn't paint it.—

Izak laughed. —Too old.—

—I should've started with the platform. That's the trouble. I'm a fool, man.—

Izak was on his bike, but not in the saddle; it was tipped to one side and he was sitting on the central bar, supporting himself and the machine by a leg thrust out on either side. —You can still do it. Climb up the other side, man.—

—I know.—

They both gazed at the structure a moment.

—Are you going to paint the tank?—

—You don't paint these. It's asbestos—some special stuff you don't—

—Yes, I know asbestos, man. Like for the roof.—

The Indian began to climb again and this time gained the platform. Once up, he stretched his legs behind him, face-down on the ledge like an athlete doing push-ups, and carefully fished with an arm over the side to pull up the paint tin.

—You going to do the platform?—

He didn't answer but shook his head very slowly.

Well what was he going to do up there then? Izak could see by the way the head was shaken the Indian had decided on something. But just at that moment Izak's attention was distracted by one of the farm children who came along the road with a tiny tin of syrup balanced on her head. She wanted him to give her a lift back, pleaded and nagged. —I'm tired, Boetie.—

—How are you tired, Sesi, look at that little thing, it's not heavy.—

—But my foot's sore.—

—What foot? What sore foot? You just want to go on the bicycle, I know.—

When he looked up again a band of brown was begun round the top of the tank. It was not a very large tank, shaped like a barrel, and by standing on his toes—the red rubber soles of his sandals showed—the Indian could reach up the brush to the rim. He was going to paint the tank after all? No. When he had eased himself all round it and finished the top band, he squatted and with some difficulty, because squatting took up more room than standing on the platform, made the same band, the width of the paint brush, round the bottom. Now he was starting to write—no, draw something on the belly of the tank, where it faced Izak and the road. Izak began to pass remarks and show off, gently, not going too far, laughing. —What are you doing? What's that you're making there? It's a face! What is this? *Ag* come on, man—

The Indian only shook his head again slowly; he knew what he was doing.

—What thing is it?—

When the sign was gone over a second time to thicken the outlines, he drew himself aside from it and turned the dark glasses once again: —Don't you see?—

The outline of an egg, standing upright, was divided inside by four lines, or rather one vertical line that half-way down subdivided, branching off a shorter line to either side at an angle. The Indian hung there a moment beside his work, swinging one foot. Then he came down in only two movements, the second a clear leap, easy as a cat from a roof, and began wiping his hands on a bit of rag. He did not look up at what he had painted.

Izak knew that egg. He saw it on the motorbikes. Even on shirts. It was smart. People wore it like you wear Jesus's cross. It was, he saw now, what was shiny hanging at the end of the chain on the Indian's bare chest. But he did not know what it really meant, as he knew the cross and also the six-pointed star that the people of the Church of Zion had on their flag. —It looks nice there.—

The Indian still did not look up at it. He had not seen how his handiwork looked from the ground, as Izak did.

—I'd like to buy me one. You must get one for me in your shop, ay.—

The Indian laughed and shook his head again without looking up at him, either.

—Oh, please, man, I like to have one (he patted his breast, where it would lie). How much you selling for? Why you don't get it for me—

—We don't keep it in the shop.—

They didn't talk together any more after that, because the Indian didn't talk. Izak hung on for a while zigzagging the front wheel of his bicycle in the dust and watching him return to the job of painting the struts.

—You'll break a leg— It was the voice of Dawood, the most recently-married brother, speaking Gujerati. The painter glanced down a second behind his dark glasses: the farm boy had tired of waiting for conversation and gone away; the little sister had the married brother by the hand, as if she had dragged him there.

—What's that for?— Dawood was tussling with the child, laughing.

—It's the peace sign.—

—I *know*, stupid—

Two days later, stirring one of the cups of milky tea that was brought to him regularly from the house, the father spoke from a silence between them. —Jalal, why do you have to put that (still holding the teaspoon, he flapped the hand from the wrist) up there.—

He answered in English without a smile. —For fun.—

—But two feet high, everybody sees it from a mile away.—

—What d'you expect me to put up? The South African flag? The moon of Islam?—

—You wear it hanging round your neck—all right—

—What's wrong with it. What's the difference round my neck or on the water tank.—

—Yes, it's all right for the white boys, they've got no other troubles. The hippies. White students at the university. And it looks red—the colour of the paint, I mean—

The young man's face closed in on the other in cruel amazement, grinning and spitting—*Red*! *Red*! You believe everything you read in their papers, everything they tell you on the radio. You swallow it all down. Day after day. If they tell you it's communists, then it's communists. Red! And let me tell you something, that paint's your paint, it's brown bloody paint from the store-room. Red! If they tell you *Koolie*, then it's *Koolie*, hey, why not—you believe what they say is true, don't you.—

205

He shouted as if he and his father were alone.

His father never forgot the presence of the old man; in his place, in his chair. He spoke as a man does conscious of witness, of giving account to an invisible code.

—Never mind. You've got all these Dutch farmers up and down this road and they see it. You never know when someone notices and starts something—I know about these things, believe me. They don't worry us, we don't worry them, that's the best way. Leave it like that. ...The police van is up and down this road every day—

—So the police are going to come and say you're a communist, we're communist Koolies, that's what's going to happen, ay?— That's the hammer and the sickle up there, *you* say—they've told you—*you* and *they* say—

His temper and his nerve flew apart under his own words. They took a hammer to the coloured photograph of himself smiling on the day he got his matric results that hung with all the wedding pictures in the sitting-room. He was smashing himself. —*They* know—*you* believe— Suddenly aware—urgent as an alarming internal spasm prefacing uncontrollable diarrhoea—that tears were about to come, he burst through the dark passage that led from shop to house and shut himself in the room he shared with brothers.

They were at school. There was no key but he pushed the corner of a bed across the door as he had done at other times. He heard his mother breathing on the far side and making small polite noises in her throat. But she would hang about, afraid actually to speak. He lay on his bed and smoked. There were no tears. He thought where he might go. To cousins in Klerksdorp. His mother's aunt in Lichtenburg. An uncle and cousins in Standerton. Even Dawood's wife's people near Durban. Plenty of places. To work in the same kind of shop and hear the same talk.

His mother smelt the cigarette and went almost soundlessly, although she was of majestic size, turned away, down the narrow passage.

The telephone answering device has twice recorded an attempt to reach him through a personal service overseas call.

He could, in his turn, record an instruction for calls to be diverted to the number at the farm. But he does not. There is no one to answer at the house, unless he happens to be inside when the phone rings. And it would mean that anyone else—if there is anyone left, by now, who may not have given up trying to invite him to dinner—would be able to foreshorten the distance (business in Australia, skiing in Austria) at which absence has placed him, in their minds, over the holidays.

There's no way of knowing whether the call would have been reverse charges. Even if you wear your jeans to rags and go barefoot the possibility of telephoning across the world without having to pay marks you unmistakably as belonging in pig-iron, I'm afraid. You are branded by it.

—I just wanted to say Happy New Year and all that—

I notice on the phone you always leave out—avoid using—any form of address that establishes your relationship to me. You don't call me anything. But that doesn't change who you are. —Oh jolly good idea, how're things? Has it been a cold Christmas there? Having a good time? I've been very quiet, taking it really easy—slept the New Year in, believe it or not, in bed at ten o'clock more or less—

And then? A silence while distance is something audible if not palpable: that faint supersonic ringing in the ears, of long distance lines, those wavering under-sea voices that are always there, forlorn sirens of other conversations thinly tangled across millions of miles. Can you hear me? Think of something to say next.

—It's not Terry who wants to speak to you. I do.—

That's also not impossible at this juncture, although we usually communicate through the lawyers, having long ago found that this was the best way to avoid friction that might be harmful to him. But that was when he was a child. Look at him now, a young man fully equipped by Eros himself with the beginnings of a beard. —I know why it's you.—

—He wants to stay and I intend to keep him here.—

—I knew that was it. Why else should you phone me?—

—I have no intention of seeing him forced to go into that army for a year. He has his principles and I don't see why you shouldn't respect them.—

—Yes, and you are going to keep him there, under mama's skirts, and I can do what I damn well like about it, isn't that so?—

He's standing beside you and watching your face to see from it how I'm reacting. —Why can't the boy speak to me, like a man? Let me talk to him.—

He has nothing to say.

—But I have: to you. He's a minor. I have full custody under a court order. You should be aware of that. I shall get an interdiction served on you—

—Oh yes—run to the lawyers, as usual, you can afford the best there is and I won't stand a chance against your money—

He's thought of something he could have said to the boy, anyway. Sticking out of the open windows of the car are the shaking heads of two young saplings, one on either side. Their roots, each in a big fist of soil carefully gloved in sacking and plastic, are on the back seat of the Mercedes. —The trees I told you I was going to plant—remember?—they've been delivered by truck but I don't trust the nursery with these beauties. You know what they are? Spanish chestnut. Specially imported variety. A hundred rands each. My present to myself. God knows how they'll do, but I'm going to have a go. Have you bought yourself roast chestnuts in the streets? That's the best part of the bloody miserable New York winter.—

The road is so familiar that it exists permanently in his mind like those circuits created when electrical impulses in the brain connecting complex links of comprehension have been stimulated so often that a pathway of learning has been established. He knows where the speed-trap traffic cop hides himself. He reads without actually looking at it every time the hieroglyph someone's scrawled on the Indians' rain-water tank. He is aware before he sees her floral rabbits and donkeys displayed on the bonnet and roof of her old station-wagon, that the arty woman who sells stuffed toys will be at the bend where the freeway ends. Particular vehicles, probably encountered many times, using the route as frequently as he does, have become half-expected pointers if not landmarks. Even faces. The other day he thought someone smiled at him from a bus-stop on the road. He could drive it in his sleep; sometimes does; he awakens in the middle of the night in town and for a moment thinks he is at the farm, he wakes camping out in that room at the house and thinks he hears the telephone ringing in the flat. The fancy heads of the little trees are dipping and bobbing in the air-stream created by his passage; people in passing cars give his the second glance that is drawn by anyone exposing out of context a component of private existence—those Boers who will tie anything from a woman's dressing-table to a farm implement on top of their cars, or the location black cycling along with a primus stove on the handlebars or—once—a goat tied on his back.

How many times has he gone to and fro, ironed out the path of the first time he went to look at the place and decided it was a good buy. Scoring a groove over and over again, ineradicable. If there is a first purpose there will also one day be a last. It probably will be something like…something not more than a new grease-trap for a drain that Jacobus's asked for, or a supply of drench for the cows. That's the reality of the place, my dear; keeping it up. It would be crazy to suppose the call might even have been you, but not entirely inconceivable. The sort of thing you would do. Even if it had been reverse charges—that might well strengthen the chances that it would be you, after all, my money is useful to count on when one's in trouble. You are always sailing close in to trouble—with a loud-hailer for SOS in one hand. Well, you are female and that's your charm, or part of your charm. You start off by re-establishing it: —You still keep that beautiful place I once saw, Mehring? If you knew how homesick I get for Africa! Not the people—the shitty whites, god knows—but the country.—

—It's flourishing—the rains are almost too good this year. You should have come out more than once.—

—I know. You didn't ever take me again—oh you would have—but we never seemed to get the right chance, did we…?—

Through the sirens calling and the deep seas drowning the cable that sways between us, you know how to put a hand on me.

No ordinary pig-iron dealer so far as you're concerned. The flesh is present at either end of the line; in fact, that's a live wire clutched to the ear in the right hand, a sparking wire at whose touch each nipple breaks out of its little worn brown parcel of slack skin. Lovely goose-flesh.

—I'm planting European chestnuts for the blacks to use as fire-wood after they've taken over—

Oh that makes you laugh—I know! That's what you really like about me, about us; we wrestle with each other on each other's ground, neither gives an inch and when we fall it's locked together, like lovers.

Whatever you think of me as an employer of black labour you are confident you can entrust yourself to me. Always have been.

—Trouble. I don't want to say too much over the phone—

—Ask away. Ask me for something. That's what I'm here for. How else will you explain to them you know me? Out with it.—

—I wouldn't do it, but there are people who matter more to me than anything in the world—

—Stop beating about the bush.—

—I wouldn't suddenly phone you again out of the blue if it were not—

Of course you would not. Of course you would not phone.

Jacobus admires the trees although they are nothing to see, this small, because he is told they are special trees. He asks a great many questions about them; he thinks this is the way to please, he knows how to handle the farmer. It is also a way of showing that he is in charge of the digging of holes that is being done by Solomon, Phineas and himself.

—Ah, is coming fruits, that's nice. And now is plenty, plenty rain, is going grow quick.—

—Not fruit, nuts. You know what that is?—

It is difficult to find an accurate comparison for chestnuts. None of them is likely ever to have seen an almond or walnut tree,

210

although these grow in people's gardens in town. Groundnuts—
those they know, a common crop not here but in the middle- and
low-veld; but groundnuts grow attached to the plant's roots.

—Yes I know nuts.— Sweat clouds Jacobus's matt-black neck
(blacker than the rest of him, as a white man's neck turns redder
from long exposure to the sun) like condensation on a bottle of
dark ale, and he is talking abruptly, all the time, each utterance
chopped short by the blows of the pick he's wielding.

—Peanuts, you know peanuts. Well, something like that only
these are very big, they're big as small new potatoes, and they
grow in bunches on the tree.—

—Big like potatoes!—

—New potatoes, little ones.—

—And I'm sure is taste very nice.—

—Oh yes. You can cook them and eat them like mashed
potatoes, too.—

Jacobus translates this bit of information and repeats it to
Solomon and Phineas as they swing and rise, swing and rise with
their picks, but they do not respond.

—I think I can taste that nuts next year.—

That wily character knows he is exaggerating, he may not speak
the language but he understands the conventions of polite conversation all right.

—Oh it will be many years before these have any nuts. You and
I will be old men, Jacobus.—

—No! How can we be old? You are still young.—

—No, no. These will be big trees, very big, when you are very
old and walk with a stick.—

—Well, is all right. Is all right, when Terry can get them, when
he can get marry and bring them nice for his wife, his little
children?—

The farmer stands over them while they dig. It's necessary because there must be no skimping: the holes must be deep, the
earth must be properly trenched to a good depth. He cuts the
thick twine round the neck of the packing on each tree and carefully folds back the plastic skin and the sacking beneath it. The
clump of roots and earth (this earth has come all the way from

Europe) has dried out a bit despite all precautions. Some frail capillary roots look like wisps of fibre from an old mattress. He tests them between finger and thumb; both limp and brittle. But he will not allow himself to investigate the bigger roots, visible though embedded in the European earth; the trees must take their chance. Handling them will only make things worse. Two hundred rands down the drain.

Jacobus is quick; no hesitation escapes him. His spade (they are beginning to shape the holes now) pauses. —But is coming all right when we plant. Plenty rain this month.—

The first hole is ready and they move on to make the next. It was difficult to decide where to place the trees. They ought to be near the farmhouse, really—a farmhouse as one thinks of one. Two great round chestnuts dark over the stoep on a Transvaal farm. It would be something extraordinary. But on the other hand indigenous trees would be better in such a definitive position, Yellowwood, Eugenia or something—as a general rule one should plant indigenous trees wherever possible, not even ordinary exotics like eucalpytus and poplar; he has the companion volume to the wild-flower book, a book of indigenous tree species. Anyway there really isn't a farmhouse yet; that place could perhaps be fixed up one day but it hasn't the right character, doesn't look as if it were ever intended to be a real farmhouse. The curve where the road from the entrance to the property turns up towards the complex of farm buildings seems right; a sort of dignified approach to where, one day, a farmhouse and its garden would be differentiated from the farm proper, preside over it. 'Turn right when you come to the big chestnut trees.'

He stands with his hands on his hips, for balance, looking down into the hole. Whatever else they may or may not be able to do, they know how to dig. There is laterite on some parts of the farm, but not here, and the spades have cut down clean and deep. The cross-section of close-packed soil laid bare has its layers of colours and textures stored away. Broken in upon, the earth gives up the strong musty dampness of a deserted house or a violated tomb. At one layer roots frayed by the spades stick out like broken wires. He leans down to tug at one—the young trees must not have to compete for nourishment with the root system of some other growth. But the roots don't yield, and he can't see where they can come from. There's a vertigo that goes with pits; not that this one could take him in and conceal him entirely; it's not more than four feet deep, even crouching, his head would stick out like an unwary rabbit's. But there are some for whom it would be large enough; those tribes who bury in the foetal position.

They have dug one good hole and it remains to make sure they don't think they've done enough hard work for the day and slack off on the next. The rhythmical grunts with which their picks are flying up, over there, and hooking into the ground with a thud, doesn't mean they won't try to get away with going down only three feet.

They've stopped. Jacobus is making a show of heaving at something; it's a rock they've struck. On the desk at the office in town there is a grey-brown stone that bears marks of having been shaped, a kind of petrified whittling, that he once picked up when they were ploughing. The secretaries all ask about it. Like Jacobus, they feel obliged to show interest in what interests him. He is able to explain exactly. —You know what that is? That's a hand-axe. It was used like this—here, open your palm. You know how old that is? That's a stone age implement, from my farm.— But this is nothing but a boulder that has come to light.

The chestnut trees are buried up to the bole in a mixture of bone-meal, well-dried manure and the soil the digging displaced. All the colours of the layers are mixed up, now, there will be a fault—negligible, on the natural scale—where the two small trees now stand like branches children have stuck in sand to make a 'garden' that will wither in an hour.

There are a number of other positions he could have chosen. He sees that, walking over the farm with his trees in mind, superimposing two large chestnuts in flower (pink or white?—he forgot to ask the nurseryman, but perhaps one doesn't know until the first blooming) at various points in his landscape. The irrigation ditches are full of water. Heavy grasses sag into it in wet swags. Frogs flip themselves like thrown stones from an (absent) schoolboy. For the first of seven summers the river is at its full summer height, and he can hear its accelerated pace, its raised voice above the sounds of birds and reeds and grasses, behind the yells of one of the herdsmen chasing an obstinate cow. He can hear it all over the farm. It's not easy to get near. The third pasture is deceptive. A glossy, rough, matted acid green with here and there patches of grass flowering bronze straw stars looks luxuriant and solid enough to take an army over it without being so much as trampled. But there's no foothold. As you put the weight of a boot on the grass it lets you into water; it's all marshy, down there. And even in the middle of the day mosquitoes are active and find your neck. He has to retreat from the reeds, where he can hear waterbirds quarrelling somewhere in there, safe from everything—there must be hundreds of them this year. The mealies are going to be magnificent, at this rate. Up on higher ground he hears himself crashing through them as if he were coming towards himself, about to come face to face with... He stops dead, they creak and rustle, their sap rising to right themselves after his shouldering. It could only be one of them—a farm worker, that is, a familiar black face among black faces, up here. Maybe one of their children on guilty childish business, searching for birds' eggs. He doesn't move and the other doesn't move; it's as if each presence (himself and the sound of his own breathing) waits for the other, as concealment. Again he's almost tempted to speak, the sense is strong; to make an ass of himself, saying aloud: —You're there. It seems to you that it is to you that observations are being addressed: The mealies look as if they're going to be magnificent, at this rate.—

The hairs on their leaves rasp at his clothes. The cobs are clubs pressed against the central canes, with a tassel of silky green fringe tagged at the top. To demonstrate, to test a cob he has to slice with his thumbnail through the tight bandage of ribbed leaves that encases it like a mummy. Through the slit the nail suddenly reaches and penetrates the white nubs so young they are not yet quite solid, and their white milky substance flows under the nail and round the cuticle. Even here, there is a great deal of water: coming out of the mealie-field, he has jumped a ditch and landed on a bank that gives way. His left leg plunges before him down into a hole, he is one-legged, lop-sided, windmilling his arms for balance, and he regains it only by landing with one palm hard on the wet, tussocky ground. He doesn't quite know what to do next, for a moment; he stays there, in this grotesque variation of the position of a runner poised for the starting shot. He could have broken a leg. But he is unhurt. He must get his leg out of the mud, that's all. It has already seeped in over the top of the boot and through the sole and holds him in a cold thick hand round the ankle. A soft cold black hand. Ugh. It's simply a matter of getting enough leverage, with the other leg and the rest of his body, to pull himself free. As he heaves, the mud holds him, holds on, hangs on, has him by the leg and won't let him go, down there. Now it's just as if someone has both arms tightly round the leg. It's suction, of course, that's all; the more he pulls the greater the vacuum. He would get out of his boot if he could, but the leg's caught nearly to the knee. He pulls and pulls; down there, he's pulled and pulled. It's absurd; he's begun to giggle with queer panicky exasperation.

And then, he's been let go. That's exactly how it feels: something lets go—the suction breaks. He has to stump up to the house with an elephantiasis of mud on one foot. It's heavy as lead. It feels as if part of him is still buried.

Jacobus is full of concern, of course. The good old devil half-carries him to the tap, tries to scrape the mud away with a spade and, making a hell of a mess, twice the mess necessary if he'd been left to deal with it himself, washes the clotted earth clear of the shoe. Alina, on Jacobus's excitable and confused instructions, finds a pair of veldskoen in the house and brings them. They are a little too short, the old shoes of a half-grown boy. But they will do. That's what comes of having two places; you never have what you need, in either.

The sun has turned to a thickening blur of radiance and the heat is intense. It'll come down again, this afternoon.

—Too much rain, Jacobus.—

—Too much rain, master.—

...the heaven was hard and it did not rain. The people persecuted him exceedingly. When he was persecuted I saw him and pitied him, for I saw men come even by night and smite his doorway with clubs, and take him out of his house... And on another year, when they saw that the heaven wished to destroy the corn, they hated him exceedingly ... I heard it said that it rained excessively that it might cover the dead body of Umkqaekana with earth. I heard it said they poisoned him and did not stab him. I heard it said that those people were troubled, for their gardens were carried away by a flood.

The weather came from the Moçambique Channel.

Space is conceived as trackless but there are beats about the world frequented by cyclones given females names. One of these beats crosses the Indian Ocean by way of the islands of the Seychelles, Madagascar, and the Mascarenes. The great island of Madagascar forms one side of the Channel and shields a long stretch of the east coast of Africa, which forms the other, from the open Indian Ocean. A cyclone paused somewhere miles out to sea, miles up in the atmosphere, its vast hesitation raising a draught of tidal waves, wavering first towards one side of the island then over the mountains to the other, darkening the thousand up-turned mirrors of the rice paddies and finally taking off again with a sweep that shed, monstrous cosmic peacock, gross paillettes of hail, a dross of battering rain, and all the smashed flying detritus of uprooted trees, tin roofs and dead beasts caught up in it.

From the Moçambique Channel a mass of damp air was pushed out over Southern Africa, and as the other factors—atmospheric pressure, prevailing winds—did not head it off, turned to rain. It began one afternoon but unlike other cloudbursts common on the highveld after a hot morning, did not stop at sunset. The rain went on all night—a really good rain, people remarked, steady and soaking—and continued most of the next day. A set-in rain; one of the three-day rains that, in a good year, mark the beginning of the end of summer and ensure that the grazing will last out well into winter. After three days it did slacken, but the tarpaulin of cloud bulged low with more, and by afternoon it had begun again, a rain steady as ticker-tape. A dark rain, a tropical rain, not the summer storms of a high altitude often lit by the sun still shining in another part of the vast sky.

The English-language evening paper published a picture of a pet dog being rescued from a flooded storm-drain by the fire brigade. In the city, black men put specially-shaped waterproof covers on their hats. On the farm the children huddled along to school in plastic bags that had held superphosphates. The streets of the location returned to the vlei of which it had once been part, and the white policemen at the local station had time to send off entries for several commercial radio competitions: there was a drop in crime.

In the bus queues at the location gates people stood under more sheets of plastic, scavenged from the packing in which the factories nearby received materials. The distended buses lurched cautiously round from the gates to the road, their windows steamed-up inside and streaming outside. Location taxis, old and huge, were the first to be stranded by water on the plugs or in the distributor. But soon there were cars from the city, as well, with grimacing white men in raincoats dirtying their handkerchiefs in an attempt to dry off some vital part of the engine, or waiting anxiously for a passing black, bent drenched over a bicycle, to stop and help push the car out of the way of traffic. The traffic moved slower and slower; came to a stop. Sometimes there had been an accident, someone had skidded and caused a collision, and helplessly, clumsy in a chain-mail of rain, a string of cars collided nose-to-tail behind the first, as the coaches of a shunting train buffet each other. Once it was a transport vehicle blocking the way, a huge tented thing from the abattoir. Water streamed over marbled pink statuary of pig-carcases; the attendant workers in their yellow sou'westers clambered about, black seamen trying to batten down canvas against high seas. The sense of perspective was changed as out on an ocean where, by the very qualification of their designation, no landmarks are recognizable. The familiar shapes of factories lined the road somewhere, if they could have been seen and if what the tyres went over as if greased, engaging with a tangible surface only on intermittent revolutions, was a road somewhere. At the three-way intersection a sheet of water formed through which most vehicles could venture successfully the first few days so long as more rain was not falling too heavily at the time, making visibility nil. When there were children in these cars they shrieked with pleasure and fear at the lack of sensation—the impression of being carried along without any kind of familiar motion; it seemed arms that bore them let go, yet they did not fall. Red of their lips and tongues and bone and blubber-white of their noses pressed gleefully against the windows made melting, distorted images loom up to the cars behind: flesh disintegrated by water. On the Friday the sky held for a few hours and there was a tender area of glare where the sun must have been buried, a grey pearl in jewellers' cottonwool or an opaque insect-egg swathed in web, and in the lunch-break white youths from the Fiat assembly plant rolled the legs of their jeans and waded, goading one another in Afrikaans. By four o'clock, when the factories were closing for the week, rain so close and heavy it actually pummelled the flesh of the black backs on bi-cycles, came from over the Katbosrand hills. The artificial lake might be only a few inches deep in places; it might be over the axles of cars in others. Everywhere the dim-lit submarine habita-tions waited. A young man stripped to his underpants emerged from one as if daring a line of tracer bullets, arms over his head, knees comically bent, kicking up water in water, against water, and bolted back again. Some vehicles were slowly reversed, eddying round their own axes, and crawled off up the roads again. One—in a great hurry perhaps, or merely bored and impatient—began to edge round the lake. The car wavered, tipped, obviously floated, then found solidity again, and from the lalique glimmer of its lights, could be judged to have regained safely the slight rise on the far side of the hazard. Another crept out and the people closed in the car nearest it heard the determined change to second gear. But this time, just as it had come through what must have been the deepest water, because there, too, like the first car, it was seen to float a moment and then engage with some solid surface again— just as it was about to gain the rise, something burst, out there: one of the many tributary streams that fed the vlei from miles away, unseen, swollen unbearably for six days, ruptured like a blood-vessel and shot mud-red into the lake, the final violent, infinitely distant whip of the cyclone's passing, the final fulfilment of the weather outlook for the Moçambique Channel. The car swung sideways, tilted, and was sped over the drop to a gulley below the right of the road, now a waterfall and in moments a tangled heaving river, bearing away, bearing away. It made its escape tearing through the eucalyptus between the cyanide mountains, frothing a yellow saliva of streaming sand. A man got out of one of the stationary cars and staggered a few yards, arms out, in the direction that the car had disappeared. He clearly had difficulty in keeping on his feet. He staggered back again, arms stretched in the direction of shelter.

Safety, solid ground.

That little gully: who would have thought it. Mehring read about these things with the intense, proprietorial excitation with which one learns that a murder has taken place only two doors away from a house one has lived in for years—in an ordinary house on whose mat the newspaper has been seen lying each evening, a house from whose gate the same dog has barked the countless times one has passed by. That little gully. There ought always to have been a paling there—a drunk might have gone over some night, swerving too quickly. But who could ever have imagined that the trickle of water that sometimes dried up altogether for months on end so that that gully was nothing more than a culvert full of khakiweed and beer cartons thrown in by the blacks, the trickle of water that in normally rainy weather was never more than a gout from the big round concrete pipe that contained it under the road, could become a force to carry away a car and its occupants. 'Without a trace', the reports said, 'before the horrified eyes of astonished witnesses'; the search went on for three days during which hundreds of people drove as near as they could to the washed-away road and walked the rest, scrambling along behind the police who were dredging the water. These fans and aficionados of an unnamed sport were so enthusiastic a following that more police were deployed to keep them back; finally the area had to be declared closed to the public. In addition to a nine-year-old wedding picture of the missing couple, a Mr and Mrs Loftus Coetzee, supplied by their relatives, there were pictures of the disappointed crowd with their children and umbrellas. Mr and Mrs Loftus Coetzee were found drowned in the car from which they had been unable to get out, deep in the new river that had made its bed for them; the reason why their car had been so difficult to find was that the water had carried them to, and flooded, oné of those wide pits between the disused mine dumps that had long been a graveyard for wrecked cars and other obstinate imperishable objects that will rust, break, and buckle, but cannot be received back into the earth and organically transformed.

Although he had every reason to visit the scene—he was cut off from his farm by the washaway, after all, it was greatly to his interest that repairs to the road should be begun at once—he kept away until that business was over. The telephone wires on the farm itself must have been down; the exchange said they could get through to other farms on the party line but his place couldn't be raised. He phoned old De Beer and got Hansie, who said the only other road—the long way round, 60 kilometres by way of Katbosrand Station—didn't make sense because the vlei had risen so much the approach was impassable from that side, too. But Hansie thought everything was all right on Mehring's place; one of the boys from there had got across at some point and reported that apparently no stock had been lost. De Beer had forbidden his boys to attempt any crossing since then because one of the women had been fool enough to try and she was drowned—washed up right away down at Nienaber's.

That ordinary little gully—no more than a ditch, really. There were road-menders' barriers with lanterns looped from them in a half-circle along the great bite into the road where it had collapsed under the impact of water. Water no longer flowed over the road but down there—even from the distance at which he had parked his car and now stood balanced on the fender to see—it was still a bile-coloured river dropped back from the banks of its spate which, ragged with the bared roots of eucalyptus, dripped like torn gums a yellow and rust-red slime from the chemicals in the mine waste dumps. There was easily room for the Mercedes to edge along the side of the barriers. Easily. But the road-menders' boy with the red flag started prancing about frantically and the provincial traffic policemen kicked their motorbikes aggressively alive: it wasn't worth it. He made the whole thing appear a feint, he merely used the space to turn the Mercedes back to face town, and left them standing. Who would it have been who went over to De Beer's? Jacobus? No, he would have sent someone else, one

222

of the younger boys—Izak or Solomon. At least the sense to realize it was necessary to send some reassurance through a neighbour; God knows how long before the telephone people would get round to putting up the telephone poles again. His secretary had been to see the telephone manager, but the obvious thing to do was to use a contact with the Minister of Posts and Telegraphs. He sat on a Board with someone who knew the man well. But that would mean a lunch and the admittance—evidence—that he himself was back; back from wherever it was he couldn't be found. —To think it could have been you, coming from your farm; you're on that road all the time.— He said, mocking the secretary's satrap or sincere concern for him—But I'd never do a thing like that, my dear! Never!—

At night the noise of frogs was the drugged, stertorous sleep of the drowned earth. The pastures and fields were water-meadows; under a hot sun the area of water, that was greater than the area of burning had been, shrank back every day, leaving a stained and sodden margin. On the highest ground, the hooves of the kraaled cattle squelched imprint after imprint, one cancelling-out or breaking down the swelling ridges of the other, kneading a rich black mud and dung that oozed a brown buttermilk. The ash-heap of years of cooking fires had washed down and pasted grey all over the compound yard. The fowls were wet feather dusters. The L-shaped row of breeze-block rooms was reflected in puddles and if the walls were struck, gave back no ring of sound, solid with damp. The persistence of the rain had found those places in the roofs where sheets of corrugated iron did not overlap properly or rust had filed through, and water had overflowed the pots and buckets placed to catch it. Under the sun, all that the inhabitants possessed was spread out over the fowl-runs, the eucalyptus trees whose wet black bark was peeling, the fence of the paddock where the calves were kept. Blankets, torn shirts, remains of white men's clothing, a blazer with the badge of a white school, some stained object recognizable as Izak's cap, mattresses with their fibre appearing to grow out of them, shoes stiffened by wet into the shape of the feet that had worn them as white people commemorate their children's first steps by having their baby shoes bronzed, the cochineal cobwebs of drenched bright thin head-scarves from the Indian shop—here was an inventory of everything the farm workers owned. Witbooi's references from previous employers were spread on stones to dry, weighted at all four corners under smaller stones. Drops blown from the trees and dangling crystals from the fence shook down to magnify, then blotch still further, the lettering TO WHOM IT MAY CONCERN.

Jacobus's gumboots leaked. The uppers on the left foot had come away from the sole; he had worn them out during the drought, forgetting the purpose for which they had been provided, and now they could not serve it. The telephone would not serve him, either. He spent long periods in the house, turning the handle; the thing was dead, it was not merely the refusal of the white man at the other end to take any notice. At last he went from the telephone through the rooms of the house in a way he had never done before; he opened the cupboards as possessions must be sorted after a death, putting objects aside like words of a code or symbols of a life that will never be understood coherently, never explained, now—here was a box of stones (what did they want stones for); here that stick whose handle opened out into a seat (yes, the farmer had once stuck it into the ground and sat on it, watching a fence being put up); here was a nice radio, bigger than Izak's, and they just leave it in the rubbish as if it were nothing to them, the son had forgotten to take it back to his school at some time. He found a pair of gum-boots that must have belonged to the son, too; they were all right: he could work into them his soles the wet had made pink and lined as a washwoman's hands.

He drove Phineas and Solomon, Witbooi, Izak and Thomas hard about the reconstruction and repair necessary on the farm. A calf had wandered off and drowned, but only one; the other one hundred and forty-nine of the herd were intact. A cow calved and developed mastitis and he had found the right medicine for that, in the house, and filled up the syringe and injected it the way he had seen the vet do. He had had the lucerne and teff that was on the flooded side of the barn moved to the verandah of the house, where the drainage was good even if the rain slanted in under the roof. He would get everyone busy soon digging the irrigation canals free of the muck that blocked them. Whoever it was who came to the farm when the road was open again, when the telephone worked again, would see how everything had gone on without instructions just as it did under instruction. Nobody would be able to accuse him or prove anything against him, whoever it was who came next, who came first—farmer, police, vet, one of those inspectors who might be from the government, asking about the people working on the farm or the cattle.

All along the vlei, broad river of islands of reed and willow, the lands remained underwater. No one could get near; no one went down there. The yellowbill duck with their neat, clear markings, the pin-stripe black and grey on the pinions, the flash of sheen-blue as they opened their wings to air them, the shaded purple over the gorge, sailed themselves; calm barges. The black coots shrieked and quarrelled and skittered behind screens of half-submerged reeds. As the water gradually fell back new sand and mud shoals rose, where the flesh of the earth had been furrowed aside by the strength of water. Obscene whiskered balloons of dead barbel were turned up to iridescent-backed flies in the steamy sun. The crystal neck of a bottle stuck out of the mud; pappy lumps of sodden fur with rats' tails. A woman's ring or perhaps only the tin loop that lifts to tear open the top of a can of beer glittered in there among the trident-marks of birds' feet. Other objects appeared and sometimes disappeared again, flushed, rolled up by the waters for a day, and then slowly sinking down to the mud they had come from, that covered them with a coating of it-self so that even while visible they seemed to remain of the mud, the leg and broken back of a chair protruding bones through the thick skin of the mud, the door-panel of a car curved like the chest-wall of a living creature under the same thick black skin. A pair of shoes appeared. They held still the shape of feet, like the ones put out to dry up at the compound. They held more than the shape; they were attached still to a large object, a kind of long bundle of rags and mud and some other tattered substance more fibrous, less formless than mud, something that suggested shreds, despite its

225

sodden state and its near-fusion with mud and rotted cloth—something that differed, even in this advanced state of decay, from any other substance, as a wafer of what was once fine silk retains unmistakably its particular weave and quality, its persistent durability in frailty, even when it is hardly more than an impress of cross-woven strands, a fossil imprint against the earth that has buried it. Bits of actual woollen cloth were bonded with the bundle; if such things could have been read by the eyes of birds, which perhaps do not see colour but only tones of dark and light, despite their remarkable sight, the fragments would have been seen to be recognizable as pin-striped, the pin-stripes of a man's jacket. Bits of another kind of wool, greyish-black, had floated up with the bundle and caught here and there on the mud-bank. Some were stranded quite far from the head-shaped object at the opposite end to the pair of shoes; but on the top of this object, that resembled a hairy coconut (almost human) washed up on some deserted African beach, were traces of more of this wool, and from the object's withered greyness shone, gleaming white as the nose-bone of a child pressed against a window out of the rain, a naked nose that had cast its flesh. And a jaw of fine teeth, long, strong and even. Set rather prognathously, in the forward-jutting rounded arc that, in life, would make a wide white-toothed smile. One of them.

Yêbo, my baas.—

There's Thomas, the night-watchman, at the gate, although he must be off duty by this time in the morning. Perhaps he heard the car from afar (as usual; at last) and has come running with his dog to show he's been on the job, flood or no flood. He has his balaclava cap and is wearing his single little gilt ear-ring: —Yêbo baas, yêbo baas— An all-hail rather than an ordinary greeting; the ridge along the dog's skinny spine rises and the beast capers round the old man in response to the ring of his voice. —Yêbo, my baas.—

Jacobus is standing near the house in the pathway of the approaching Mercedes. His hands, at his sides, are palms forward, open. His mouth is open, his face wide, but not with a grin. He will have his tale to tell, all right.

The horn is sounded playfully, the car will pretend to run him down as if to say, yes, it's true, the road's restored, here I am ... But Jacobus isn't going to move; this is no time for levity, apparently: one must respect their sense of ceremony.

He is bringing the car to a stop in the usual place, next to the shed where the farm implements are kept and sees now that Phineas and Solomon and Witbooi—the whole bang shoot, or nearly—are lined up, too. Poor devils, they must have had a scare, quite a tough time; anyway, there are rations in the boot, mealie meal and beans, that'll be welcome. He is conscious of the movements involved in getting out of the car because all are watching him. Jacobus has his hands suppliant in front of his body now, loosely linked and lifted.

He says—We think something is happen.—

—Well, Jacobus, how is everything! How are you!—

—Everything it's all right, yes. Ye-es. Everything coming all right.—

—Everybody safe on the farm? Eh? Phineas—Solomon?—

There is an outbreak of murmurs of assent, grins, movement—they come alive, bashful and eagerly responsive.

227

—We wait every day—Jacobus is saying—Every day. We think perhaps something is happen. I'm trying phone—

—It still doesn't work, mmh? I tried to get you this morning. And then I thought no, the road *must* be open by now—

—Try, try phone. No one is come, nothing. Some days I'm say to Phineas, it's better you try go to Baas De Beer—

—I know, I phoned him. But that was dangerous, he shouldn't have gone, you know that a woman was drowned, over there?—

—The water!—Phineas says. —That water was too much. I'm swimming, and it take me. I go in there by our trees, but I'm come out other side right down there, far far from De Beer—

Everyone is animated, now. Jacobus is suddenly gasping, laughing, as if he has just come through some such experience successfully. —We was worry too much. That woman was gone—gone. Nothing. Can't find nothing. And only one cow, that small one, the calf from Sheba—

—What happened to it? Dead?—

Solomon is talking: —When I'm see she not there, we looking there there, not find.—

Jacobus gives his head a quick, vigorous scratch that expresses overburdened confusion. —And the rain is coming too much. Ye-es. All the time, all the time. We looking everywhere but tomorrow we see she's get in mud, the feet is stick, and then lie down in that furrow there just behind the pump-house—

—Never mind. Only one. Not too bad Jacobus, in that flood.—

All give their crooning, groaning note of sympathy and agreement.

—And was nice, fat, that one.—

—Can't be helped, Jacobus.—

They sound regret and accord, deep from the chest again.

—You should see what the water did to the road. I tried already a week ago to get through. Impossible. Half the road fell in. Some people were drowned. The car was washed away, they were inside. Nobody could find it; the police were looking, everyone was... —

—We think perhaps something is happen—Jacobus says. He has punctuated the account he has listened to by nods that show

228

he knows all about it. —We don't know who is car that is going. We don't hear nothing. No one is come to us.—

—*Couldn't* come, you understand that? Even the other road, from Katbosrand, you couldn't get through on it. I couldn't come.—

—No phone, nothing. We think perhaps... —

There will have to be some kind of bonus for them. All of them. They really seem to have coped rather well. There's a cow making a good recovery from what old Jacobus had the sense to recognize as mastitis, and, what's more, to treat with the right injection. —How did you know how to put it in, Jacobus, eh? You're a clever doctor now, eh?—

He doesn't need much encouragement to mime, step by step, exactly how he filled the syringe, etc. —Always I'm look nicely when the doctor he's here for the cows.—

—I'll save plenty money, now, eh, Jacobus, we won't need the doctor any more.—

He's grinning almost shyly with pleasure, very bucked with himself.

There'll have to be some bonus, yes; in the meantime—a full pack of cigarettes is a nice gesture. Even though he cups his hands to receive, as is customary, it passes almost from man-to-man in the atmosphere of a crisis successfully overcome.

—How long since I was here, Jacobus? Must be nearly two weeks.—

—Is more two weeks we are alone here.— He's determined to make a drama out of it. He drops his head on his breast and moves it mournfully from side to side.

—Well, you looked after everything *very nice*. I'm very pleased with you. All the boys. D'you hear?—

Jacobus and he have moved on together past the farm buildings—the others have drifted off out of a kind of delicacy they have, primitive as they are. Jacobus represents them: —Thank you master, ye-es, thanks very much, master.—

Of course some measures sensibly taken in the emergency will be allowed to remain for ever, now that it's over, unless it's made clear that things can't just be left like that, normal procedure must be returned to. The bales of feed on the verandah of the house: they ought to have been back in the barn by now. Unless it's seen to, the stuff'll never be put back and indeed when there's another load of teff it'll be dumped there, too. That's how they are, the best of them. The house will simply be taken over as another outhouse. There's nobody living there to complain. Next thing, there'll be parts for the tractor nicely stored in the kitchen: all the veterinary medicines he must have taken out of the cupboard when he was rummaging for penicillin for that cow are still laid out on the dining table. He's cleared some of the irrigation furrows, though; they're hardly that—all little overflowing rivers, now. One of the women is doing her washing conveniently in one of them, a heap of bedraggled grey blankets. Everything probably got quite a soaking, up at the compound; but the rooms are cement blocks, they should have been fairly weatherproof. The picannins are enjoying themselves. The game is to float plastic beer containers —some sort of race.

—They know they mustn't leave those things lying about when they've finished playing, eh, Jacobus.—

He's shown the place where the calf got stuck in the mud and died. The more it pulled, the faster it was held. He makes a note to bring new bearings for the pump; a good time to repair it, while it's not in use. Jacobus has said that all the pasture on the vlei side of the farm is useless at present, the cattle will get foot-rot if they are allowed to graze down there—but probably that's all nonsense, what's needed is to drain the land. —That's all right: you can get the boys to dig more irrigation canals—you make some more furrows, then the water runs away.—

Jacobus considers a moment. —Is too much water. Too much.— He goes through the motions of pitching a spade, lifting earth, and then standing back, the imaginary spade has dropped, he is dismayed: —As soon you digging, the water's coming again. Even in that camp up there, not so near the river, when I'm start dig, is filling up.—

—No, no, that doesn't matter. That's nothing. If you find the proper place, the proper slope, after a day that big water will have flowed away. Then slowly every day the earth will drain, it'll dry— come I'll show you where—

The third pasture, for instance, is half-emerged from water already; he can even make out, from where he has had to stop because he hasn't gumboots on (he thought there was a pair at the house but they've disappeared) the tops of the stones that mark the place where a sheep was roasted. He can't go any farther than this but Jacobus is instructed to go down all the way along the vlei and find out how deep or shallow this ground-water is. It's ridiculous, just leaving land to turn back to swamp; water can't be more than a few inches in most places, by now. Jacobus says nothing; which means he's not too keen, doesn't want to slosh around in the muck, no doubt he's had enough of it, but that's too bad. The place must be got going again. For everything in nature there is the right anti-dote, the action that answers. Even fire is not—was not—irrepar-able, organically speaking. Look how everything came back. How the willows must be laved by all that water, now! How brilliant, beetle's-wing-green their leaves are...that ash, partly their own destroyed substance, must have fed them, in the end. Nature knows how to use everything; neither rejects nor wastes.

Down there Jacobus is taking giant's steps. He wades and plods; he is too far away for his pauses and pressings-on to be interpreted. It's not possible to walk much, wearing ordinary boots. All one can do, up here, is stride carefully from hummock to hummock, avoiding water as children avoid stepping on the lines of paving. He gives up; he's simply standing now, and for the first time since he arrived, for the first time since the flood, he is exposed to the place, alone: it comes to him not as the series of anecdotes and imagined images it was while he was being told how it looked and what happened there in the past two weeks, but in its living presence.

A bad smell. A smell of rot.

No, not bad: ancient damp, vegetal dank, the fungoid smell of the pages of old books, the bitter smell of mud, the green reek of a vase where the stems of dead flowers have turned slimy. Twice in the short distance he has managed to cover he has seen a clot, a black coagulation aborted out of the mud. Prodding with a stick shows these to be nothing but drowned rats.

His gaze is the slow one of a lighthouse beam. Something heavy has dragged itself over the whole place, flattening and swirling everything. Hanks of grass, hanks of leaves and dead tree-limbs, hanks of slime, of sand, and always hanks of mud, have been currented this way and that by an extraordinary force that has rearranged a landscape as a petrified wake.

A stink to high heaven.

Yes, it *does* smell bad. The sun is a yeast. The whole place is a fermenting brew of rot, and must be; that's life, that deathly stink. As there were the foetuses of hippos there's a lump of dead rat. (Alas, young guinea fowl chicks will have gone the same way.) He feels an urge to clean up, nevertheless, although this stuff is organic; to go round collecting, as he does bits of paper or the plastic bottles they leave lying about. He has been so busy tidily looking he hasn't noticed Jacobus has turned back and is coming straight up the third pasture through the shallow pools and mud and is almost upon him again.

Jacobus is in a hurry. He's running, so far as this can describe the gait possible in such conditions, over such terrain, stumbling and sliding, lurching, slipping. There's the sensation that the eyes of the old devil are already fixed on him before they can be seen, before the face can be made out. When it is near enough to separate into features he becomes strongly and impressively aware that there is something familiar, something that has already happened, something he knows, in their expression.

Jacobus is panting. His nose runs with effort and a clear drip trembles at the junction of the two distended nostrils.

Jacobus is going to say, Jacobus is saying—Come. Come and look.—

'*And who was Unsondo?*'—'*He was he who came out first at the breaking off of all things (ekudabukeni kwezinto zonke).*'—'*Explain what you mean by ekudabukeni.*'—'*When this earth and all things broke off from Uthlanga.*'—'*What is Uthlanga?*'—'*He who begat Unsondo.*'—'*Where is he now?*'—'*O, he exists no longer. As my grandfather no longer exists, he too no longer exists: he died. When he died, there arose others, who were called by other names. Uthlanga begat Unsondo: Unsondo begat the ancestors; the ancestors begat the great grandfathers; the great grandfathers begat the grandfathers; and the grandfathers begat our fathers; and our fathers begat us.*'—'*Are there any who are called Uthlanga now?*'—'*Yes.*'—'*Are you married?*'—'*Yes.*'—'*And have children?*'—'*Yêbo. U mina e ngi uthlanga.*' (Yes. It is I myself who am an uthlanga.)*

No, no

No, no. The struts of the Indians' water-tank are broken on one side, the rain's done it, undermined the thing, it's about to collapse. No no. The place was bought for relaxation. We lay there shut up in the house on summer afternoons while you said you were having your hair done; I parted your legs while you were in the bath and soaped you with my own hands because, as you once so graciously admitted, I'm not without tenderness, no ordinary etc., etc. Tank's going to fall unless they do something about it, they won't, peace will end up face-down in the mud. Peace hurtles along on a thousand motor-bikes, is worn on the sleeves of leather jackets that pocket flick-knives, and is drawn in red ink on a satchel containing books on unnatural violation of the male body, or plain buggery, that's the real name of what you're curious to know more about. No, no, no. What's the point? What can be left, after ten months? If those *boere* bastards had done what they should, it would never have been there. They couldn't even see to it that a proper hole was made. Scratch the ground and kick back a bit of earth over the thing like a cat covering its business.

But no. No, no. It was dumped there in the first place, not taken away, in the second, and is certainly not the responsibility of the owner of the property. A dead trespasser nobody claims. Why should anyone? No, no. There are a hundred-and-fifty thousand of them in those houses passing on the right, rolled out by speed behind the high fence under the smoke. The women in the bus queues at the gates are busy with a flash of implements and crude coloured yarn while they stand. They're tough. Sheets of broken water around their feet; and the passing car flings it in their faces. They're used to anything, they survive, swallowing dust, walking in droves through rain, and blown, in August, like newspapers to the shelter of any wall.

Recognized by the shoes and apparently what's left of a face, with the—that's enough! Why hear any more, it's not going to do anybody any good. That's enough. A hundred-and-fifty thousand of them, practically on the doorstep. It was something that should have been taken into consideration from the beginning, before the deed of sale was signed. They'll plough down palaces and thrones and towers, you said, smiling defiantly, in the ring of voice that I know means you're quoting some poem; you waited to see if I would recognize the lines, knowing damn well we pig-iron 'millionaires' don't read poetry, and that makes you feel superior, particularly if it's one of your left-wing geniuses no one's ever heard of. And you laugh: —Roy Campbell, South African fascist.— —No ordinary S.A. fascist, I'm sure— I've amused you, again. It disposes you well to me; as I walk about the room in the house that is exciting because we know that from outside it looks as if there's nobody in it, I feel your gaze on my penis that's thrust out a stiff yearning tongue, helpless, even though I'm moving casually enough around fetching a cigarette or pouring a drink to bring to the bed. Others have examined the thing, of course, as you are doing. Some woman once said that the tip or head looked just like a German helmet; that dates me: it must have been during the war—I was only sixteen when it began. What can be left that is recognizable after so long in the earth. The vlei never dries out. It is always wet, down there, moist anyway. There are worms in that ooze. Spaghetti with bulges of pink; not spaghetti, more like those tubes that are part of the innards of a chicken—the solid white line on the road is preventing him from overtaking a frozen chicken delivery van ahead. Rats, and water-rats. There are no jackal. They are nature's scavengers. They keep the veld clean. De Beer has not seen a jackal for more than ten years. —Oh no. *A helmet*! It's exactly like the middle of a banana flower. Even the purplish colour and the slight moist shine. You know how the banana flower hangs sideways from the plant?—

It's not an image that will go down well with whoever the lucky man is now in London left-wing circles; none of them's likely to be familiar with the flower of the banana palm. What could be recognizable? What's left of a face with a—no, no. Let's not hear the story. The vlei will have done its work. Whichever end of the cycle is taken as a starting point, decay or germination, moisture is the right condition. Things rot or grow; rot and grow through becoming some organism other than the one they once were. Rats turn to jelly, a black jelly like coagulated blood, that is the consistency conveyed by the point of a stick. And here's just where it disappeared without a trace before the astonished eyes of horrified witnesses. The van carrying frozen chickens has pulled up at the red traffic light exactly at what must be the place (the temporary fortification of planks and barriers where a proper concrete support and balustrade is in the process of being constructed at the side of the road, marks the spot). Waiting for the light there is time to follow over and over, painted on the back of the van, the lines of a huge chicken, wearing a top hat and monocle, with a cartoon bubble anthropomorphically attributing to it the suicidal boast ONLY HIGH SOCIETY BIRDS LIKE ME ARE GOOD ENOUGH TO BE ARISTOCRAT FRESH FROZEN CHICKENS

—No one will remember where you're buried.— Ah, it's not as easy, not as final as that. Couldn't recognize the place when it was burned and then when the reeds and the grass grew so high again, just as if nothing had ever happened. Couldn't recognize—'find' isn't the word, no one ever searched, it was forgotten, even they never mentioned him again, not even Jacobus. A stink to high heaven. Everything was sweet and fresh and beautiful, my God, lying there. The grasses nearly met overhead and moved under the weight of a body, gently feeling at it. The sun went behind a cloud and a cool palm of shadow rested a moment on cheeks warm from sleep; easy, always, to drop off down there after a late night or a long journey moving through emptiness, casting a rigid flying shadow over seas and forest and deserts without touch: never coming as close as the single silver-blond stalk that sinks and rises in the breeze to the ear or nose of the sleeper. —O Mehring, how you romanticize, how you've fallen for that place.— A stink to high heaven. It was not final; the only thing that is final is that he's always there. It was never possible to be alone down there. Never lonely. Never feel lonely. It may sound crazy— No, put it another way. A funny thing— You don't have to be a believer in a lot of superstition and nonsense—there's a difference between thinking to oneself and thinking as a form of conversation, even if there are

236

no answers. Poor bastard, whoever those bastards were they didn't give him time to speak. God knows what he hasn't said. What he could have told; might have said. They have difficulty in expressing themselves. Only the face and the nose—that's enough! Whether the old devil really said 'nose' or whether the picture of the thing is growing with not being able not to think about it, whether the detail has been added—enough. A stink to high heaven: the burned willows have grown again and the reeds have become thickets of birds, the mealies have stored sweetness of lymph, human milk and semen, all the farm has flowered and burgeoned from him, sucking his strength like nectar from a grass straw—

An awful moment looking at a green light and not knowing what it means.

Jeers of horns are prodding at him. Blank.

A shudder of tremor comes up the back of his neck to his jaw and he jerks to engage the gear. Unnerving; but it happens to everyone now and then. The single syllable chatters away crazily at his clenched jaw. No no. No no. Back to town. He has not waited to hear more. Let them do what they like with it, whether or not the word was 'nose'. Everything at the intersection which he is now crossing like any other competent driver who's had a dozen cars in his lifetime and to whom the wheel in his hands is second nature, asserts the commonplace and ordinary reassurance of what are the realities of life. The things he takes so for granted that, his mind on business or other preoccupations, he doesn't normally even look at. There they are, the blacks on foot yelling at each other conversationally, the chicken van, a family car pulled up so that papa can buy candy floss for the children, an overloaded location taxi crawling, a bus sending up diesel fumes, three Lambrettas identically mounted by youngsters with girls clinging pillion with the appearance of those beetles who mate while in motion, flying along, one clamped upon the other's back. Nothing has happened. Good god, tomorrow he will settle a dispute with the Industrial Council, and he has decided to turn down another directorship, this time of the new platinum mines—he has more directorships than anyone could wish for, apart from being chairman of two boards. As much money as he needs and knows what to do with, what's more. The road back is commonplace and familiar enough to bring anyone down to earth. The white working man knows he couldn't live as well anywhere else in the world, and the blacks want shoes on their feet—where else in Africa will you see so many well-shod blacks as on this road? There is a bus-stop for them (beer cartons strewn) and here, ten yards on, a bus-stop for whites employed round about: just as counting sheep puts you to sleep so ticking off a familiar progression of objects can be used to restore concentration. A prefabricated shelter at the whites' bus-stop and from the background of a well-known cigarette advertisement someone stands forward and—again—he has that peculiar inescapable sense that eyes are fixed on him as target or goal. No. A girl's face; a young woman is standing there, and the eyes claim him and, nearer (he has slowed automatically, out of distraction rather than curiosity) he can see clearly that although she is not actually smiling the corners of her rather big mouth are curled in a suppressed greeting. No no. He's not quick enough to accelerate; she's raised a hand, not too high, a gesture that detains—'Just a moment'—rather than imperiously signals 'Stop'. No. The Mercedes rolls to a halt, it has lost its puissance; she seems to be approaching at the same pace. —Oh can you p'raps lift me again? Thanks so much.— He does not take in the face at all. He sees only that the road and traffic, in miniature but clear, are reflected across her eyeballs as in one of those convex mirrors at amusement halls.

What could be a more routine incident? A car has stopped and picked up someone who wants to go in the same direction, into town. In less than a minute the action is concluded and the car is moving on with two people in it instead of one.

The driver says—You know me, then?—

—Oh yes. You lifted me and my grandad. You don't remember.—

He listens but what is really holding his attention strangely for a few moments is the wide, flat-topped pyramid of a mine-dump to which he has deliberately turned his gaze as another normal landmark. There: has it not even a certain beauty? There are beautiful, ordinary things left. People say they are unsightly, these dumps, but in some lights... This is a firm dump, that the rain has not softened in substance and outline, but that the wonderfully clean sunny air, sluiced by rain, gives at once the clarity of a monument against the glass-blue sky and yet presents curiously as a (remembered) tactile temptation—that whole enormous, regularly-crenellated mountain seems covered with exactly the soft buffed yellow and texture of a much-washed chamois leather. That's it. It is *that*—the imagined sensation of that lovely surface under his hand (the tiny snags of minute hairs when a forearm or backside cheek is brushed against lips)—that produces, unbidden by any thought that normally prompts such an unconscious reaction (God knows, his mind is far enough from these things, this morning) the familiar phenomenon in his body. It's not what the doctor calls a 'cold erection' though: pleasureless, something prompted purely by a morbidity in the flesh, what they say happens when a man's hanged. It's more like warmth coming back to a body numbed by cold or shock. Subliminally comforting.

—He never shuts up a minute. Jabber, jabber. I could have died. He's always like that. Being old, you know.—

—He seemed a nice old man.—

She says, and from the voice he gathers she is smiling, not ill-naturedly—He's all right. He keeps himself going and that. Lively.—

—You never said a word, I remember.—

—I did say thank you I'm sure.—

—Yes, that's all right, you said thank you.—

—My, I was glad to see you coming along now. How many times I've been soaked these last weeks on the way from work.—

—You recognized the car.—

—I knew it was you. I've seen you before. Passing. Often, before that time.—

—Yes, I'm on this road a lot. I could drive it blindfold.—

She's laughing, giggling—Ooh, don't do that, I'm scared stiff in cars. Once I grabbed the wheel when I was with someone and I thought we was going to crash—and I can't even drive. I'm terrible that way; nervous in a car. And specially today, I left home so late for work this morning without even a cup of tea. It's unfair having to go to work Saturday morning, I wish I could find me a five-day week job.—

—Learn to drive, you won't be nervous anymore.—

She babbles like a schoolgirl but now answers with the bridling hardness that sort of girl acquires young. —What's the use without a car.—

It is this tone that makes him glance sideways, at last, and she's busy in her big shabby white bag stained pinkish with handling, so there's an opportunity. No no. He would never have known he had seen her before with that old commissionaire. But she couldn't have invented the tale; how could she have known it. It's the same little girl. Not little at all, in the sense of the word one means it. She could be twenty-five or late twenties; there's something about the odours and small sounds that come from the bag—cigarette tobacco from crumpled fags, the strong whiff of cheap cosmetics, a jingling of objects and the fussy clicks of the bracelets colliding on a capable-looking sunburned hand—that suggests perhaps a divorcee looking out for herself.

She catches him, suddenly full into his glance. Really not bad; large brown eyes of the kind that seem to have no whites, all painted up, of course, coated eyelashes and lids, a brown oval face with a mole between upper lip and nose, a high shiny forehead under a rather tortured mop of dull dark hair. A cheap mass-production of the original bare tanned face he likes in a woman.

His attention is back to the road but on the margin of his vision there is her head on one side—Oh man, couldn't you p'raps just stop a minute by the roadhouse, I really need a snack or something—

God no.

He flicks the indicator to signal the left turn and she's folded her hands together and looks to the front, immediately satisfied, like a child given a promise of sweets. Turning his head to make sure no bicycle will come up on the left, the glance doesn't encounter the face but takes in, in passing, a tiny gold cross tipped lop-sided by its position between pushed-up breasts—yes, she's one of those, dangling them for the boys on Saturday night and down on your knees at the Dutch Reformed Church on Sunday. It really isn't

240

necessary to get out of the car for her, she won't expect it: he's not a fumbler, he produces money as easily as he makes it, and from nowhere has two rand notes in his hand, gesturing them as she opens the door.

—And what for you?—

—No, nothing.—

—You sure?—

—Nothing for me. You go ahead.—

Standing at the window of the roadhouse where the black waiters come to pick up orders they serve to cars she plumps the back of that hair with one hand while she waits, and turns a foot on the heel of one of those clogs, like orthopaedic shoes, the women are wearing these days. He has only just in check a confused impatience ready to rise if she keeps him waiting for her bloody hot dog—why stop, anyway, there must be plenty of buses for these people. He never would have got into this if he had been thinking what he was doing. But she's been given a packet almost at once, and she's coming hobbling over the fine grey stones that surface the court of the roadhouse, smiling, though not looking at her benefactor. The smile is for any man who may be watching her progress. He sighs to release the tension of cold impatience it has not proved necessary to summon.

She gets in beside him and arranges herself and slams the door and the car turns to the road and waits to insert itself into the nearest lane of traffic again, here where the mine-dumps and the remains of the old eucalyptus plantations create a sort of industrial rusticity on either side of the road. She has not opened the packet that has brought into the car a whiff of warmth and grease, but leans forward to put it into the open glove shelf and as part of the same movement puts her hand on his thigh as she settles back again. He is waiting for the opportunity to regain the road. The hand is on his leg. His eyes flicker regularly in reaction to the unbroken passing of cars. When he sees his chance and sidles swiftly into the line the woman's hand is still on him.

—By the old mine-dumps. The trees are nice, there, you can just take that little road down—

He has seen it. No, no. Jacobus can't be stopped. Shoot him

down in his tracks; still he comes on. He has flipped the indicator to signal and she's still talking—Yes, it's quite all right, go ahead; even with the rain and that. You can go, you won't get stuck, it's all right, all sand, not mud.— As the sound and sensation beneath the car's wheels change as it leaves the ridge that ends the tarmac and begins to impress the mixture of red earth and yellow sand that is the dirt track, she is making encouraging remarks—Okay. Okay. That's fine ay, that's fine.—

The arty blonde who sells stuffed toys from her station-wagon sees it: a black Mercedes with a man and woman turning off the main road just before the freeway and driving down into the old plantation. He saw the elbow crooked from the hip and took, beyond the flashing emblem whose prism is always there the bonnet's length before his vision, the stare of sunglasses. Oh no. There is no sound but chatter beside him and the soothing swish of tyres over wet sand where they fit smoothly into the worn hollows on either side of a spine of grass. The eucalyptus are not thick— they have suffered many successive fellings to provide timber props underground in the mine and the present growth consists of thin trunks growing out of the sides of the original boles—but there has been so much rain that their tough, clean wintergreen smell comes in very strongly through the window. The track is just a hundred yards or so below the freeway; from that point, the city is not more than ten minutes away, that's all. The track must date from the old days when these mines were still in production; what is the purpose of it now? It can't lead anywhere, but it has remained open. From here, not too far in, where he has not exactly come to a halt but paused, foot on the clutch, because where is he going? where does it lead to?—from here you could be in town in ten minutes. A silent place. It might be deep in the country, in a real forest with real mountains enclosing it. A boy could people it with Red Indians or cops and robbers, it looks like a place to run and hide; but four lanes of traffic and a freeway are just over the trees, and behind the yellow mountain a scrapyard, a brickfield, foundries. No no. That's enough. Once let them near you—the old man had his gold-braided cap in the car window and his hand on the door that time before he could say no—there's no limit to what they want. With your money, what is there that they dream they could not do and what is there they do not expect of you. Damn it all, no.

—There's nice.—

Two words stay the movement that will put the Mercedes into reverse gear.

—Why don't you eat.— They beg on street-corners and spend the money in the next bar; that's what they'd do with it if they had it. No no.

—I nearly forgot.— The hand is lifted from him and rakes into the shelf for the packet, displacing at the same time something hard that rolls out onto the floor of the car. —Look at that!— She's dived for it. A glass marble. It has been lying there as it lay in the dust and fluff (smell of cat) where I found it for you; it lies in the stranger's hand that was on my thigh but did not touch me, an egg stolen from a nest, as you showed a brown agate egg in a stranger's adolescent hand, a whole clutch of pale, freckled eggs that will never hatch. The car door is standing open on the passenger side. Hampered by her shoes, she is strolling a little way ahead.

—Come—she says—Come and look.—

She has half-turned, the face beckoning, the white packet of food in the hand that holds the white bag. She stays like that while there is a moment when neither moves, she half-turned among trees and he seen through the open door of the car, and while he gets out on his side and slowly closes his door softly, with no more than a click—distinct—between the two of them. No no no. But nothing stops Jacobus running or rather trying to run, like that. What for? What need of haste when everything is over long ago, dead when it was found. Violence is a red blossom for you to put behind your gipsy-ringed ear, a kaffir-boom flower you wear in London as your souvenir of foreign parts, like those Americans who leave Hawaii with hibiscus around their necks. But violence has flowered after seven years' drought, violence as fecundity, weathering as humus, rising as sap. If it had not been for the flood, the best year for seven years. No no no. The scent of the trees is light and cool. Their narrow leaves browned by wet cover the earth like the shed wings of a horde of insects. They do not crackle underfoot because of the damp. She has taken off the coat (raincoat? people have got used to

243

expecting rain every day) that she wore unfastened in the car, and spread it on the ground, the thing is spread-eagled with its arms out, only a head seems missing.

—This's nice.—

He has no idea what he is going to say. —You could eat in the car.—

—Toasted bacon and egg—she says appreciatively. She has wrapped the white paper genteelly round the lower half of the sandwich, whose fatty smell is sickening against the freshness of the eucalyptus, but she speaks with her mouth full, showing bits of egg on good teeth, inoffensively. She's young. She pats the raincoat she is sitting on; she's kicked off, or perhaps it's simply fallen off—one of her clumsy fashionable shoes.

—I don't want to sit.— What he desperately needs to convey is that she is presumptuous, that he is being held up on his way to wherever it is she, living in another milieu, cannot know he is going.

—It's nice here— She has stretched out, she's making a wood of the place, a picnic out of it. She lies back, both shoes off, ankles crossed, propped up on one elbow and eating the messy sandwich, lazily smiling and enjoying the air.

—You should have eaten while I drove.—

She pats the raincoat beside her.

He sits, turned slightly away from her. The green of the trees, the suède-yellow mountains, the clean air are deceptive: this is a dirty place, an overgrown rubbish dump between mounds of cyanide waste, that's all. There are bits of rusty tin and an old enamel pot lying nearby. A porridge of old papers splattered against the trunk of one of the trees. He hears her licking her fingers.

—My, I was starving, man. You saved my life.—

—Come on. I must go.—

She lies there lazily, flat on her back now. She is wearing a tight pink cotton sweater with long sleeves and a round low neck. She pulls down her mouth, warm and relaxed and glistening with the business of eating, and squints, frowning, over her cheeks at her body, brushing crumbs from her breasts. She smiles again, making a play of sleepy, half-closed eyes.

—Get up.—

She put out an arm to be pulled, then, he cannot ignore it; and on her feet completes the movement (as when her hand came to his leg in the car) by leaning her whole body against him, belly to belly, breast to chest. The mouth tastes of bacon and the contact of tongues and lips and opposition of teeth becomes, as always, the inhabiting of a place unlike any other place, a sliding and kneading between smooth resilient walls of pleasure that open ahead and close behind without room for anything else, without thought, without identity. Then he puts her away from him, let her fall if she will. He's going back to the car, the road, the freeway.

—Oh just a sec—she begs—I must find somewhere. You know: I've got to go. Just wait one moment for me.—

The raincoat's still on the ground. He has the impulse to lie there, exhausted, to flop down with his head hidden on his arms, and the leaves would be near his eyes. Not a pleasant place. The car looks abandoned. He does sit down again, but more or less on his hunkers, elbows on knees, and sees the car as it would appear to someone coming upon it, in this place. The toy-woman knows, she sees cars turn off into the plantation with couples in them. Others: that mess of wet paper, cigarette packs. No one knows who the people are who come here; the short journey, the destination, are unrecorded in the pattern or documentation of their lives. It doesn't count. A stretch of waste ground that no longer serves its original purpose and for which a new one has not yet been decided, apparently; most of the mining ground round about has been surveyed and declared as townships of one kind or another, quite a profitable operation. No one knows and one goes away and never comes back to this place again although it is not more than a mile from the freeway. Unless something happens; it is the sort of place people might dump a body. One could be murdered here. *We think something is happen.* The Mercedes swept over the road into the culvert, and everything was kept in order, everything was maintained more or less as usual, as far as they know how. They were ready for the next white man. If it were not to be me, it would have been someone else. The next buyer. Perhaps they thought I was dead; they know another one will always come. They would take

245

off their hats at the graveside as they'd take them off to greet the new one. —We think something is happen.— But it can only happen to me. They have been there all the time and they will continue to be there. They have nothing and they have nothing to lose. She's come back and she's lying beside him, pulling with propriety at her clothes. She's a woman like all the other women, no better and no worse than the smooth, clear olive-coloured face, the dark hair and the Romany eyes she suggests as she lies quite quietly and intimately, sidled against him where he has stretched out on his spine. Without a cushion his head drops back too far for comfort and he has both hands folded under it. —It's nice here. It's nice here.— She giggles and murmurs, because that's the way she thinks she will please; she's taken her pants off in the bushes of course. No no. She's opened her whole mouth over his, taking his lips entirely into the wet membrane inside hers, and his eyes staring up close like a jeweller's loupe brought to her face show that the hairline isn't clean at all, it's a fake, it's not the same at all, there are short rough curly hairs interspersed with blemishes and pimples that encroach on the face as sideburns—

While his tongue plunges down her throat to choke the bitch, stuff her, in the closed-up house with the whisky bottle on the floor and the cologne in the bathroom, his gorge rises in revulsion. No no. The grain of the skin is gigantic, muddy and coarse. A moon surface. Grey-brown with layers of muck that don't cover the blemishes. She pulls away; she pretends that's that, she knows how to excite; they're panting, eyeing each other, and—suddenly—he has become aware as of a feature of a landscape not noticed before, of a pair of strong male calves in woollen stockings exactly on a level with his eyes, behind her shoulders some yards off in the scrubby growth the eucalyptus have put out. Between the leaves a pair of solid calves is in squatting position, facing knees-on but a little to one side so that a black pocket-comb is plainly visible stuck between a great calf-muscle and the ribbed turnover of a sock.

If it were not for the comb—so undeniably the sort of detail that no unnerved imagination could supply—there could not possibly be anyone there. There cannot be anyone there. But there is. Someone has been there all the time. It would be possible to be entirely surrounded, cops and robbers, in this place, without knowing it. But how ridiculous. No, no. Examining the trees without moving, without indicating anything, he has seen another pair of squatting calves—or is it the first that have changed position or crept to view from another angle. She's lying with her breasts lolling apart under the cheap cotton sweater as her legs are rolled apart under her skirt, exposed knees dark-skinned and rough as dirty elbows. Her mouth's open and wet for anything, with a knowing smile, a bit jaunty. A heavy jutting mouth; nothing like, at all. —Come. What you bring me here for, then, man.— Her manner is easy and shrewd. How could anything ever have come of it, a bloody love-nest twenty-five miles from town, you were so 'intelligent' you saw through the whole thing, of course it amused you, the first time you saw me looking in at the windows—Why not just leave it all as it is?— Her eyes are glittering, quite nasty, but she's grinning, more amused than rebuffed. The burly calves are not there; that is to say, not to be seen, but there all right. Someone has been watching the whole time and is watching still, waiting to see—what? When the bitch went off into the bushes, was it to signal or conspire? Oh God no. That hair's been straightened and that sallowness isn't sunburn. That's it. Perhaps. It's a factory girl he's been lured into the woods with; a poor factory girl doing a grade of work reserved for coloureds. A Sunday newspaper story. A dolled-up super-market caricature of the tanned, long-waisted lucky ones who, aping pigment, provide in turn a model for one like this, who has it, to follow: a double fake. She's a trap, then; she waits by the road and brings white men here for whatever those *Boere* call them-selves, the miscegenation squad or the vice squad, to follow. She could be Portuguese; one of those little silent immigrants who can be trusted not to speak. It doesn't calm him that she has the accent of a bilingual country, that her mistakes in English clearly come about because she is Afrikaans-speaking. It doesn't help that so much is illogical and not feasible in fact; if she's a trap, you bloody fool, how is it that she was with the old man with the gold-braided cap, the one she says was her grandfather, the first time she made him pick her up. It is all nonsense, horrible nonsense, it can't happen to him, but here he is, in this place, this dirty mine

247

plantation, his car stands there, can't be denied, she's lolling on a raincoat on the ground—

He's struggled to his feet while someone's there, right there, watching him. But he shouts first. The habit of authority speaks for him—if he's about to be set upon, robbed, killed, castrated (they could also be a gang, here in the plantation, waiting to leap upon men in *flagrante delicto*, unmanned when most manly) he will challenge. —What d'you want?— He hears his own yell.

The man in woollen knee-stockings, shorts, with an open-necked shirt and an ugly ginger sports-jacket is ten yards off. His slow-thinking red face with cropped reddish-blond stiff hair, brighter than the dull fuzz that shows against the light along his forearms and above the tops of the socks, looks grave. He stands and they gaze at him, caught between the trees as if he were a creature framed in its natural habitat. A thug in shorts. One of their rugby-forward dicks. Or a mine detective maybe (same breed), patrolling the property—they used to employ them to keep an eye on such places, trying to catch people who were involved in illicit gold-dealing. (This mine has been closed for ten years...) The creature clears its throat. —You better go— It speaks in ponderous policeman fashion.

The man and the woman are both fully dressed, unless you count the fact that her shoes are off—exactly the perfectly innocent shedding of town shackles allowed any picnicker. The raincoat serves to make the damp ground a place to sit on, that's all. There is even the paper that has until recently wrapped food, crumpled into a ball and flung aside by her, just the way others like her have already fouled the place before her: witness that disgusting mess against the tree, eh.

—Yes? What do you want here! Yes?— He is shouting but can scarcely hear his own voice for the beat of his heart thudding like a pick into the swelling thickness of his chest muscles. These are the bastards who shovelled him in as you might fling a handful of earth on the corpse of a rat, just to cover the stink. —Say what you want!—

—It's not safe here.—

Is that all? Is that the best you can do, thick-headed ox, guardian of the purity of the master race?

—What business is it of yours? Who are you? What d'you think you're doing in this place?—

He stands his ground because those are his orders: dispose of the body, and so you dump your rubbish on somebody's private property; that's the easiest thing to do. About as civilized as the blacks who knife each other for you to bury.

—What do you want?—

The man suddenly squats down again, confidentially, although he hasn't come any nearer. —They find you people here, they rob you.—

—Who? What the hell are you talking about?—

—I'm telling you. They leave you naked. You won't have nothing.—

—We are fully clothed; we came to eat our lunch.— How shamefully, not able to stop himself in time, he has stooped to pick up and demonstrate the pathetic evidence of the crumpled ball of greasy paper.

—They sell it in the location. You won't see it again. Your watch, your money.— He speaks very low, almost wheedling, his head down and his eyebrows raised because he's peering up. He dares to shuffle a little closer. *That's some kind of signal!* Stupid not to keep a gun in the car! The others will burst out from behind the trees where they have been watching and listening: not even a strong man, not yet fifty, kept fit by sauna baths, massage, and exercise on his 400 acre farm, will stand a chance. And at last it will be in the papers, it will all come out, distorted, decayed, but just recognizable, a face with a—enough. —*Trouble*—you said: the prominent industrialist associated with the economic advancement of the country at the highest level who helped his leftist mistress to flee abroad. He tried to interfere with me (that's the phrase that's used) when as a young prospective immigrant girl I sat beside him in an aircraft. He propositioned me in a coffee bar, trying to persuade me to sit in the dark with him at a cowboy film. If I had had my father's money I would have known better what to do with it than to pick up a prostitute and take her behind the trees. We phoned again and again, but no wonder, he was caught with a black girl, that's what he was doing. She hasn't even got up, the bitch. She lies there looking on, she doesn't even bother to draw her legs together. She has friends who matter more to her than anything in the world, because they pay her, yes, she has her kind of loyalty and it's bought. He's going to leave her to them. He's going, in a matter of seconds—mustn't give himself away by so much as glancing towards the car—he's going to make a dash for it, a leap, sell the place to the first offer, jump in, the key's there in the ignition, and drive off reversing wildly first through the trees, the open door on the passenger's side swinging and crashing, breaking branches and tearing leaves. He's going to run, run and leave them to rape her or rob her. She'll be all right. They survive everything. Coloured or poor-white, whichever she is, their brothers or fathers take their virginity good and early. They can have it, the whole four hundred acres. She'll jump up and scream after him, sobbing and yelling, and they'll come at him at the same time, that one will tackle him round the legs, grabbing him as he passes, holding fast from the ground like a fist out of hell, and bring him down to them...no no no. No no, what nonsense, what is there to fear— shudder after shudder, as if he were going to vomit the picnic lunch, it's all coming up, coming out. That's a white tart and there was no intent, anyway, report these gangsters or police thugs terrorizing people on mine property, he's on a Board with the chairman of the Group this ground still belongs to... No, no, no. RUN.

—Come. Come and look, they're all saying. What is it? Who is it? It's Mehring. It's Mehring, down there.

Witbooi offered to make a coffin. They used a tarpaulin in the meantime, weighted with stones from that place where the whites once cooked meat. Izak helped saw the planks at the work-shop near the house; Alina brought tea and porridge and stayed to talk, but not loudly, because of what it was the two men were hammering together. Jacobus had phoned the farmer in town at his office and asked for money for the wood. It was granted without questioning or difficulty, yes, all right, get it from the Indian and tell him he'll be paid. Jacobus knew, through Alina's daughter's husband (Christmas Club) that the India had wood stored from some building he had been doing. But the farmer didn't want to hear about it. He was leaving that day for one of those countries white people go to, the whole world is theirs. He gave some instructions over the phone; Jacobus must look after everything nicely.

Jacobus and Alina and one of the other women went to the Indian store together, with the pick-up, to fetch the wood. The women cried and said there was no money for a wrapping-cloth and wouldn't the India give them some material, anything, any piece of old cloth? He felt sorry for the poor devils, human after all, who must have lost a member of their family, and got one of his sons to cut a length from a roll of Japanese cotton that wasn't a good seller. They said God would bless him.

The funeral took place on high firm ground on a fine Thursday afternoon. Solomon and his brother had dug the grave. The coffin that now held properly what it should was put on the hay wagon hitched to the tractor and driven by Jacobus slowly enough for all to follow on foot. Plovers flew up peeping, shrilling, darting and diving ahead, raising their usual excitable alarm in a serenity of sky and land that took no note of them. The tractor rolled on. At the appointed spot, those people who had not followed were gathered; old Thomas the nightwatchman did not sleep that afternoon, and the children stood by. The women and old men from the location

251

who weeded the lands were there. So was Phineas's wife, but her followers were not with her. Thursday is the day when the women members of the sect of Zion meet in groups on the veld round about the location, and one of these appeared, led by a man in a long white coat with blue sashes criss-crossing it, carrying a tasselled staff, and accompanied by a man with a drum. He struck the drum softly once or twice: the sound of a sigh in space, the great sun-lit afternoon that surrounded the gathering. There was a moment of absolute silence when everyone was still, perhaps there was no need of speech, no one knew what to say, and then the one with the staff began to declaim and harangue, sometimes lifting a foot in the air as if to climb some invisible step, waving his staff. The women of his group, round white hats starched and ironed into the shape of four-petalled flower-bells, sang a hymn. He prayed aloud again and once more they sang, and Thomas's voice joined them in thin but perfect harmony. The eyes of the children moved with the spade. Phineas's wife's face was at peace, there was no burden of spirits on her shoulders as she watched Witbooi, Izak, Solomon and Jacobus sink the decent wooden box, and her husband shovel the heavy spatter of soil, soft and thick. Without consulting Jacobus, Witbooi had privately provided a pile of medium-sized stones to surround the mound as he would mark out a flower-bed in a white man's garden.

The one whom the farm received had no name. He had no family but their women wept a little for him. There was no child of his present but their children were there to live after him. They had put him away to rest, at last; he had come back. He took possession of this earth, theirs; one of them.